Pilgrimage

One Woman's Return to a Changing India

Pramila Jayapal

SEAL PRESS

Jacket design by Joseph Kaftan
Jacket photograph by Thomas Holton
Author photograph by Anne T. Keeney
Maps by Diane Cowin
Text design by Alison Rogalsky

Excerpt from "The Waste Land," by T. S. Eliot, from *Collected Poems 1909–1962*, is used with permission of Faber and Faber Ltd, London.

Library of Congress Cataloging-in-Publication Data
Jayapal, Pramila, 1965–
Pilgrimage : one woman's return to a changing India / Pramila Jayapal
1. India—Politics and government—1977– 2. India—Social conditions—1947– 3. Jayapal, Pramila, 1965—Journeys—India. I. Title.
DS480.853 .J39 2000   954.05'2'092—dc21   99-052946
ISBN 1-58005-032-8

Printed in the United States of America

First printing, March 2000

10   9   8   7   6   5   4   3   2   1

Distributed to the trade by Publishers Group West
In Canada: Publishers Group West, Toronto, Ontario
In the U.K. and Europe: Airlift Book Distributors, Middlesex, England
In Australia: Banyan Tree Book Distributors, Kent Town, South Australia

For Janak,
my miracle boy

Contents

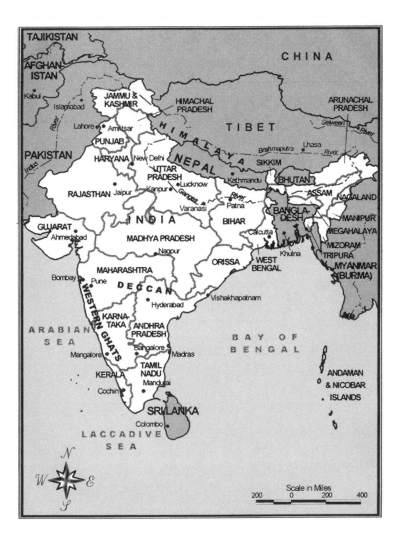

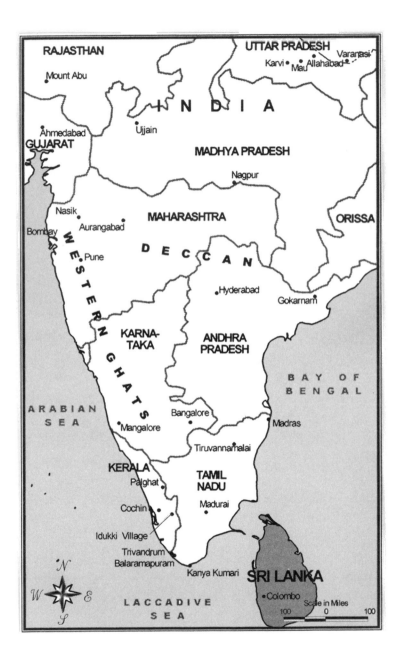

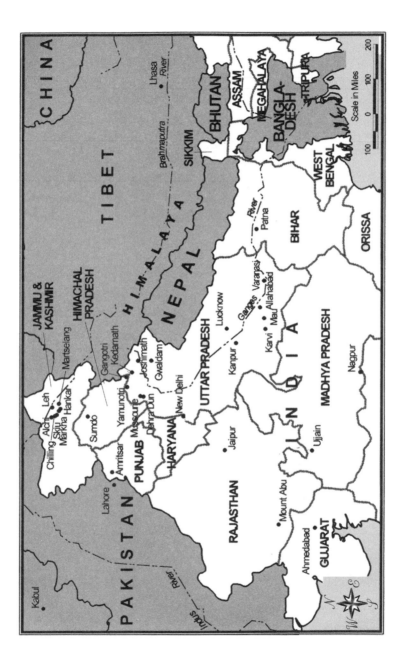

Pilgrimage

Introduction

In April 1995, after twenty-five long years away, I returned to live in India. Born there, I left at the age of four for Indonesia, Singapore and eventually the United States. This return to my homeland was made possible by a two-year fellowship I had been granted by the New Hampshire-based Institute of Current World Affairs to write about contemporary societal issues in India. I had intentionally made the topic vague, partly to allow myself the breadth to write about whatever I wanted and partly because I sensed that whatever I thought I wanted to write about was bound to change. Embarking on this fellowship was the perfect extension of my past years working in international development. On a more personal level, it was also the natural next step to my years of questioning about the role India plays in my life. Behind all of the professional reasons to return to India was my intuition that my discovery of India would center on a discovery of self, and that ultimately my professional and personal lives would fuse together in inexplicable and powerful ways.

I had not always known that I would want to live in India again. In fact, I had spent my childhood rejecting India, my teenage years struggling to compose an "American" identity and my twenties focused on building a private sector career in the unlikely fields of investment banking and marketing. From college to investment banking to a top graduate business school program, my path seemed to follow the perfect ladder to success. And yet, it was not enough. Twenty-somethings talking in loud voices about billion-dollar deals, nights spent working in fluorescent-lit cubicles, and promises of hundred-thousand-dollar salaries did little to make me feel whole. Few people I met had any interest in India or the rest of the world (except Japan and its stock market); I rarely talked about India, other than to try and explain why I had no Indian accent. Rather than highlighting my foreign upbringing and Indian birth, I focused on ridding myself of them and on fitting into a corporate culture where dark suits and a certain acceptance of corporate values were to mask any underlying differences in race, ethnicity, class or gender. I could not rid myself of the nagging sense that there was a woman within me, waiting to emerge, a persona that included a complexity of new images of homeland, identity, life values and work.

I ultimately left the private sector and traveled for several months with my husband Alan through parts of West Africa and India. There, far from "civilization," I met the most civilized people I could have imagined. They were inspirational, these people, men and women who had a strong sense of place and identity. Many were social activists who had committed themselves to improving their communities; they had discovered their life's work and were acting on it.

I came back to the United States energized. I had a vision for myself: to apply my work in the private sector and my graduate degree in business to the non-profit world. There were business skills to be used in productive ways in this other sector, something I could contribute that would be useful. I began working for a Seattle-based international health organization whose mission was to improve the health of disadvantaged people around the world, particularly women and children. I managed a $6 million loan fund that provided small, affordable loans to otherwise "unbankable" health projects, which included small rural clinics, AIDS/HIV prevention and information efforts, and women's savings and credit groups that linked health with credit. Because we made loans around the world, I traveled extensively to Africa, Latin America, Southeast Asia and, of course, to India to evaluate projects and offer advice to these grassroots efforts. As much as I loved working in the field, I began to feel more and more like an outsider. I wondered what wisdom I could actually offer on these two-week, or even two-month trips to communities I did not belong to. Parts of the international development world felt as strange to me as the private sector, driven almost exclusively by notions of economic progress and often far too homogeneous in ethnicity and class. Programs and policies were typically made from five-star luxury hotels rather than the villages the policies were meant to serve, and like me, many of my colleagues had little real sense of the people they represented.

As a foreign woman of color, I often found myself regarded as a spokeswoman for the communities we served, particularly for those in India. But this felt false and uncomfortable to me. I knew more about India than many of my colleagues, certainly, but far too little to represent it in truth. It was also becoming increasingly clear to me that the development world had far more to learn from these populations than to teach them.

I decided I had to go back to India, the place I felt best qualified to represent, and immerse myself in learning. After years of trying to distance myself from the country, then trying to interpret her for others, it was time simply to discover her.

I returned to India with no answers and often not even the right questions. As I explored the vast country, I also explored myself, the nuances of my feelings and the spaces from which those feelings emerged. I peered at myself in all of my distinct forms: as an individual, a woman, an Indian and, yes, a product of a Western education. It was often a struggle to reconcile these seemingly disparate personas.

Looking at myself in these modes stretched my mind and body in ways that were alternately painful and stimulating. My head throbbed from thinking; my eyes felt dull from overstimulation; my body was tired and grimy from the physical strains of living in India. I watched as the old me shed its protective barriers and exposed itself, warts and blemishes often uncomfortably vivid.

A few days before I left for India, I had scrawled in my journal, *Truth is an eternal conversation about the things that matter.* I had recorded no author but drew heavy blue lines around this statement as if to stamp it not only on the page but also on my mind and soul as I traveled throughout India. The truth I searched for was about India, about me, about everything I would witness there—these were all vitally important in piecing together my individual puzzle.

During my two years in India, I met people for whom life still revolved around family, community, spirituality and land. I began to understand how far from these real values our lives in the West have strayed. These people taught me that life is ours to live but not to dictate; ours to question but not necessarily to receive answers; ours to appreciate but not to expect. From them, I learned that our only task is to fully live in the present. Past and future are creations of our own minds; they last only as long as we think about them, dissolving into nothingness the instant we allow them to.

These attitudes were grounded, in part, in a long lineage of Indian spiritual teachings, from such great texts as the Bhagavad Gita and the Upanishads, to the teachings of the sages Mahatma Gandhi and J. Krishnamurti. But it was more than this, because many of the villagers I met who inspired me the most had never read these teachings. Yet they had a real sense of the space they occupied in the world. This sense fundamentally changed the way they interacted with their surroundings. They were more centered, more connected, not only to the physical place but to the spiritual place within them. We in the so-called "developed" world fool ourselves too often. We allow ourselves to be surrounded by human-made things and forget that we are here by grace, not by right.

Success and accomplishment in India were viewed completely differently than in America. To be sure, this too is changing with the influx of global forces, but across the country, I met men and women whose success appeared in their inner strength, calm and resilience. They persevered through conditions I could not have imagined because they truly understood who they were relative to the world. They maintained a sense of mortality and humanity. They cultivated an inner wisdom and clarity that radiated brilliance. Their success was a part of their search for truth, rather than a diversion, as "success" had been for me for most of my life.

ॐ

When I returned to India that spring of 1995, I found it easier to write about issues rather than feelings, the logical result of too much education based on the analysis of fact. My feelings were personal and therefore not valid, I believed. My education and work experience had trained me to believe that objectivity was a preferred quality in a professional (and even personal) context. Writing about personal experiences and reactions, then, felt strangely unsafe, stripped of any protective veneer. Some superb writers helped on this front. Edward Said's *Orientalism* and anthropologist Ruth Behar's *The Vulnerable Observer: Anthropology That Breaks Your Heart* reminded me that even the best objectivity is filled with subjectivity, that perhaps marking ourselves as "vulnerable observers" is the only justice we can do to those people and places we write about, to our readers and to ourselves.

Ultimately, I also realized that this entirely personal perspective is the *only* way to begin to understand India. As much as one might want to manufacture absolutes, there are none. I now know that India's greatest gift to me was her capacity to evoke emotion, to push me to question my feelings and through that questioning, to understand the ways in which I try to make sense of the world as well as the limitations of those ways.

I spent my two years in India vacillating wildly between romanticizing and criticizing the country. My most intense struggle centered on reconciling what seemed to be two completely different Indias. One India—culturally rich, artistically divine, spiritually enlightened— nurtures and propels individuals to spiritual greatness, to create architectural wonders that show genius and a palimpsest of rich history etched in stone, to return to the simple and the real rather than the plastic and chrome. The other India is the blackest of holes out of which few can crawl. This India mocks poverty by piling it on destitution. It laughs raucously at the intention to take one's life into one's own hands by dealing cards that could not win even the best gambler a penny.

India, as a friend of mine likes to say, can be both a physical hell and a social heaven. On the one hand, it pulses with life, with humanity, with small wonders: the early mornings when the countryside is fresh and cool, when men and women squat on their haunches in the grass and brush their teeth; the lush green glow of ready-to-harvest rice paddies, where long white necks of geese rise regally out of the fields; the monsoon rain as it beats out its rhythm on the roof; the jingle of bright glass bangles on a woman's wrist; the graceful welcome of the village women who warmly led me into their homes. It is a place where people openly express their humanity; where connectedness matters; where there is a belief in being part of a larger social order. But on the other hand, India can be impossibly difficult: throngs of people, cars and animals; constant electricity outages; piles of garbage, broken sidewalks and rutted streets; and the unbearable unfairness of poverty, gender and caste discrimination.

I found that I had to work hard to allow myself to feel what India laid out at my feet, to confront that my emotions were as much a product of my own frailties as they were of those I was watching, to push myself to accept without resignation, to prevent myself from tuning out the world around me, to resist the temptation to alleviate physical discomforts that often felt overwhelming.

I am, in many ways, a product of a modern world in which we use (and have been used by) technology to both simplify and complicate our lives: seeking the easiest and fastest ways to travel, to communicate, to exist. All too often, this means enclosing ourselves in imaginary bubbles that protect our sense of physical and mental space. To be physically uncomfortable in India does not just mean traveling down a bumpy road in a decrepit old bus; it means being completely present to the smells and sounds of life on the bus: the feel of a sleeping woman's head as it drops onto your shoulder, the pressure of a man's hand on your back as he struggles to keep his balance in the aisle, the belching of someone who has just finished a good lunch. There was no room in India for the physical or mental space that is held so sacred in America. I could not enclose myself in a world made of my own choosing in order to forget that a completely different world existed just outside.

In an oblique way, my time in India allowed me to create a new space in my mind and soul for absorbing and rethinking old ways of viewing the world. All of the logic of my Western education, upon which I had based so much, seemed to take me a very short distance to any real understanding of myself or of the world around me.

William Blake once said that Reason is just Satan, that it snuffs out imagination and freedom and emotion. Living in India lit for me again that candle of imagination, of passion, of connectedness. I found that I could logically analyze issues until, as an individual, I was confronted with a reality, a practical enactment of an issue that placed me as a player in the scene. Then the analysis had to be adjusted to include emotions and circumstances, the lack of absolutes. Often these situations were outside my past framework of understanding, and they left me with few consistent answers. This is the only truth there is, I realized.

Living in India rejuvenated my spirit, brought alive parts of me that had faded into the background of a modern life that is sometimes too efficient, where emotions are shielded by good manners, where space exists so bodies do not touch on buses or trains. In India I touched and was touched every day, by people, by scenes, by thoughts in my continuously bubbling mind. With each experience—whether I was accepting pickles from a woman who had nothing else to give or watching a group of men willingly push our broken-down car down a deserted road—I learned that even twenty-five years away from India could not break the basic threads of human commonality that bound us together from birth. It was good to be back.

PART I

❦

Shades of Gray

Coming Home

April 20, 1995. I am in New York's Kennedy Airport, waiting to board my flight to India. A Pakistani woman and her four children are sitting next to me. She wears the traditional black purdah, but her children, the product of cross-cultural exposure, are dressed in blue jeans and button-down shirts. I smile at her, and she smiles back. There is an immediate recognition that we are from the same part of the world. Over the years of traveling back and forth from America to India, I have noticed that older Indian and Pakistani women gravitate toward me. They are confident, despite not knowing me, that they have found a fellow friend who can help them negotiate the airports between here and there.

I assure my Pakistani friend that I will help her, too, and suddenly, as I watch her children, my eyes fill up with tears. I have not cried yet, not even when I left my husband in Seattle, too filled with excitement to be returning to live in, not just visit, India for the first time since I left at the age of four.

I brush away my tears self-consciously. I realize that I am crying over leaving the familiar—America, my husband, my friends—for the unfamiliar: India. I am crying *because* India feels unfamiliar and I wish it did not. I am crying over the realization that I am strong-willed and independent in America, but I am unsure of who I will be in India. I am crying because I am afraid I will not fit in the very place that is supposed to be home. I am crying because I know my life is changing and I am not sure how it will look at the end.

๑โค

When my mother was pregnant with me in 1965, my parents lived in Jaipur, the capital of the northwestern Indian state of Rajasthan. In Rajasthan, as in many parts of India, boys are generally considered much more desirable than girls. My mother and father already had a daughter, my older sister, and all of their neighbors and friends kept assuring them that this child would be a boy. My parents tried to tell them that they actually wanted another girl, but no one believed them. They tolerated sympathetic looks that seemed to say, *Poor things! They must prepare themselves like this in case there is another disappointment.*

My sister, just under three years old when she first put her hand on my mother's stomach and felt me kick inside, had an old *ayah*, nursemaid, who looked after her. The ayah also felt it her duty to reassure my sister and mother that the next baby would be a boy. *Chota munna aayega*, she would say with only a trace of worry. *A little boy will come.* My sister repeated this mantra until I arrived, and so I was nicknamed Munna, little boy.

My father was the consumer affairs manager for an international oil company. Working for a foreign company in those days was considered the ultimate measure of success. My sister and I grew up hearing my father's stories of how, as a young man just out of college, he would stand beneath the windows of the tall company building in Bangalore and vow that someday he would be sitting at a desk looking out one of those very windows. His family, although not poor, was never wealthy, and my father's success in eventually becoming the general manager of the company's Bangalore office was our family's version of the American dream, complete with its not-so-subtle messages: dream, work hard and achieve.

My mother was a dreamer too. She immersed herself in poetry—in Keats, Byron and Shelley—and earned her master's degree in English literature. Once her children grew up, she spent her time teaching and writing. She credited her love of literature to her father. My grandfather Achan (which means father in our native language Malayalam and was the name my sister and I called him) had entered the police force as a young man during the British rule of India, eventually ending up as director of vigilance and anticorruption for the southern state of Tamil Nadu. He mastered British English and developed an obsession for the English language, gathering dozens of dictionaries and books on etymology and the origins of idioms and common phrases. His favorites were such works as Hobson Jobson's dictionary, which documents the singular "British Indian" usage of words and phrases. Achan also adopted many British customs such as starting every meal with a homemade soup, drinking tea from a silver tea set complete with a floral tea cozy, and wearing British-style Bermuda shorts.

In their own ways, then, both my mother and father had established their ties to the West even while growing up in India. They moved in an up-and-coming social circle of Indians and foreigners, an energetic, party-loving group as enamored with Western movie stars like Jimmy Stewart and Audrey Hepburn as with their Indian equivalents, Amitabh Bachaan and Hema Malini.

In December 1969, a few months after my fourth birthday, my father was offered a transfer to the company's new office in Jakarta, Indonesia, to establish and run its marketing department. It was not a difficult decision. Both my parents had a wanderlust and the opportunity to "go abroad" (as it was then called) was not to be missed, although undeveloped Jakarta at this time barely qualified as "abroad." It was a small town with lush green gardens in the city center, colorful outdoor markets and one luxury hotel (which today stands worn and old) that sat behind a circle displaying a powerful statue holding the freedom flame of Indonesian independence.

The international school I attended in Jakarta was one of the finest in the region, the natural destination for the children of ambassadors, missionaries and other expatriates. In the company of children from forty-three different countries, I believed the world was small enough that I could put my chubby little arms around it and hold it close to my heart. We young students asked each other where the other was from as easily as we greeted each other in Indonesian. Countries became more to me than simply geographic borders; they were the faces, accents and homes of my friends. By humanizing countries in this way, we humanized the world.

But growing up with the children of wealthy foreign diplomats and oil company executives had its consequences. I was surrounded by children who lived in beautiful houses, had multiple servants and as many cars. The Americans, in particular, who comprised about 40 percent of the school's children, had the nicest homes: mansions filled with plush furniture that was color-coordinated with the curtains; cupboards stocked with goodies like potato chips and peanut butter imported through the American commissary—an elite store that, like the American Club, was only for Americans. They also took the most exciting vacations to magical places like Disneyland, flew off to Singapore on shopping sprees at the drop of a hat and brought back fancy brightly colored bicycles, games and toys. I began to think that this was what life was about, equating wealth with good. I quietly went about rejecting my Indian roots for the more glamorous Western life I saw around me.

I pulled out my "Indianness" only when required. Once a year, for example, on United Nations day, I would hoist the Indian flag and trade my fashionably torn jeans for a sari, deftly wrapped around my skinny body by my mother's long fingers. When my parents requested, I would accompany them to various Indian functions or attend Indian Independence Day celebrations. I refused to learn Hindi or even to speak our native Malayalam (although I still understood the latter). I asked few questions about India, as I was more interested in America's mysterious, alluring image, studded with exotic amusement parks and enormous shopping malls and, perhaps most important, exuding an aura of freedom, defiance and worldliness.

The annual family vacations to India were dutiful trips, enjoyable in the doing but boring in the telling. Despite some wonderful memories of my grandparents' home in Madras on India's southeast coast, where we spent much of our time, my vacations paled in comparison to those of my friends. As I grew older, India became worse than boring to me. It became positively unappealing. The heat, the filth, the squatter toilets—any feeling of adventure and novelty that these had once held for me as a child now dissipated into the most judgmental disgust.

The summer after eighth grade, however, my mother took my sister and me to visit the old ruins in Delhi and the historic city of Agra, which houses the Taj Mahal. We walked through the crumbling fortresses of the early Muslim kingdoms in South Delhi, wandered the overgrown gardens near the Red Fort in the original city of Shahjahanabad (Old Delhi), gazed up at the minarets on the Pisa-like tower of Qutb Minar, listened to our footsteps echo on the marble floors of the Taj Mahal and heard the romantic stories about the love that the great Mughal emperor Shah Jahan had for his wife. I felt an overwhelming sense of epochal history, tradition, culture, religion— the beginnings of a sense of curiosity about the country I had left behind. Although I soon reverted to my fascination with America, the trip gave me a new appreciation for the country of my birth.

When it was time for my sister to go to college, my parents intensely discussed whether they could afford the cost of an American education. They ultimately decided to take the enormous financial risk because they believed that America offered opportunity and the best education possible. They promised that when it was my turn, they would send me to America as well. Sometimes, to tease me when I was misbehaving, my parents would threaten to send me to Valliamal Girls College, located a few blocks from my grandparents' house in Madras. My sister and I would see the young women pour out of the unfriendly Valliamal cement building, their hair neatly braided into two long plaits, their blue pinafores still crisp over their clean white blouses, even at the end of the day. Compared with my international school in Jakarta—where there were no uniforms and children sported the latest Western fashions such as denim cut-offs and T-shirts emblazoned with saucy sayings—the Valliamal women represented a stifling of creativity, a prudishness (there being no boys on the premises) and a lack of opportunity.

My parents' joke was funny until the year before I was to go to college, when our finances became shaky. Faced with the real possibility that I would end up in India—maybe even at the dreaded

Valliamal College—I began to pray to our family goddess, Ambika Devi, more often. Our house in Jakarta had an L-shaped porch bordering a small garden framed by hibiscus and frangipani trees. At the far end of the L was our *puja* room, the place where we worshipped and prayed. In the calming dark, I could see the brass prayer lamps glinting below the framed picture of Devi. Never having been particularly enthusiastic about religion before, I now began praying five times a day. I begged Devi to allow me to go to America and to escape the braids and blue pinafores. As my mother often reminds me, Devi always listens.

The vivid distinction I pictured between Valliamal and American colleges accurately represented my opposing images of India and America: India, repressive and backward, and America, creative and advanced. I could not have known then that I could push India away only for so long before it would tumble forth out of the dark closet to which I had relegated it, challenging me to confront its essential role in my life.

✺

I shift in my uncomfortable plastic chair at the airport. The Pakistani woman asks me to look after her bags while she and her children go to the bathroom. She sweeps away, the children gripping the purdah's cloud of black cloth.

I pull out a black laminated folder from my carry-on bag. Before leaving Seattle, my husband and another friend had thrown me a surprise farewell party. They had asked each guest to create a page of words or pictures of their wishes for me as I undertook this adventure. I now carried these pages with me, knowing that I could draw from the energy of their creators when my own spirits were down. Here in the cold, impersonal waiting area of Kennedy airport seems like a good time.

The first page has a picture of my husband Alan and me from the summer of 1990, just months after we had finished graduate school. We were in the Canadian Rockies, at the top of a long, winding pass in front of snow-capped, jagged mountains, surrounded by lush park land. The camera captured us sweaty and smiling, obviously pleased at our surroundings. Alan has been more supportive than I could ever have hoped of my quest to live and study in India. We have decided that I will go first, and he will join me six months later. He needs the extra time at work, and I, although a little nervous about it, think it will be good for me to spend time there on my own initially.

I continue to flip through the book of creative pages. The tears are coming again, but I do not notice them until they drop onto the pages. There are more eclectic and inspiring wishes: Edward Abbey's *Benedicto*, Winnie the Pooh on "Where is home," and a Nootka poem called "Weave and Mend."

I see my Pakistani friend approaching, and I quickly put the folder away. It is mine alone, and I wish to keep it from other eyes. I do not want to answer any questions because I do not have the answers. I do not even feel capable of answering the seemingly simple questions.

Just an hour before, I had been standing in line at the ticket counter waiting to check in for the flight. An Indian man behind me smiled his greeting and said jovially, "So, going home?"

I thought for a minute, then softly replied, "Yes, going home." Home.

Liar! a voice inside me screamed, *How can you call it home when you have not lived there for twenty-five years?* How indeed?

Life had come full circle since I had arrived alone in the United States at this very airport.

☙

I was sixteen years old when I moved to the United States for college in September 1982. It was only the second time in my life that I had been to America; the other visit had been for two short weeks with my family a few years earlier, and I remembered little of it. This time I was alone.

I stood in the Kennedy Airport immigration lines, an interchangeable number with any of the hundreds of other foreigners waiting to be granted entry into the United States. Like the others, I could be denied entry at the will of a customs officer who had woken up late, missed his cup of coffee, or had a hangover. My heart pounded, a feeling that would inexplicably return every time I entered the country for the next fifteen years. Never mind that I always had legal papers or that eventually I would become a "resident alien," the horrible term for a United States legal resident who is not a full citizen. That pounding heart was my constant reminder that I did not really belong in America.

My entry was innocuous, however. With a loud stamp on my passport, I jumped into a new world. Standing with my two old, fake leather suitcases, I shrank into the endless tile and concrete of the airport. In one corner I saw a couple embracing passionately, she in tight black jeans and high-heeled shoes, he with his thick broad arm circling her waist, pressing her into him. Their lips melted together and I turned away, embarrassed to witness their private reunion in this public place.

I had selected the college I would attend, Georgetown University in Washington, D.C., out of a catalog. When I arrived at my dorm room, my roommate was already there. Gina was from New Jersey. She had chosen her side of the room and filled the shelves above her desk with the contents of the fifteen bags of luggage she had brought. Gina's mother and grandparents had driven with her to settle her in her new home. As I listened to their voluble conversation, I stashed my collection of cotton summer clothes on a single white laminated shelf in my cupboard. The rest of the empty shelves depressed me. I closed the door quickly to shut out the feelings of loneliness that were rising in me.

I had not yet reconciled India's significant role in my life, but in a new country I desperately needed an identity. It felt incomplete, false somehow, to say I was from a country in which I had lived for only four short years. Instead, I took to giving a ten-minute speech about my origins to anyone who had the misfortune to ask where I was from. Yet, India was still, almost by default, my origin, my heartland. So that first day, Gina and I walked into the Georgetown neighborhood, and I bought a big poster of the Taj Mahal. Above my bed in the dorm room, the Taj Mahal gave me a story to tell about who I was.

My identity was confusing to my friends at Georgetown, as it has always been to those around me. I speak fluent English, tinged with an unplaceable American accent. With an ear trained not just to hear different accents but also to hear the unique colloquial ways in which people express themselves, I could masquerade as the quintessential American—on the telephone, that is. The telephone would not give away my obvious foreignness, my jet-black hair, dark chocolate eyes, brown skin.

I still had to learn the small things about living in America, like how to dress in the winter. I had to learn that sweaters were never tucked into jeans, that I could not wear white after Labor Day, and that I should keep my shirt collar inside the neck of my sweater. I had to learn to wear socks and shoes instead of sandals and to tolerate the angry rashes that broke out on my feet from being constantly enclosed. I had to learn to smile politely while those around me referenced television shows and commercials I had never heard of.

On the first day of classes, Father MacFadden decided to use me to make a point. He was a Jesuit priest, over six feet tall, with a hint of a belly, gray hair with a bald spot in the back and glasses that rested on his nose. Father MacFadden always looked down at everyone, literally. Even if sitting, he would tilt his head back just so he could look down through those glasses. On this day, Father MacFadden was explaining to his new group of students that each of us views and hears things differently. We draw our understanding of a phrase, an issue or event, he said, from the context we bring to that situation. He turned suddenly in my direction.

"Pramila, what do you think of when you hear someone say the 'Prime-Time Players'?"

I was caught off-guard, unnerved by the smiles of those around me who seemed to know what the Father was talking about. "Certain important countries in the world?" I said doubtfully. The class erupted in giggles. I could feel the heat rushing to my face. I had proved his point. I could not have known, no matter how much I had read from my home far away in Jakarta, about *Saturday Night Live* and the Prime-Time Players.

❧

The flight to India via London is announced. I walk to the plane with my Pakistani friend, taking one of her many bags for her as she struggles along with the rest, her children hanging on her skirts. As we walk, I suddenly realize that like my Pakistani friend who speaks little English, soon I will be living in a place where I do not speak the language fluently. Although I have been taking Hindi lessons, it is not my native language. More unsettling is the thought that people will expect me to speak Hindi because I look Indian. I am entering a world where I may fit in some ways, but in others, I will be more of an oddity than I was in America.

My flight row companion is another Indian woman. She is returning to her home in India's Punjab region to "look at suitable marriage matches" for her son. "He has a green card," she confides in me, "so he can have many choices." Her son, a computer engineer, has lived in America for some ten years. "But," she says delightedly, "he still wants me to choose his Indian wife. One girl is quite fair. I think she will be the one." Skin color, I am reminded, is of supreme importance in many of these marriage matches. Being fair is worth several steps on the marriage eligibility ladder and in general esteem. Even my grandmother would click her teeth disapprovingly when I exposed myself to too much sun: *So dark, Munna. Why do you do this?* I always find irony in the fact that being dark is desirable as long as one has to work at it rather than inherit it.

My companion chatters on and I listen, relieved that she does not ask me who I am or why I am returning to India. It is too complicated to explain. For her, America is still what it has been for me the past thirteen years: opportunity. In my emotionally fragile state, I do not want to try to explain why "opportunity" is no longer enough for me, why I must now go back to India.

My mind is moving back and forth through time as if there were no boundaries. The pictures meld together, their frames dissolve. Looking out the airplane window, I can still see the land below. I remember how enormous America seemed to me when I first arrived, not just because of its physical mass, but because it is so sparsely populated compared with Asia.

In India, even in her most remote parts, the human touch is everywhere, perhaps a straggly scarecrow built by human hands in the middle of a vast corn field, perhaps an Indian flag hoisted above a small shack, perhaps the glaring infringement of a bold red and white advertisement for Coca Cola on the way to a sacred temple. At times this omnipresent human presence feels invasive, but at other times it feels comforting, alive, real. In America I sometimes feel like an actress in a movie; in India I am in a documentary, seeing reality's intensity.

Now, in the confined spaces of the airplane, my return to India seems as strange as the idea that humankind is able to cross continents in funny-looking steel birds suspended in midair. It is raining outside, and the raindrops are sucked by intense vacuum pressure to the windows of the plane.

I remember my fascination with America's seasons when I first arrived. From India and Indonesia, I knew about rain: monsoon rains that pounded rooftops with a comforting thunder, torrential rains that flooded the land and quenched the sun-dried earth of the summer, cool rains that soothed our bare feet as we ran home through beckoning puddles. I knew about heat too—blinding sun, clammy skin and baking ground. But winter, spring and fall remained mysteries to me.

As the sultry heat of Washington, D.C., turned cold, the leaves began to change color and fall, lining the Potomac River with reds and golds. I picked up the leaves and saved them and, in the most naïve gesture of wonderment, mailed them to my mother in Jakarta. I wanted to share my amazement that a single landscape could look so completely different two months later, that lush green foliage could turn to dried gold that fell to the ground and was eventually swept into huge piles. My mother laughed when she received the leaves, brown and crushed ugly things devoid of what I had seen and wanted to share.

I saw snow for the first time my first year in college. Georgetown's basketball team had just played and lost to the University of Virginia. I returned home from the Capital Center stadium in D.C. on a bus full of half-drunk, irate, disappointed fans. The sky turned gray, the clouds swelled and darkened. In my dorm room I turned up the radiator and threw on a nightshirt just as my friend Tyrone, who lived in the room below me and had never seen snow either, knocked on the door. "Pramila, it's snowin'!" he said in his New Orleans drawl. "C'mon! We gotta go!" I pulled on a pair of jeans, a sweatshirt and shoes (no socks), and together we ran outside. The snow was coming down, falling invisibly until it reached the rays of the street lamps, where it gained shape and form. The white feathers dusted Healy Tower, the steeple in the middle of campus, with powder. Even our ugly brick dorm suddenly seemed beautiful.

That night, I was the wide-eyed newcomer, an Indian girl seeing snow for the first time, oblivious to those around me laughing as I stood beneath the snow, tongue outstretched to catch the falling snowflakes. They landed, cold pricks on my warm tongue, disappearing down the back of my throat, only to be replaced by more and more and more. My mouth was sore from staying open, my face covered with melted snow, my hair dotted with white. Tyrone and I giddily whirled around, finally lying down on the gently sloped hill in front of our dorm to make snow angels. As we waved our arms up and down and opened and closed our legs, our angels took shape. At that moment, anything was possible. Covered in snow, with frostbitten fingers and toes, I laughed and laughed for the newness of it all, for the miracle of snow, for America.

෯

The plane lands in Bangalore. This is where my parents live, where I will stay and rest for a short time. I have arrived alone. Both my Indian and Pakistani companions have departed at the previous stop in Bombay. I have had two hours to myself, lost in groggy, jet-lagged thought.

I step off the plane and smell India, her masses, the hot sultry air brushed with the scent of jasmine and diesel fumes. I feel vulnerable, soft, as if someone could stick a sharp pencil in my flesh and cause me to pop. My arrival is momentous, but yet so ordinary. I am sure that I wear my jumble of feelings on the outside, reflected in my face, embedded in my eyes. But, no, I am quite wrong. No one is looking at me. No one, it seems, except me understands that I have finally come home.

Revisiting Kerala:
The "Model" State

Just outside my parents' veranda, in an undeveloped lot, there is an enormous rain tree. In the West Indies, where the tree species originates, it is also called the "singing tree." The name apparently comes from the chirping of cicadas that have made their homes on the trunks of the tree. The cicadas secrete a watery fluid that looks like raindrops as it is released down the tree trunk, giving the tree its common name.

I could not see the fluid coming down the trunk, but it seemed to me that the tree's enormous drooping branches were themselves green rain, stretching from sky to earth. From my parents' flowered couch, I would sit in the early mornings with a cup of coffee and listen. The busy city rush had yet to start, and I could hear the crank of an old water pump, the clinking of pots from the homeless families who had settled into that empty space, the rustle of the rain tree's branches as they swept across the moist grass.

It was April, and the cool weather was just coming to an end. The mosquitos began to show themselves, and the earth dried and crumbled beneath my feet in the unbearable midmorning heat. I had been spending time in Bangalore simply absorbing and reconnecting with my parents. It had been, I realized, thirteen years since we had even lived on the same continent. Although they were excited to finally have me near them again, they worried about my decision to return to India.

"Are you sure?" they kept asking when I had told them of my plans to apply for the fellowship. "It will be difficult for you, you know.

You've not lived here for such a long time."

They were even more anxious about my intention to live as simply as I could manage, to go to villages, to keep as little distance from the masses as possible. To them it seemed an extraordinary choice to make. Although they may have appreciated my reasons, I know that they often wished I would leave this kind of learning to someone else.

∞

Two weeks after I arrived, I received a call from my friend Viji. Viji runs a nonprofit organization that gives loans to groups of economically disadvantaged women who have organized themselves into small savings and credit groups. The loan fund I managed in Seattle before coming to India had funded Viji's group, Friends of Women's World Banking India, to make loans that tied together health issues and women's credit. Through that process, Viji and I had developed an immediate friendship. She had been delighted when she heard I was moving to India. "Come with me," she had said in her exuberant way. "I will show you everything!"

Viji invited me to go to Kerala with her to visit some of her projects. It seemed somehow fitting that my first trip would be to my home state, a state I had never lived in but had often been proud to claim as my family's origins. Viji and I would, together and separately, travel through different parts of Kerala, giving me a unique opportunity to get a glimpse of a variety of issues and projects. I jumped at the chance, and we agreed that I would take the night bus a few days later to the southern city of Cochin.

Kerala's narrow finger of land stretches some thirty-nine thousand square kilometers along India's southwest coast, making it one of the country's smallest states. According to Kerala's mythology, Varuna, the god of the sea, granted Parasurama, an avatar of Lord Vishnu (one of the Hindu trinity), the gift of as much land as he could cover by throwing down his *parasu* (ax). Parasurama threw his ax into the sea, causing the water to recede from Kanyakumari to Gokarnam, forming the strip of land that is now Kerala. It is a topographically beautiful

and diverse slice of India, with coconut palm-lined beaches bordering
hilly ranges of the Western Ghats, fertile natural forests. Small and
large streams, lagoons, rivers and waterfalls (in the highlands) inter-
mingle with rubber and tea plantations and acres of land planted with
ginger, cardamom and pepper.

Kerala has long been hailed as a development model, often held
up to the rest of the "developing" world as a possibility, a goal toward
which to strive. Kerala's statistical record is impressive: In 1991 its
literacy rate was 91 percent versus the national average of 52 percent,
and 87 percent of females were literate versus the national average of
36 percent. Life expectancy, infant mortality and death rates all ri-
valed those in many Western countries. Family-planning campaigns
have been extremely successful there, resulting in an almost zero population growth rate. Public health care is excellent, with primary care
clinics within reach of most of the state's population. Kerala's successes in the development world provided me with a compelling
counter during my years in development work to those who pronounced all of India an economic and social disaster.

Although I had never lived in Kerala, I had visited it many times
growing up, staying with my paternal grandfather and aunts and
uncles. The most memorable part of these visits was going to our family temple in Peruvemba, outside the city of Palghat. Most families
have in their house compounds some sacred grove or *kavu* where either snakes or deities are worshipped. Our family temple was built by
my mother's great-grandfather when some laborers working in his fields
came across a black stone which started bleeding after their plough
hit it. My great-great-grandfather brought an astrologer to the site
who declared that this stone was the goddess Bhadrakali (also known
as Ambika Devi) in *swayambhu* form (self incarnated in the stone). My
great-great-grandfather built a small temple at the spot as a gesture of
respect to the goddess, and She became our family's goddess. Although
our puja rooms always had pictures of many different gods and goddesses, Devi remained the central deity of our worship.

The temple gained importance, partially because one branch of
our family is said to have oracles who at certain festival times become

possessed with the spirit of the goddess and utter prophecies. According to family lore, my great-great-grandfather himself is supposed to have had "visitations" by the goddess and prophesied many events.

Built in traditional Kerala style, the temple was small and simple, surrounded by a low stone wall and with no roof other than the propitious ashoka tree under which the stone had been found. The ashoka tree marked the entrance to the temple and was housed in a circular pavillion along with several stone *nagas*, frighteningly real statues of long, coiled snakes representing the ancient serpent deities of India.

As a child, going to the temple was a special treat, even a privilege. Walking into the temple, I immediately felt awed. I spoke in whispers so as not to disturb all the spirits who lived there. The small sanctum sanctorum, the temple's innermost sacred room where the *pujari* (priest) performed special pujas, was dark and cool. Inside it, I was wrapped in calm. The pujari's chanting fell over my head and shoulders like smooth, clear water. By the end of our puja (which was never very long), I felt refreshed, light and protected.

⚛

It was a matter of particular pride for me that I belonged to the *Nayar* caste. Nayars (actually a cluster of about 131 separate castes) constitute about half of Kerala's population and are famous for their adherence to the matrilineal system whereby property and family name were passed down through the female. Interestingly, Nayars, respected for their roles as landlords, farmers and professionals, were actually part of the *Shudra* caste, traditionally defined as the caste of laborers. However, Nayars found themselves in key roles providing certain services to *Brahmins* such as stringing flowers for temple prayers, managing money transactions in land and business affairs and even protecting the royalty. As a result, many people often assumed Nayars were from the higher castes of either *Vaishyas* (merchants and tradespeople) or *Kshatriyas* (warriors).

Many women's studies scholars believe that the matrilineal system is one of the primary reasons that women in Kerala hold a higher status than women elsewhere in India. Because girls were the automatic inheritors of property, dowries were relatively uncommon compared with those in patrilineal systems, which existed throughout the majority of India. (Unfortunately, this matrilineal inheritance pattern no longer exists.) Similarly, partly because girls were needed to carry on the lineage, female infanticide was uncommon in Kerala, unlike in other parts of India. Other problems, such as child marriage, bride burning and the ostracism of widows, were also largely absent in Kerala. Women outnumber men in Kerala, creating a sex ratio similar to that of industrialized countries where males and females have equal access to food and health care. (In sad comparison, India's sex ratio as a country is about 93 to 100, a ratio that highlights the approximately twenty-three million Indian females who are "missing," either because of the selective abortions of female fetuses, the passive murder of female babies through neglect or the death of women and girls for other reasons.)

Nayar customs regarding marriage were also unique. Marriage was not considered an institution but rather a convenience to produce children. Like most Keralites, I was married by the *talikettu kalyanam* rite, in which my husband tied a *tali*, a tiny gold ornament shaped like the leaf of a banyan tree, around my neck. Although this is now the official marriage rite, it was originally a prepuberty rite that simply matched a girl with a boy but did not require cohabitation. The word *kalyanam*, originally meaning an auspicious event, now means marriage. Traditionally, even after the talikettu kalyanam ceremony, the woman would reside in her family's house and the man in his. She was not economically dependent on him, nor was he required to provide for either her or their children. Rather, the woman's uncle (her mother's brother) was responsible for providing for his niece and her children. This tradition of living in the family house rather than depending on in-laws, as is the case today in many marriages across India, provided women with a sense of continuity, security and independence.

According to the traditional system, Nayar men and women were identified by their mother's house name (usually shortened to two initials), which precedes the first name. (By this system I am P. K.

Pramila, short for Pudusery Kolaikal, my mother's house name.) The father's name does not enter the picture. Although this practice is changing, I am still asked by our family priest when I go to the temple for my mother's name as the means of identifying my lineage.

The women in my own immediate family corroborated the truth about Kerala women's strong status in family and society through jokes, history and their own examples. My sister and I grew up regaled by stories of how Nayar women would put the shoes of their husbands outside of the house when they had tired of the men. According to my mother and grandmother, husbands would see the shoes outside and meekly take their things and leave.

All the women in our family were highly educated; my grandmother's sister was a pre-eminent gynecologist, one of the first Indian women in that field; my mother and her sisters all had master's degrees in various fields from medicine to English literature. Being raised with women's power gave me my own sense of identity as a woman as well as a sense of the possibilities of and for women. When I tired of the many questions from my Western friends about the terrible situation of women in India, I used the stories of Kerala women as my defense. Acknowledging the discrimination against women in most of Indian society was always painful for me; holding up Kerala as an exception gave me some small comfort.

Visiting Kerala with my friend Viji would give me the chance to really explore this state that I claimed as mine. It seemed an auspicious start.

ॐ

It took twelve hours to travel from Bangalore to Cochin by bus. My father, horrified that I should choose this mode of transport as a single woman who could afford to fly or take the luxury train, insisted on inspecting the bus the day before I was to travel. To my great amusement and slight annoyance, he drove to the bus terminal, inquired about exactly which bus would be making the journey to Cochin and then climbed on board to inspect the seats. He returned home slightly mollifed and mostly resigned.

The bus was packed, primarily with "Mals" returning home. "Mals," my mother informed me with a twinkle in her eye, were Malayalees (from Kerala) who had certain distinguishable characteristics: darker skin, hair slicked back with coconut oil that shimmered in the sun, large kohl-lined eyes for the women and neat braids for girls that hung down the center of their backs. "Your hair is not long enough," my mother said laughingly, "but otherwise, you look like a definite Mal."

I arrived in Cochin just as dawn was breaking. The streets were silent. I took a cycle-rickshaw to the hotel where I would stay with Viji, drinking in the coconut trees, whose long fronds hung down above relatively clean roads, squat buildings and wide medians. Later that day, Viji and I wandered through the colorful streets arm in arm, stuffing ourselves full of hot roasted peanuts from rolled newspaper cones. Our trip would take us into the villages of the Idduki district, Viji told me, a hill region that borders the Western Ghats. We would also visit Balaramapuram, where hand-loom weavers were trying to revive their old craft, and Trivandrum, where the fisherpeople's association was having a meeting that we would attend. After a week, Viji would leave and I would continue on my own in Kerala for a few weeks. We would meet again after that in the capital city of Trivandrum.

Over a luscious shrimp dinner cooked in typical Kerala style, with coconut milk and lots of cilantro, I asked Viji to tell me about some of her other projects in Kerala. With Kerala's reputation as a leader in development, wasn't there less to do here than in other states? Viji's answer was mixed. In some ways, she said, literacy had made Kerala groups more aware of what needed to be done. Still, there were the same problems here as elsewhere—unemployment, corruption, gender discrimination.

Ironically, the combination of a highly literate work force, strong labor unions and the lack of an industrial base requiring highly skilled workers have contributed to extraordinarily high unemployment rates in the state. In 1995, for example, 27 percent of Kerala's labor force was unemployed and 60 percent of those unemployed were educated— often through the college level. Kerala's unemployed account for 10 percent of the nation's unemployed, even though its population accounts for only 3.5 percent of the nation's population.

Although a socialist mentality existed in Kerala long before the Communists formally came to power in the first free elections after state formation in 1957, this Communist government had the greatest impact on labor laws and activities. The majority of labor reforms were introduced after 1957. Kerala was the first state to provide unemployment and disability compensation, welfare funds (that function similarly to Social Security in the United States) and retirement funds. India's Trade Union Act of 1926 provided that a union could be formed with a minimum of seven people and encouraged the formation in hundreds of industries, from the Head Load Workers Union (people who carry goods on their heads) to the Autorickshaw Workers Union to the Cashew Workers Union.

Kerala's liberal worker policies—quite revolutionary for their time—have made it more difficult for Kerala to compete with neighboring states for business. I spoke about this situation to my uncle, who had been the Joint Commissioner of Labour in Kerala before retiring recently. "It is much more expensive for companies in Kerala," he said. "The wages for workers are high, and the employer has to pay so many benefits. For example, we are now seeing a lot of cashew factories, a mainstay of the Kerala economy, moving across the border to Tamil Nadu. There they can pay their workers half of what they must pay here, and they don't have to worry about unions or other benefits."

Because of the state's high literacy rate, Kerala (unlike its neighboring states) must also worry about the quality of businesses it needs to attract. Most Keralites are overqualified for small, unskilled factory work. Unable to find work in Kerala, scores of able-bodied young people move to the Gulf countries or elsewhere, often leaving their families behind. Those who stay in Kerala frequently feel they are stagnating. For example, at a small dairy cooperative in Kavalangad village in the hills, I spoke with Babu Joseph, a village society convener with degrees in botany, zoology and chemistry. Unable to find a job, Babu eventually became a moneylender, borrowing from the bank at 20 percent and relending it at 40 percent. To Babu, Kerala's highly educated labor force was a big joke.

"Come and see how to generate unemployment," Babu said wryly, "Kerala, the development model!" He continued: "We produce and then it goes somewhere else to be processed and comes back to us costing so much more. Look at rubber. Kerala produces 90 percent of the rubber in the country, but none of it is processed here. It is all exported to the factories in Rajasthan. We sell it for 50 rupees a kilo, and it comes back to us in the form of rubber products that cost twenty times the cost of raw rubber. In Rajasthan the workers will take 7 rupees, whereas in Kerala you would have to pay 50–100 rupees per day. We, the educated labor force of Kerala, can't understand how they can accept that kind of money. We mock them, but at least they have jobs. We don't."

If Kerala continues to be unable to attract new investment, the state's revenue deficit, which has quadrupled in the past ten years, will continue to grow. Trying to maintain progressive pension funds and social services without an accompanying increase in investment revenue will surely become unmanageable. For many villagers the fact that all their products, from milk to electricity, have to be imported from neighboring states has made life very expensive in this supposed land of plenty.

⚙

My weeks in Kerala were fast, confusing, exhilarating. My initial image of Kerala's physical beauty and progressive history and social traditions was accurate, but as we traveled throughout the state, I felt increasingly uncomfortable about singing Kerala's praises as a complete development success. Yes, there was no question that political awareness was high, that health care was good, that villages were cleaner. Coffee shops in Kerala's big cities were filled with both the young and old, arguing over the latest political events. In the development projects I visited, people were banding together to fight alcoholism and environmental destruction, to improve consumer awareness and to combat various forms of social inequality. Walking down the streets of Trivandrum in the early morning cool, I would see rows of young men sitting on the steps of the closed, shuttered shops, reading newspapers. All boys and girls were in school. People seemed to understand the need for hygiene and small family size.

Yet there is another side of Kerala that is rarely reported to the outside world. In this Kerala, unemployment, lack of fulfillment and unhappiness have resulted in hopelessness. In this Kerala, it is estimated that a suicide attempt is made every fifteen minutes, and that half of these attempts are made by young people between the ages of eighteen and thirty. In this Kerala, women (who we may imagine have a good life here) account for two-thirds of all suicide attempts, and at least half of these suicidal woman are spouses of alcoholics. Suicides in Kerala account for 50 percent of all suicides in India. In this Kerala, liquor sales have risen 200 percent in the past decade and a half, outstripping the population growth of 17 percent in that same period. Half of the alcoholics in Kerala are between the ages of twenty and thirty. Like suicide, alcoholism appears to be a young person's problem.

ॐ

Many of the Keralites I met were wonderful lyricists, idealists and believers. Yet, it was these same people who brought the other side of Kerala from simply depressing facts to real struggles. These believers, with their convictions in social justice, showed me most clearly that there was still much to be done in Kerala. To rest on the laurels of past success and ignore Kerala's present challenges would be a sure way to wipe out all the state's social gains.

In Idduki village I sat on the covered porch of my host family's house with our next-door neighbors. We watched the sheets of rain from a fierce storm blow in sideways and batter the long skinny trunks of the coconut trees that lined the property. In the lovely, silent aftermath of the furious rain, Basil, the neighbor's seventeen-year-old son, sang us beautiful Malayalam *kavitas* (poems) about the destruction of the environment, the cutting down of forests, the extinction of wildlife species.

In Balaramapuram, three socially committed twenty-five-year-olds had formed the Balaramapuram Weavers Association. Kumar, Rajan and Satish held master's degrees in politics, economics and engineering, but they had decided to come back to their villages and help the weavers rejuvenate their art form. "It is not just about art," Rajan told me intently. Until recently, Rajan had been a *sanyasi*, renouncing the world and its trappings for higher spiritual awareness through a life of contemplation and asceticism. He believed passionately in the virtues of Gandhian practice and in 15th century ways of life, when art and social justice were woven into the very fabrics that were made. "I wish we could go back to those times," Rajan said, "and rely on ourselves and our communities instead of on outside synthetic materials and sources. Those are our roots."

There was also John, a well-known environmentalist and poet-turned–social worker in the small village of Kothamangalam. He described battles in which he had been lashed by the police between his fingers with a *lathi*, a large bamboo stick bound with iron, dragged along a hot tar road and thrown in jail several times. John had been instrumental in organizing people to successfully protest the construction of four major hydroelectric projects in Kerala, and the police, even in this highly educated state, had never approved of his actions. When I asked John whether he thought Kerala was indeed the development model it is often described to be, he smiled.

"Tomorrow," he said, "I will take you to the hills to visit the *adivasis*, tribal people." John wanted to start a small project there to cultivate and sell herbs. The land was fertile and the adivasis desperately needed the money. He wanted my opinion of the project, and, he said, visiting these people would help me answer my own question.

On the bus ride to the hills, I learned that these adivasis used to be considered experts on herbs. Like other tribal groups across the world, they had been forced to assimilate into the larger culture, and therefore lost much of their traditional knowledge. With the rising Western popularity of herbal medicine, however, large multinational corporations have started invading their lands, where many of the herbs still grow naturally, taking away the herbs, packaging and selling them. Naturally, the adivasis got nothing in return. It never even occurred to them that they should.

John and I changed buses several times and finally got off at a small village called Nadukani, a name that means "seeing the countryside." In Nadukani there is an old pavilion. From the top, we could see the lush green fields of the lower Periyar River, marred by the concrete buildings of a hydroelectric project. From there we climbed up a steep path, overgrown with fragrant lemongrass and other wild plants. We tramped through the brush, slipping and sliding on the muddy path, slick from the recent rain. I repeatedly had to extricate my sari from the prickly bushes and wished heartily that I could simply hoist it up to my thighs the way John was doing with his *lungi*, the cloth he wore around his waist. We climbed a small hill and as we descended, I could see the tribal houses, tucked away in the terraced hillside.

About 150 adivasi families lived on these sloping, fertile, mist-clouded hills. Some lucky families had managed to keep their land, but they knew little about how to cultivate it. In places we could see signs of growth—ginger, tapioca, bitter gourd, some cardamom and pepper. In some small flat areas people had tried to make little rice paddies, but it was difficult in this hilly, loose-soiled terrain.

Several men came out to greet John. We were invited into almost every house we passed. The houses were one-room mud huts that seemed small until we saw what many families had lived in until recently—thatched huts, about five feet by twenty feet, that were now used to house cows. In each simple house we were treated with the greatest hospitality, offered heaping plates of tender, small bananas and enormous glasses of sweet, milky tea. In one hut an old man with a beautiful lined face held my hands tightly in his and smiled, ear to ear. When I apologized, explaining that I could understand Malayalam but not speak it, he consoled me graciously: "The shame is not your Malayalam, it is that we don't know English." Even though I knew it was my responsibility to know Malayalam, not theirs to know English, he made me feel immediately comfortable and welcome.

In another hut several people came to talk to us about their situation. The government had set aside grant funds specifically for housing for adivasis, who live in some of the worst conditions in all of Kerala. But when several families had applied for these grant funds, they were told that to receive a 6,000 rupee "grant" from these special housing funds, they would have to pay the government official 4,000 rupees. John was furious to hear this. Turning to me, he asked, "Did you think literacy eliminated corruption?" Turning back to the adivasis, he said vehemently, "Do not pay!" But they shrugged and said, "What choice do we have?"

⚛

John told me that I must meet Sugatha Kumari, an award-winning poet who had become increasingly involved in challenging social disorder and fighting for justice in Kerala. Sugatha's name had already cropped up several times in conversations with friends. According to them, she had championed Kerala's environmental movement, fought for the rights of traditional weavers and almost single-handedly forced the state to investigate the condition of mental hospitals. I went to Athani, the women's shelter in the capital city of Trivandrum that Sugatha had founded, and met Chitra, the director, who arranged a meeting for me.

My appointment was at Sugatha's house one sunny morning at ten o'clock. My rickshaw dropped me at a small metal gate, beyond which stretched a long curved lane. I followed it past a big house to another small cottage. In the quiet morning air I could hear birds chirping and the distant squawk of chickens. My knock on the carved wooden door was answered by a woman who ushered me into a modest, sparsely decorated sitting area.

Sugatha emerged from a side room in a simple blue cotton sari, her long black hair flecked with gray and wet from a recent shower. She grasped my hands tightly and welcomed me. She had just returned, she said, from a sleepless, all-night journey from a remote area where a mining company was destroying a natural rock formation. This destruction would mean the end of fresh, pure water to the nearby villagers. Sugatha was helping them plan their resistance.

Despite the visible tiredness in her face, Sugatha looked ten years younger than her actual sixty years. She had a quiet calm about her. We sat silently for a few minutes, and then, partly to stop myself from staring at her graceful lined face, I asked her why she had chosen to become involved in social issues at all. She put her hands on the sides of her head and closed her eyes. Then she opened them halfway, looked off to the side and said, "Well, I'm a poet, you know. I suppose that means I'm quite mad. That's why I got involved."

Sugatha also had a good example in her father, who was both a poet and former Congressman. She described him as a freedom fighter, an often lonely crusader who tired of politics being about politics and not people. I had heard of him before, a principled man who lived almost as simply as a sanyasi, by most accounts.

As a child, Sugatha had written a few poems about trees and forests, but her real transformation into an environmentalist came in 1979 when she read an article on the planned construction of a hydroelectric project. The project proposed building a dam across the Kunthi River, which runs down the middle of India's oldest natural forest, the Silent Valley. The dam would create a reservoir in the valley to generate electricity; it would destroy the habitat of several rare species of flora and fauna, seriously damage the soil and drainage of the area and involve the cutting of huge numbers of old-growth trees. The Silent Valley project would eventually become one of the fiercest environmental disputes the country had ever known.

Sugatha gathered together a group of her writer friends to protest the construction. Along with others they launched a highly successful movement to preserve the Silent Valley and other natural areas from destruction. Using poetry and emotion, they motivated thousands of people to join the struggle. Sugatha herself wrote a poem called "Maram" (Tree) that lavished praise on the individual parts of the tree—from its tender leaves to its sunken roots—in the same way that one might pray to a temple deity. Ten thousand copies of the poem were distributed throughout Kerala. Ultimately, the dam project was shelved and the Silent Valley preserved. The battle became an inspiration for hundreds of other environmental struggles across the country for the next decade.

Over the years Sugatha and her friends have fought court cases, generated publicity, staged demonstrations, and held meetings. They have won some battles and lost many. "It's all right," Sugatha said, talking about these disappointments. "We need soldiers to fight losing battles as well. There is no question in my mind that people are at least thinking about these issues now, which is so important."

I asked Sugatha to tell me more about Athani, the women's shelter she had founded for "problem" girls and women. Some of the women were recovering from mental illness but could not go home because of the stigma attached to their condition. Others continued to have serious social and psychological problems. Often battered, abused, tortured or raped, the women in the shelter came from all economic classes and castes. One girl from a high Brahmin family had been raped by a family member but managed to keep it a secret. When she got married, she confided in her husband. His family then refused to accept her and threw her out of the house, despite the husband's protests.

Earlier that week, when I had visited Athani, Chitra and I sat with the resident women and girls in a circle on the floor. They sang to me, shy but curious, trying to catch a glimpse of me without looking directly into my eyes. For those few minutes together singing, they seemed to forget their scars. They held hands with each other, their grip so much more precious because of the betrayals they had already experienced in their young lives.

When I asked Chitra whether she felt life was better for women in Kerala than in other parts of India, she shrugged. "How can I look at these girls and say life is better? What good does literacy do for me when I am too scared to go and stand on a street corner by myself in the evening?"

I had heard these sentiments from village women, but I was surprised to hear it from Chitra, who fit my notion of a "strong" Kerala woman. She laughed when I shared this with her, and related a recent experience. She and some colleagues had gone to a conference about women's freedom and rights. They returned to town excited and empowered. At the train station, however, they all stopped and looked at each other. None of them wanted to go home alone without a man accompanying them in the rickshaw. They laughed with sadness at this absurdity.

I asked Sugatha what made her turn from fighting environmental causes to creating the Athani shelter. She settled into her chair and began talking.

"One night, a young man visited me. He told me that young girls from the Trivandrum Mental Hospital, which was located next to a police station, were being taken out at night and provided to the policemen for their sexual pleasures. At that time it was state law that all mental hospitals were closed to the public. Nobody could go in, and girls were not supposed to come out. One can only imagine what the conditions were like inside a place that was never subject to public scrutiny. The girls, naturally, were powerless to protest their treatment or the conditions in which they were made to live. The young man begged me to do something.

"I could not sleep that night thinking about the terrible state of these hospitals. The next day I requested special permission to visit one of the women's wards. The officials allowed me to go in because they knew I was a troublemaker and would create a huge fuss if I was not given permission."

"It was horrible," Sugatha said, her eyes glowing with intensity, her face rid of its previous tiredness. "There were rows of single cells, just five feet by ten feet. Four or five women had been crammed into each cell. In the corner of each was a small latrine pit. Because the girls did everything in the cell, the floor was covered with excrement and urine, mixed with rice droppings. Most of the women, young and old, were completely naked, with matted hair and blank, wild eyes. I walked in and felt sickened. I looked down and saw, in the middle of the room, a body lying there. It looked like a dead person, so frail and thin, completely naked. It was an old woman, maybe about seventy years old. The woman opened her eyes and looked at me. In Malayalam she said, 'The children are hungry.' First softly, then louder and louder, she repeated the cry. As she did, other women in the cell joined in, until the whole row of cells was filled with the plaintive cry of hunger. Tears streamed down my face. I put my hands over my ears to shut out the screaming and ran out of the room to the administrators and doctors. I screamed in anger and sorrow to them over the condition of these women. 'Treat them like human beings,' I pleaded. 'You treat your animals better than this.'"

At this point in the telling, Sugatha stopped, visibly moved by reliving the incident. "'Stay out of it,' they told me."

I turned my head so she would not see the tears that had collected in my eyes. We sat in silence for a few minutes, and then she began to speak again.

Sugatha went home that evening after visiting the hospital, and once again called together her activist friends who had helped in the Silent Valley fight. In the beginning, they were dubious about getting involved in a completely new area. But Sugatha was insistent. "We've seen it now, we know about it, we cannot walk away." In the end they agreed to form an organization called Abhaya (Athani's mother organization), whose goal would be to clean up the mental hospitals.

The activists then began their familiar process of organizing. They involved students and doctors across Kerala. They filed court cases, met with political leaders, wrote letters to the Prime Minister. They joined forces with the Naxalites (the Communist Party of India— Marxist-Leninists), the Gandhians, the environmentalists and anyone else who would come along. They used their contacts with journalists to get as much publicity as possible.

Eventually, the Health Minister requested that Sugatha visit all the hospitals in the state, to recommend and to help implement changes. One of the first changes she instituted was to open the hospitals to the public. The single-cell system was abolished, and women were clothed and fed properly.

While she was involved in this work, Sugatha saw the plight of women who continued to have serious social and psychological problems, no support to manage them and nowhere to go once they left the hospital. From this knowledge, she formed Athani. Abhaya had also recently built a new mental hospital, which was inaugurated by the then Vice President, now President, of India, K. R. Narayanan. It was a beautiful airy place with high ceilings, situated on eight acres of land. Many of the girls work cultivating plants, vegetables and flowers.

When it was time for me to go, Sugatha told me she wanted to introduce me to her children. We walked to the other house on the compound and talked with her son and daughter-in-law for some minutes. They offered me a ride back to my uncle's house where I was staying, which I readily accepted. As I climbed into the car, Sugatha took my hands in hers and said quietly, "I do not think we are taking the right road to development. We are imitating the rich countries in the wrong way."

Listening to Sugatha moved me tremendously. She possessed a simplicity that belied the role she had undertaken as a powerful spokeswoman for the environment and later, for the state's poor and displaced people. Her measured attitude to success and failure highlighted her strong grounding in her identity and life's work. But more than anything, I saw in Sugatha elements that I sought in myself: roots in her community, a community that she fought for with her passion and her talent, a community and environment that she knew intimately.

❀

Viji returned to Trivandrum that evening. The next morning, we woke up at 5 a.m. to go to the temples. The air was fresh and clear, and city life had started a couple of hours before. We went first to the Amman (Mother) Temple, one of few temples dedicated to women deities. There, instead of cracking coconuts for an offering as is typical, we lit firecrackers ("boom" cost 1 rupee, "boom-boom" cost 2 rupees). We left our shoes in the rickshaw and walked into the compound, the wet sand crunching under the soles of our feet. There were men in the temple, but it was filled with carvings of goddesses. In the center a beautiful gold-plated figure of Shakti, a form of Shiva's wife Parvati, was framed within an arched entranceway lit with small candlewick flames. We held out our hands for the holy coconut milk, drank it and then sprinkled the rest on our heads. We smeared sandalwood paste on our foreheads and talked in the dusky cool temple about how nice it was to find a temple devoted just to women goddesses, where even men prostrated themselves in front of the goddesses.

Next, we went to the famous Padmanaswamy Temple. Closed to non-Hindus and foreigners, it is inside an old fort and is a beautiful example of typical Dravidian architecture, with its cascading layers forming a triangle with a flat top. Even at six in the morning, the shops lining the street up to the temple were open. Tour buses carrying pilgrims from other states had arrived. The temple tank, a concrete square filled with water and surrounded on all sides by steep steps, was beginning to fill up with people bathing themselves to ensure they were clean prior to entering the temple.

I was stopped at the temple entrance, because of my *salvaar kameez*, the traditionally North Indian dress of long tunic and balloon pants, now worn throughout India. I was told that I had to wear a *veshti*, a piece of cloth normally worn by men, tied high under my chest to cover my trousers. A little annoyed but mostly amused that the salvaar kameez, which left no skin except the face and hands uncovered, was considered not modest enough for the temple, I rented a veshti in a small concrete room just off the temple, where I left my bag and camera.

Viji and I walked into the room that contained the sanctum sanctorum, the innermost room holding the famed sleeping Padmanaswamy, an incarnation of Lord Vishnu, one of the Hindu trinity along with Brahma and Shiva. (Vishnu is also called the Pervader, known for the three giant steps with which he claimed the entire universe.) A temple Brahmin pointed me in the direction to gain access to the inner room, but it cost 2 rupees. I did not go; I have never liked the idea of paying to see God up close. Instead, I stood on a small platform with huge crowds of people. Eyes closed, I was pushed and pulled with the crowd, enveloped in the smell and heat of bare-chested men and sari-clad women stuck together in devotion. Heady from this experience, I exited the platform. As I left the room, I saw a man near my left shoulder pull his arm and back away from me. He had twisted his entire body so that he would not touch me, and he was looking at me with a mixture of fear and contempt. I wondered what I had done to him. When I asked Viji, she shook her head and said, "He must be a high-class Brahmin who considers you impure because you are a woman. And especially since it is Saturday, the holy day, they are supposed to remain very pure."

I realized that it had been naïve to think that in literate, politically aware Kerala, such an incident would not happen, that somehow the people here would know better than to fear women and their "pollutive" aspects.

ॐ

I took the train back from Trivandrum to Cochin. On one side the black, pock-marked cliffs of the Western Ghats rose starkly out of rich green forests. Along the roads rubber mats were strung out to dry on clotheslines. Pineapple trees with their silvery spiked leaves were planted in patches between rice paddies in the undulating land. Above us, clouds with pinkish hues hovered over small fields of tread rubber set next to old stone houses, some with curved arches, others with gleaming wood trim. And then, out of nowhere, rose a cliff of red sandstone in the distance that sucked in the sun and reflected it out again.

The train entered the area of Kerala's backwaters, the long narrow channels of waterways that were the traditional means of transport. Here on the winding rivers, long boats with fishermen continued as they had done for decades, maybe centuries. Here was traditional life: a bare-chested old man in a white lungi threw out his nets expertly; a village woman squatted on her haunches next to the river, scrubbing her brass pot; a group of youngsters splashed each other joyfully with water. Here on the riverbanks, the coconut trees that lined the banks had been beaten down by rain and wind, prostrating themselves in front of their neighboring trees. Rice paddy after rice paddy gave a sense of stretching to eternity, of tranquillity and certainty.

At the top of the river, I could see leaves and branches being swept along, almost skimming the water like a helicopter about to take off. The river seemed placid, but there was clearly a strong undercurrent. Like Kerala, it was smooth on top and murky underneath.

I was still proud of my state for what it had achieved, proud that its history included the Nayar matrilineal system, high literacy rates and good public health care. At the same time, however, I had seen the pitfalls in assuming these factors alone would assure happiness and fulfillment. The danger in holding Kerala up as the exemplary development model is that people may forget to look at what still needs to be done, to recognize that advancing on certain fronts will naturally bring another set of issues and problems that need to be addressed.

Sugatha and John and countless other inspiring Keralites had offered proof of Kerala's billing as the most developed state in India, but they also took this reputation away in the same breath. Happiness is not simply about good health and literacy, although those are critical components. It is about meaning and purpose, about being able to contribute. Education combined with lack of opportunity is a deadly combination. It is hope for the future and despair for the present, all wrapped in one.

Modern Women

My mother says she fell in love with Bangalore in 1955, when she attended college there. She decided then that she would some day retire to Bangalore—which she did three and a half decades later when she and my father decided to leave Singapore and return to India.

Bangalore today bears little resemblance to the city my mother lived in and describes, the Bangalore of 1955. Once named the Garden City for its beautiful trees and gardens, Bangalore is now known as the Silicon Valley of India. Computer companies, young professionals and multinationals with executives seeking bearable climates have flocked to the city. The tremendous economic boom it has experienced since 1990 gave it the dubious honor of being the fifth fastest-growing city in the world in 1995. On a practical level, this meant a rise in residential property prices of 30 to 40 percent in just the six months prior to my arrival, with an average three- or four-bedroom apartment in a good part of town easily costing the equivalent of $350,000. In keeping with the new emphasis on luxury items and international tastes, up sprouted Kentucky Fried Chicken, McDonald's and Pizza Hut, modern supermarkets with imported goods from Europe and America, glitzy pubs and bars and chic exercise clubs.

To me, unchecked growth has robbed Bangalore of its charm. Infrastructure has not kept up with growth, and new buildings and housing developments have been designed in haste and without giving respect to the already existing graceful architectural lines. Bangalore's famed natural beauty is now visible only in pockets like Cubbon Park, and the air—depleted of its oxygen—is thick with construction dust and diesel fumes rather than the scent of the city's supposed plentiful flowering trees. I found it most ironic that this supposedly modern city, housing the headquarters of some of the largest multinational computer companies, still has difficulty maintaining functioning power and telephone lines, much less providing internet access. The advanced work of the computer industry, carried out in Bangalore but exported to the rest of the world, seems to have had little effect on its own home place.

⚛

Along with the multinationals and young professionals, Bangalore had become decidedly hip. My newly purchased wardrobe of salvaar kameez, which I had thought would help me to fit in, served more to single me out as old-fashioned and dowdy in Bangalore.

The young women, in particular, were trendy, dressed in blue jeans, tailored jackets and fashionable platform shoes. They rode motorcycles, partied at local stylish restaurants, boldly held hands in public with their boyfriends and worked in prestigious jobs with computer companies, banks and advertising firms. They seemed like the ultimate Modern Women. I reasoned that if they were clearly breaking out of the traditional boundaries of dress and behavior, they would no doubt be challenging the traditional ideologies surrounding the role of women. Naturally, I thought, they would be feminists.

My new friend Meghna was a perfect example. I met her at a play reading in Bangalore. Tall and attractive, with ebony hair that tumbled thickly to her shoulders, Meghna attended the Bangalore Law School, one of India's finest. We met at a popular restaurant one evening and she told me about the kinds of projects she was working on at school: women's issues, children's rights and other human rights issues. We hit it off instantly. Meghna was twenty years old. She felt passionately about issues that had taken me at least five years longer in my own development to commit myself to.

Over coffee, I pressed Meghna to tell me about her friends and colleagues, the young women she went around with and worked with. Were they equally interested in women's issues and social issues? Meghna thought about it before answering. And then, almost in surprise, said, "You know, I don't know. There are a few who think like me, especially the ones I am at college with. But some of my other friends that I have grown up with, I have no idea. We don't talk about these kinds of things that often. Why don't you come and meet them and you can find out for yourself? You could tell us a little about your work and yourself, and ask whatever you are curious to know. It could be an interesting discussion."

I loved the impromptu idea. As we arranged the details, I began imagining what these women might tell me. I began imagining that I might find out what I would have been like if I had stayed in India.

☙❧

I arrived the next Sunday afternoon with cold sodas and snacks at Meghna's friend's apartment. The women came in clusters, spreading themselves out around the room until it was full, a dozen expectant faces looking curiously in my direction. They were middle- to upper-class women, educated in excellent high schools and now studying business, law, arts and engineering in some of India's finest colleges.

They talked generally about women and men, and how they felt women were perceived in the environments in which they participated. Engineering colleges, I was not surprised to hear, were still male-dominated institutions, with about ten males for every four females. "The teachers and other men believe that women are going to get married after college anyway, so it is a waste of time to teach us," said one engineering student. "They think we are not really serious about engineering the way that men are."

It was news to me that many of the elite colleges in India still had different entrance examination standards for men and women. In contrast to any type of affirmative action policies in the United States, for example, Indian men can score 60 percent on an entrance examination and be eligible for admission, while women must score 80 percent.

"It's not just the men and the professors who are to blame," said one woman, after a slight pause. "Women don't want to compete actively with men either. Sometimes when the girls are called on in class, they say they don't want to answer the question. That just fuels the fire. Naturally, the teachers start paying attention to the boys if that happens too much."

"Yes," agreed one of Meghna's law classmates. "There is some internal conflict going on. For example, our mock trial teams, selected on the basis of tryouts, have a ratio of two women to twenty-four men! This is far worse than the actual gender ratio within our college class. Women, who do extremely well on standardized exams, do not even come to try out. I talk about it with my classmates, and we think it is attributable to socialization. What are identified as 'desirable' qualities in an Indian woman are at odds with the 'killer instinct' that one needs in law—maybe even in other professions. Vocal women are termed 'very aggressive' in a negative way. This affects your chances later of getting married and being accepted."

Over my next two years in India, I found I too had to struggle to balance how I expressed myself in Indian society. Having been educated in the West and affiliated in various ways with feminist friends, organizations and causes, I was accustomed to being considered an equal to my husband. In India, I constantly encountered very different assumptions about the respective roles my husband and I should and did play in life. Alternately amused and annoyed, I had to choose my battles. If I felt centered and stable, I could combat hostility with laughter; otherwise, I would have to keep a tight rein on my anger and resort to earnest explanation—over and over and over again, until it seemed tiring and unnecessary to explain any more.

One particularly vocal argument took place almost six months after my arrival in India, in the northern Uttar Pradesh hill station of Mussourie. Alan had joined me by this time. It was winter and the air was so cold it made my nose numb, red and drippy. We lived in a sprawling British remnant of a house, with high ceilings and no heat other than the fireplace in the living room. We would wake in the morning to frigid air, so cold that I could not expose any uncovered parts of my skin to its clutches. Clothed in a heavy bathrobe and covered with flannel sheets, I would pull my computer into bed to work until it warmed up outside. Alan, who has always excelled at cooking breakfasts, would take to the kitchen with some gusto and fix omelettes stuffed full of fresh vegetables from the market. He would serve these to me in bed with a steaming cup of coffee. One day, Pandey-ji, one of the men from the organization with which we were working, came in to find Alan in the kitchen and me in bed with my coffee and computer. He was horrified.

"This is not correct! Why is *Saab* in the kitchen and *Memsahib* in bed working?" he sputtered, using the Hindi words for *sir* and *madam*.

"I like cooking breakfasts," said an amused Alan. "Besides, my omelettes are much better than Pramila's."

"But have you thought about what you are doing? The woman should be in the kitchen, not the man. If you thought about it, I'm sure you wouldn't do it anymore," wailed Pandey-ji.

Later that day the conversation continued in the car with other members of the organization's staff. The others, who conduct gender-equity trainings in their villages, were both disturbed by and under-standing of Pandey-ji's perspective. Some secretly subscribed to the idea of prescribed gender roles, while others questioned tradition. In the end, though, it was a battle to reconcile their personal lives, which were open to societal comment and pressure, with their own desires to change tradition. One man, we heard later, allowed his sister to be married with a dowry, in spite of his involvement in a vigorous anti-dowry campaign at the same time.

࿐

"How many of you would call yourselves feminists?" I asked the women in the room around me. Silence and shifting around in the seats sig-naled discomfort at the question. Only three women raised their hands: Meghna, her law school classmate and the woman from the engineer-ing college. I registered my own surprise silently. I had wrongly assumed that these well-educated women who were in the top pro-fessional colleges would be like Meghna, fighting for women's issues, self-confident and aware of themselves as women with capabilities outside what society prescribed.

"Why don't you consider yourself feminists?" I asked. The answers came almost instantly, as if they had been sitting and festering inside, churning around until they had to come out in a big rush.

"We don't like what we think of when we hear the word *feminists*," chimed in one woman. "In fact, I almost didn't come today when Meghna told me you were a feminist!"

"Yes, me too," said another. "I thought, 'Oh God, I don't want to go and listen to some female talk about how women are better than men!' I want equal opportunity, but I think the way to get it is to just prove that we can do well in our own fields. Take the opportunities when we get them."

"Feminism is getting on a soapbox," one woman in a mustard T-shirt said.

She was interrupted by Meghna's older sister, who obviously had different leanings than her younger sister: "What are they making a big deal about anyway? Life isn't so bad. A man has to work; a woman has a choice."

The woman in the mustard T-shirt picked up her line again. "Feminists just want to argue about the spelling of the word women. They want to change it to wo-myn, so there is no men in the word! It trivializes the real issues. Why does the spelling of this word matter?"

"Language is important," Meghna argued. "It is part of an internalization process that indicates certain views of gender roles."

"Well, all I can say," replied the unconvinced woman, "is that if I have to do work for women, it would be easier to do it if I were not called a feminist."

⚘

I had known about this schism among women. Feminism is—unfortunately—viewed by many Indian men and women as an "ism" introduced by the West and inappropriate in the Indian context. Those who decry feminism in this way do not know or choose not to remember that if feminism means fighting for women's rights, it is a struggle and a process that has been at work in India in large and small ways since the nineteenth century.

Interestingly, in those days, issues such as women's education, widow remarriage, and abolishing female infanticide and purdah were fought for primarily by men like Iswar Chandra and Reshab Chandra Sen, who led the fights to stop child marriages and other such social practices. Women rarely spoke out at that time, but the few who did were strong, radical reformers and became role models and inspirations to women who would later take up the same causes.

In the twentieth century, the dynamic began to change. Mahatma Gandhi was instrumental in integrating women into the fabric of everyday life, encouraging their economic productivity through the spinning of *khadi*, homespun cotton. During the 1960s, the anti-price, anti-war and student movements led to the creation of autonomous women's groups and the resurgence of women's active participation in social issues. But it was the 1970s that marked the most prominent change in the nature of the women's movement. The National Committee on the Status of Women was established in 1971, and hailed as an historic step. Activist-oriented groups, this time led by women, began to form around specific women's issues such as rape, dowry and wife-beating. These groups were able to bring about some changes, such as the amendment of rape and other laws to deter dowry deaths in 1983. Feminist magazines, literature and workshops proliferated.

Not surprisingly, the movement also began to show signs of fracturing. In 1982, the scholar Nandita Desai described the movement as divided into three primary groups: Those women who wanted only small reforms, termed "bourgeois feminists"; those who blamed only men and the power relations between men and women for women's problems, termed "radical feminists"; and those who believed that patriarchy had certainly played its role own role in keeping women subjugated, but also understood that there were several other oppressed and exploited groups, such as Harijans, tribals and the working poor, who could and should be considered allies of the women's movement. This group was termed "socialist feminists." These groups fought among themselves and with opponents of the movement. While laws were amended and commissions were set up, there was frustration that too little ground was being gained. There were too few successes to celebrate together.

Yet, it was largely out of the growing prominence of women's issues on the political front that even more significant legislative progress has been made in recent years. In the Panchayati Raj Act of 1989, a certain number of seats on village level councils (called *panchayats*) had been "reserved" for Harijans. Then, in 1992, an amendment was added to require that 33 percent of panchayat seats be reserved for women. Hailed by almost all women's groups as an enormous step, Panchayati Raj reservations for women could be a stepping stone for women to take charge not just of their own lives but of those of their communities as well. This is not an easy process, however. In the first stages of implementation many of the women elected to the panchayat have simply remained mouthpieces for their male counterparts. However, as women are given training and realize the power they do wield when they have won an election, they begin to understand that they do not have to listen to the men and can put forth their own priorities and agendas. During my two years in India, I would see for myself this process of change and empowerment occurring with several women panchayat members.

Clearly, the idea that feminism is purely a Western concept is inaccurate. Fighting for women's rights in varied ways, from local level political representation to *sati* (self-immolation) prevention are all part of the fight for women's rights and as much a part of the fabric of India as a democracy as other basic rights. And yet, the belief that feminism is a Western concept has gained popularity because it provides some rationale for classifying feminism as a "non-Indian" idea and therefore appropriate for dismissal. The strong traditions of patriarchy in Indian culture are easily visible; changing those are even more threatening for some than the notion of eliminating caste. "These upper-class women come to our village and they give my wife all kinds of funny ideas about what she should do and what I should do," one man said angrily to me. "What do they know of our situation? My wife never thought such things until they were put in her head."

Touching the very nature of family relationships and hierarchies is a tender area; and more and more feminists are beginning to realize that for there to be any real movement in the women's rights, men *must* be involved. They must support the movement and its goals—without taking it over. Sunara Thobani, the President of the National Action Committee for Women said in a speech some years ago that "women's rights will end patriarchal power relations . . . only if women organize and empower themselves. The best thing men can do is to give the women the space to do it and to educate other men. The actual empowerment must be taken on by women."

I'd had my own battles with my own Indian and American colleagues who got so involved in ideology that they forgot that different women have different needs based on their situations. One particularly acrimonious set of conversations occurred over the place of injectable contraceptives in the contraceptive mix available for Indian women. For many years in the United States women's groups and some foundations have been adamantly opposed to promoting contraceptives that are not "women-controlled." Women-controlled, as the term is used in the West, generally refers to contraceptives that do not affect a woman's hormonal levels and are as temporary as the woman desires. The cry for women-controlled contraceptives is essentially a call for barrier methods (condoms and diaphragms) and a call against hormonal methods (primarily injectable contraceptives and Norplant, but sometimes including the pill). The concern over hormonal contraceptives (particularly injectables and implants) arose very legitimately over the abuses by governments and medical practitioners in the use of these contraceptives without informing women clients of the associated risks, and without proper procedures and follow-up care. In these cases, women became, once again, simply objects of another's decisions, forced to relinquish control of their own bodies to others.

I had readily accepted this Western definition of women-controlled methods—until I began talking with village women in India. Then I realized that the very definition of "women-controlled" needed to be discussed. Who was doing the defining? If the definition was developed by middle-class Western feminists, did it apply to poor,

rural women in India? What if they were to develop their own definition of women-controlled contraceptives? Would it be the same?

Women in America, and now many middle- and upper-class
women in India, have been imbued with certain rights and independence of thought. For these women, telling a man that she will not
have sex with him if he does not use a condom is not only imaginable,
but acceptable, because of the power and gender relations that exist
within those geographic and class contexts. Not so with village women
in India. Telling their husbands to use a condom is unimaginable, they
told me in several focus group discussions around the topic. Some
methods, like diaphragms, that required cleaning with water (a scarce
resource) and insertion prior to intercourse, were impractical as well
as unavailable. But most of all, these women made clear, they did not
have either the power or the emotional certainty to force their husbands to wear condoms or to accept their wearing diaphragms. "Give
us the injection," they would say in village after village I visited. "At
least that way, he will not know, and I can be protected from having
another baby if he forces himself on me."

For them, I realized, injectables were considered the women-
controlled method: The women could choose when to use them, they
could control their own fertility in the privacy of their own homes
with a single injection and never have to tell their husbands.

Obviously, the ideal situation would be one in which Indian
women have the range of birth control choices that exist in America,
where men and women together share the responsibilities of decision-making and prevention. But until that point, India's village women
also deserve to have their needs respected, needs that may be very
different from the needs that upper-class women living in Western
society perceive.

⚙

The conversation among the women in the apartment had turned from
feminists to that week's news that superstar boxer Mike Tyson had
been indicted in the United States for raping a woman. It surprised me
again that the room was divided in their opinions of this event.

"Women should be prepared for what comes if they wear those sorts of tight clothes," said one woman dismissively.

Meghna was horrified. "So women don't have the right to wear what they want?" she growled. "Why shouldn't men be responsible for controlling their lust?"

"Okay, she should wear what she wants," said the other, not giving up, "but why did she go with Mike Tyson in the first place?"

"So, do you condone wife-beating too?" Meghna asked, sarcastic and visibly annoyed.

"Well," said the other woman, "if a woman is educated, she should be able to get up and walk out of a marriage. If she's not willing to help herself, there is nothing we can do about it!"

I tried to stop myself before speaking but failed miserably. To Meghna's delight, I mounted a long lecture that clearly revealed my biases, which I had been suppressing until then. I cited the statistics that prove that violence against women spreads across classes and castes; that often women, even if they are educated, have never had to provide for themselves and are afraid that they won't be able to do so; that economic self-sufficiency for a single woman is difficult to achieve in India; that if she does leave, society heaps disrespect on her and she becomes a "fallen" woman, free game for other sexually aggressive men.

My preaching fell only on the ears of the small converted group of two or three women. The others tried unsuccessfully to hide the skeptical looks on their faces.

I ended my speech to silence and quickly moved to another subject. One of the women said she would like to discuss marriage. "We've already talked about bondage!" joked another.

The room quickly came to a general consensus that a job came first, then love. Few planned to marry before twenty-seven or twenty-eight, and the majority felt they would have a "love" marriage rather than an arranged one. A few women told me they expected to have arranged marriages. One was clearly comfortable with this idea, and another was resigned to it but not necessarily unhappy. "A love marriage doesn't guarantee that the guy is any better than in an arranged marriage," she said. "In an arranged marriage, everything is taken care of for you. Family, background, and so on is all going to be compatible."

The law school student shook her head. "It makes me very uncomfortable to hear that. It can't be that everything is taken care of. I feel that in an arranged marriage, one stays in the marriage or does certain things one wouldn't do otherwise because of pressure, all the contact between the families and communities."

"Yes, but at least the boy is a known evil," shot back the other woman. The women began speaking incredulously of the sister of one of them, who recently agreed to marry a man she had only met the day before.

As they spoke, I thought about the discussions I'd had over the years with my mother about arranged marriages. Her marriage to my father was arranged, but she has always told me it was her choice; this was her way of saying that the arranged marriage system also had choices built into it, at least in her case. My grandfather sent my mother's picture to my father in response to a matrimonial ad that my father had placed. These ads are still common today, and often occupy many pages of both local and national newspapers. My father came to meet my grandparents and my mother. Things went well, my parents tell me laughing, well enough that they managed to sneak away and meet alone in a café without my grandfather's knowledge. "I needed one more meeting to decide," says my mother. "Then we knew." My parents say they fell in love over the next year, through their love letters and the poems they wrote to each other. In some ways, perhaps their arranged marriage was more of a love marriage than many so-called "love" marriages today.

My mother, somewhat defensively, also tells me that arranged marriages have their own benefits: "You don't expect as much. It's not like you are floating on clouds and then have to come down and see that your idol has feet of clay, that he burps and farts and snores. After all," she says, "in America, with all your love marriages, you have a 50 percent divorce rate. People expect that marriage is perfect because you fall in love. But you still have to live with the man day to day. It can't possibly be perfect forever. In arranged marriages, we're prepared for this."

I think my mother feels that she has to defend arranged marriages, but she also spends much of her free time talking to battered and abused women who are trying to leave their marriages. I know she understands that staying in a marriage is not the ultimate indicator of happiness. At the same time, I think she is right that often we in America, buoyed by the idea that we can "have it all," want exactly that in marriage, and all the time. During a down time, we can become like kids who have spent so much time in their childhoods being entertained by various mechanical gadgets that they cannot entertain themselves. In America we are able to bail out of marriages much more easily, partly because we have the freedom to do so.

Neither of my parents ever pushed my sister or me to accept an arranged marriage. After asking and receiving my sister's permission, they arranged one or two meetings with Indian men that ended with just that one meeting. Eventually, my sister married an American Jewish man she had dated for almost ten years, and my parents were thrilled that she had found someone with whom she would be happy. In addition to genuinely liking my brother-in-law, they also liked his family and their emphasis on maintaining close family ties with immediate and extended families. Of course, as part of the bargain, they had to face the shocked whispers of their friends that their daughter was marrying a "foreigner." Years later, my parents snickered when many of these very same friends bragged about their children's marriages to Americans, Australians and Brits.

The group conversation around me was jumping from subject to subject. First, caste (only one woman said her parents were concerned about caste) and then contraception (all of them said, with embarrassment about the subject, that they would rely on their partners to provide the contraception). The discussion petered out naturally. I thanked them for participating, and they in turn thanked me for "giving them so much to think about." After the meeting, Meghna and I lingered. She rolled her eyes at me and apologized. She and I had both found she was far from representative of other women of her age or situation.

Back at my parents' house I brooded over this group discussion. These young women had been as lucky as I had been, given opportunities that allowed them to make choices beyond the norm and to develop themselves as individuals regardless of gender. I had expected, then, that they too would have a higher level of sensitivity to the plight of women, and be more concerned and active in working for gender equality, like Meghna was. Yet only a few of them acknowledged how their credentials, education and status protected them from much discrimination. The rest seemed almost unsympathetic to the issue of injustice against women, or at least unwilling to identify themselves with any struggles against these issues for fear of where it would place them on the societal acceptance screen.

Perhaps equally disturbing was the ease with which they had adopted the outer trappings of modernity—dress, careers, and to some extent, romantic notions of love and marriage. And yet, it seemed that for these women, this was as far as the "modern" thought went. They appeared as unlikely to challenge some of the traditional notions of women's place as some men I had met.

This had been no scientific focus group that yielded representative results, I recognized. But I could not deny the disappointment I felt to see the women whom I had thought would be at the forefront of the fight for women's status still struggling to break out of those old molds themselves. At the same time, perhaps I should not have been surprised.

The idea of *rights* in general, not just women's rights, is a concept that has its own struggles with other Indian cultural concepts of *duty* or *responsibilities*. In the West, individual rights are of primary importance. In the modern Western world, individual rights have often taken precedence over more traditional ideas of responsibility to families and community. The practice, for example, of putting parents in a retirement home when children and family exist to take care of them is incomprehensible to most Indians (although by the time I left India, several of these homes had begun springing up in larger cities). Discomfort to an individual in terms of physical space, financial difficulty or need for emotional independence is rarely considered adequate reason in India to shirk one's primary responsibility to take care of one's family. Oppressiveness, though, can also be well hidden under the guise of responsibility, often paralyzing healthy expressions of individual self.

Along with this contradictory mixture of rights and responsibilities add the sensitive nature of changing the role of women in society. It is threatening not just to the men who must live with the changes but also to the women who must carry them through, internalize them and be ready to be shunned by the part of society that refuses to change.

The young women I had met may not have wanted to classify themselves as feminists, but in grappling with issues of identity as women, they were fighting and would continue to fight their own small and large battles to redefine the place of women in Indian society. They would continue to struggle to create a space for themselves that was out of the box of the traditional Indian woman and yet not so far out that they would be marginalized by the center of society. The meeting had been a powerful reminder that in India the majority still believes in certain roles for women, even for educated women. Within that framework the woman's right to make choices exists, especially in the cities, but the choices themselves are still dictated by societal traditions and norms. Most difficult for me to hear, however, had been that perhaps even many educated Indian women—as much as Indian men—still subscribe to those norms.

I was reminded of the words of Kabir Das, the great Indian poet, words I would find appropriate for so much of what I was to encounter in India: *Dhire-dhire re mana, dhire sab kuch hoi; Mali sinche sau ghada, ritu aye phal hoi.* Go slow o mind, things take their own time; The gardener pours a hundred pots of water, but fruits come only in the season.

Rules

I arrived in Lucknow, the capital of Uttar Pradesh, on July 4, 1995. Thousands of miles across blue oceans, Americans were celebrating Independence Day: the right to life, liberty and the pursuit of happiness.

In Lucknow, it was 40 degrees Celsius (104 degrees Farenheit). The heat was suffocating, wrapping its big, moist hands around my body, squeezing me like a sponge until little drops of perspiration oozed out, creating a prison cell, a sauna for which there was no door and no temperature control. As Americans lit fireworks and drank beer, Lucknow's poor shrank from the sun. The lucky ones found space and slumped on the cool tile floor of the Lucknow train station, while the rest huddled in tea shacks along the road or crouched on uncovered pavements under their own unfurled checked turbans, which they had flung up like tarpaulins over their heads.

My train from Delhi had clattered along the tracks to Lucknow, through land that had been stretched dry and flat into the distant horizon, through the vast expanses of northern India, into the country's most populated state, Uttar Pradesh. As if in a messy playroom, odd tidbits were scattered throughout the land: haystacks, mud huts with rounded tops, a plaster statue of someone holding an Indian flag.

I had hurtled into the heat wave from the beautiful beaches of Kerala and the cosseted environment of my parents' modern Bangalore apartment. Now, here in this miserable heat, I wondered, Why? My friends and family in Bangalore had asked me the same thing, but I had not listened. I was absolutely convinced that my journey required me to leave familiar and comfortable surroundings for those that were the opposite. I felt added pressure to start this process because in three months, my husband would join me, dramatically changing my experience. I was now able to blend in as an Indian woman, but with my six-foot-two-inch American husband, I would no longer.

Before winning the fellowship that brought me to India, Alan and I had decided together that we wanted to spend most of our time in North India. Part of this decision was driven by language. Hindi is the most widespread of languages, although it is still only spoken by about 40 percent of the population. Hindi is also the language of the most impoverished states, where the issues of development and social justice that I wished to examine would be most pronounced.

Uttar Pradesh, the northeastern border of which forms the curve into which Tibet and part of Nepal are nestled, seemed the right choice. With its population of approximately 140 million, U. P. is equivalent to the fifth largest country in the world. The people in this "cow belt," as the area is commonly known, are predominantly poor farmers who are sandwiched next to each other in a fight to eke out a living from small swatches of land, or more commonly, as laborers on other people's land. The state is topographically diverse. It contains enormous distances of flat Gangetic plains as well as some of the country's highest mountains. Religiously, it is known for its pilgrimage sites, such as Varanasi and Hardwar, which lie along the banks of the sacred Ganga Ma, or Mother Ganges, as the river is called.

Lucknow was as good as any place to start. People spoke *shudh* (pure) Hindi here, and it was a relatively small city with some remnants of charm from its days as the capital of Avadh (or Oudh, as the British called it). During its golden time, Avadh churned out wonderful artists and poets, and its capital was an important center of Shi'a culture and Islamic law. The Avadh rulers built stunning monuments of sandstone, complete with minarets and ornate carvings, many of which stand in crumbling ruin today but still provide a sense of the city's splendid history and culture. The Muslim Avadh rule ended in 1857 with final capitulation to the British.

It had sounded romantic, the buildings, art and culture. But now, here in Lucknow in the middle of this heat wave, I began to think I had made a terrible mistake.

People had always told me that South and North India were like two different countries. I had nodded, as if I understood. But it was only when I lived in Uttar Pradesh that I saw the fault line that lies between the vast expanse of India south of the Deccan Plateau and the even greater space of India north of it. The month I had spent in Kerala villages had lulled me into forgetting that economic poverty is always relative. The South Indian woman may be relatively poor compared with her North American counterpart, but she is rich, very rich, compared with her North Indian equal.

Uttar Pradesh, unlike Kerala, is far from being hailed as a development model. It is not a unique experiment, neither successful nor even hopeful. The state houses a fractious and brimming population, is replete with volatile caste and religious politics and is tragically flush with economic poverty. Like most of India, 70 percent of the population live in villages.

When I first arrived in Lucknow, I saw poverty spread out, deep and thick and sticky. As I put a foot out to test its composition and texture, this poverty caught me and pulled me in. And I fell, spinning downward, seemingly powerless to interpret what I saw, to convert it into anything but an immediate reaction to my surroundings.

It began, my despair, on my arrival in Lucknow with the oppressive heat. It continued when I checked into my depressing concrete box at the government-operated Gomti Hotel, with its two single beds, ragged brown carpet, rickety laminated closet and the family of roaches that lived around the bathroom drain. It gradually crescendoed as I stepped through pile after pile of litter and rot on the streets, inhaled that odd mixture of garbage odors, street food and stale human sweat, and tasted my own salty fear as it poured out through my pores and rolled down my face onto my lips.

But it was the pigs that put me over the top. They lived in packs near garbage piles. They nosed their way through the waste, snorting and snuffling and streaking themselves with dirt and grime. They produced babies by the dozen and slept piled on top of one another. There was no beauty here, no joy, no hope.

Extreme poverty and filth were only one part of the problem; the other was my reaction to it. I was an Indian, here to prove my Indianness, but I was unable to control my despair, even disgust—just the reaction I had often silently criticized in others. I acknowledged my feelings with guilt, for the Indian "I" was not supposed to feel these things. How could I possibly tell others I felt this way, when it would only reinforce their often stereotypical notions of India?

Seemingly small things, like transport, became moral issues for me. In the South, public transportation came mostly in the form of buses, motorized three-wheelers or auto-rickshaws. These auto-rickshaws had a motor in front; the driver pulled up on a chain crank, and with a deafening example of serious noise pollution, one was off. Lucknow's public transportation system included tempos, a slightly more earth-friendly version of auto-rickshaws. Tempos, essentially minivan versions of the auto-rickshaw, could cram in ten to fifteen people and plied only set routes. But in order to go quickly to a destination not on a tempo route, the only choice was a cycle-rickshaw.

The motor in a cycle-rickshaw was a human being, made of flesh and blood and susceptible to heat and cold. He (I never saw a female rickshaw driver) cycled his passenger along in a carriage that contained a shiny bright vinyl seat, made for small Indian bottoms and tipped slightly forward in an aerodynamic stroke of genius. This tilt forced passengers to sit perched on the front end of the seat, arms stretched to the side, ready to take a dive, feet firmly pressed into the rusted tin bottom of the rickshaw.

Cycle-rickshaws came to symbolize the extent of my discomfort with my status compared to those around me. While my Indian friends easily flagged rickshaws and haggled for a rupee cheaper price, I stewed in confusion. Should I walk or ride? I could not get comfortable with being pulled by a man old enough to be my father, his bare back covered with little rivulets of sweat glistening in the middle of muddy brown banks of back expanse. As he pulled, I was supposed to sit in my seat with an umbrella pulled up over the carriage to protect me from the sun. He would cycle up a hill, this old man, painfully slowly. And I, tempted to jump out of the rickshaw and walk, was glued to my seat by the knowledge that doing so would be a loss of face for the driver, an acknowledgment on my part and his that he was too old and too unfit to carry my body up the hill. What obstinate pride it was, and how I both respected and hated it. My compensation was to pay more than had been agreed on, but even this felt as though I was cheapening his value by putting an extra five-rupee price on his effort.

For a while, I stopped taking cycle-rickshaws and walked everywhere, arriving at places sweating profusely and having to explain to my disbelieving Indian friends that I just could not take cycle-rickshaws. For the most part, they laughed at me and told me I had lived too long in America. Finally, one friend, a social worker for Oxfam, convinced me that I was simply assuaging my own guilt but I was not helping the poor old man on the rickshaw who needed the money and was willing, even proud, to do his work.

In an effort to manage the overwhelming confusion that I felt in Uttar Pradesh, I began to make rules. One area that I forever made rules about was my response to beggars. Beggars in India, particularly in larger cities like Bombay, Delhi and Lucknow, are embedded into the pavements, stuck to the floors of train stations, strung to traffic lights where cars must stop. In Lucknow's old city of Aminabad, an enormous mazelike market with different alleys for different products (pots and pans, petticoats, meat, vegetables) the beggars were everywhere: A girl, not more than eight years old, carried a tiny baby slung over her shoulder like a sack of heavy clothes. The girl's hair was brown straw, a nest of tangled strands. She walked unsteadily in shoes several sizes too big, their soles half off, flapping and slapping the pavement as she walked. A boy, maybe fourteen, leaned against a concrete pillar on the side of the road, a cigarette in the corner of his mouth. His eyes were worn and distant. I could only imagine that it was the nights sleeping in gutters, hitching rides with men who take their payment in unspeakable ways, and the constant struggle to survive that had pulled his skin tight across protruding cheekbones. A woman in a torn, thin sari sat cross-legged, cradling a baby in one arm and pulling lice out of her daughter's hair with the other hand. A blind man wearing a traditional Muslim cap carried a begging bowl up and down a main shopping arcade. He thumped his cane down purposefully but gently, brushing the toes of the *paan* (a tobacco, spice, lime and betel concoction) sellers and the well-dressed fashionable young women on a shopping trip. While walking, he chanted to Allah, the God who will save him from this life when it is time.

Each of these beggars was different, and yet they each had that singular face of poverty, of despair that I came to know in the big cities of India. And I, no matter how I traveled—on foot, or in a car, where they pressed their noses against the tinted window and created little circles of fog—passed them and felt that sharp pain of injustice, of confusion, of uncertainty. What do I do? Do I give or not?

It was both my curse that I had to pass them and my blessing that I could do so. No matter the action I chose—to give or not, to acknowledge or ignore—I would still pass them while they stayed there in that same place, begging until they could afford to move or they were kicked out by the police for littering the street or they could no longer stand the heat or dust or cold or smell.

I made my rules and then broke them. My first rule was that I would only give to the very old and the disabled. I reasoned that there are no benefits for the elderly in India; and if they are too old to work, what are they to do? The same situation exists for the disabled. This rule lasted until I began to understand that many of the disabled have actually disabled themselves so that they can get more money from begging. Begging with a stump instead of an arm is simply more lucrative. And lucrative is important when one is fighting for one's life, a life that no one else values much anyway.

I made my rules because I could not bear to look at someone with nothing and not know what to do about it. But begging was only a subset of poverty, and poverty an incontrovertible part of India. Every time I looked at a beggar, I was forced to think of why it was that the beggar was begging and I was in the position of giving. Rules made me feel that it was okay not to give, because this decision was made according to a rational process. That is, until I realized that for every one of my rules, there was an answer. If someone was desperate enough to cut off a limb to get money, was that not proof enough that they needed the money? And if I did not give to this maimed man, did I really think that would contribute to a decrease in the number of people who disabled themselves? I found that hard to believe.

But what made me most uncomfortable was simply that I could choose. To give or not give was my own personal luxury. My discomfort, I began to feel, was a small price to pay given the magnitude of my privilege, that luxury of choice.

Mark Tully, the well-known BBC reporter based in India, once wrote that whenever his visitors would ask him in a sympathetic voice how he coped with the poverty in India, he would reply, "I don't have to. The poor do." He went on to write about how he sleeps in a comfortable three bedroom flat, while the taxi drivers who live opposite him sleep in their cars in winter or on a rope bed in the summer. And they are the lucky ones.

Living with poverty means sleeping in the huge settlements of shacks crowded next to each other and sandwiched between piles of garbage and the filthy Jamuna River where even fish cannot stay alive. Living with poverty means feeling a tinted car window being raised and with it the skin of your nose, feeling despair when the car moves away, leaving you in the same place, the same empty-handed situation. No, it is not difficult for us middle- and upper-class observers to live with all the poverty in India, because we do not.

The agony and the beauty of living in India is just this: that one is challenged every day to look at life not in absolutes but in relatives. That ultimately, each one of us can understand only who we are as individuals, and perhaps, with great diligence, how we fit into the rest of the world. That we can balance the emotions India brings out only by discovering our own sense of equilibrium, by being willing to use those emotions to go deeper into our souls and psyches rather than the infinitely easier route of ignoring or denying them.

And, so, I would make and break rules until I finally understood that there could be no rules in this game. I could not impose reason where there was none, rational thought where it did not apply. For what rational man would cut off an arm for a few rupees? What reasonable world would put him in this position in the first place?

I ended up giving to people when I felt like it. It was completely capricious in many ways, and in others much more real. I gave to people when I caught sight of something in their eyes, when I was in a good mood, when I was in a bad mood, when I felt it was my duty, when, when, when. I broke down all my premeditated structures and responded only to each single moment. There was truth only in that present.

ॐ

Those months in Lucknow were difficult, and yet this was what I had come to India to experience. That made it no easier for me. I saw despair in everything. I wrote long missives in my journal, trying to release my anger, my pain, my fear. Admittedly, the extreme heat made things much worse, but the fact was that urban North India was stricken with a degree of poverty that I had previously witnessed only in passing, and I had never lived in proximity to it for any period of time. Urban poverty is far more depressing to me than rural poverty, because poverty in urban areas is not just a poverty of economics but a poverty of spirit. People have migrated to cities, dislocated themselves from their communities and support structures in pursuit of dreams, dreams that are then rejected, shredded, mocked. They are left living in slums with only the remains of their ambitions.

One muggy day, I went to visit several of the Lucknow slums with Prabhakar, the founder of Angkur, a youth group that works in slum areas, and one of his collegues, Ranjana. Prabhakar was a charismatic, intelligent young man from a wealthy family. "My parents and brother don't understand what I'm doing with my life," he said to me, with a lopsided grin. "But I won't stop it anyway."

Prabhakar and Ranjana told me that about 40 percent of Lucknow's population live in slums that receive no services from the city. Every so often, just before election time, savvy politicians will come to the slums and promise the residents services in exchange for votes.

The politicians may get the votes, but the slum dwellers rarely get the services.

None of the slums we visited were hopeful, but the last one was unbearable. Pools of dirty, green stagnant water lay next to muddy paths that in the rain must have been impassable. Scores of huts, just five-foot squares, not even tall enough to stand up in, were packed next to each other as tightly as space would allow. Many of these housed families of six and more. Roofs, if the huts even had them, were made of plastic sheets, twigs tied together with rope, any available materials. These were held down with weighted objects—pieces of a broken clay pot, a steel plate, old clothes. Stinking garbage, probably months worth of it, was piled in heaps, now grazing piles for pigs and cows. In front of the slum on the roadside of the main bustling road, there was one water handpump to serve the entire slum population. Here, women and girls were forced to undress in public so that they could bathe. They gathered around the pump as was their ritual, fighting for their turn at the water.

Just across the street was the enormous fancy headquarters of the 20-billion-rupee conglomerate, Sahara International. About twenty feet from the slum, at the road crossing, Sahara had found it in their interests to build a beautiful traffic circle, complete with blooming flowers, a lighted fountain that turns on automatically every night, and a large sign proclaiming "Our *Bharat* (India), our country of which we are so proud."

"We have asked them to support the slums and at least build some more pumps for them," said Prabhakar, noticing the direction of my gaze, "but they refused. They build houses, but not for the poor."

By the time I went home, I was exhausted and sick to my stomach from the day's happenings and sights. I took a long shower, rubbing my body until it was red, trying to erase the memory of that day and feeling guilty for trying to do so.

�❧

To understand life in Uttar Pradesh, it is important to understand a little about caste structure and politics, because despite the claims that many educated Indians make that the caste system no longer exists, I found that caste plays an enormous part in daily living and politics.

Briefly, the Hindu caste system consists of four *varnas*, or levels: *Brahmins*, (members of the priestly class charged with the duties of learning, teaching and performing rites and sacrifices); *Kshatriyas* (the warriors), *Vaishyas* (the tradespeople or merchants) and *Shudras* (the laborers). Untouchables, or *Harijans* (literally, "children of God") as named by Mahatma Gandhi, fall below even these four varnas. Within each caste, there are several *jatis* or sub-castes that vary from region to region.

Caste exists today in a much more structured fashion in the villages than in the cities. One benefit of the new concept of opportunity which has made particular headway in cities is that it implies, even necessitates, mobility within castes. Although there are limits to this mobility (even in cities, it is improbable that one would find a Harijan performing a Brahmin's duties), caste ends up being secondary to survival. If survival necessitates that a Brahmin drive a cycle-rickshaw or a member of the laborer caste work alongside a Harijan, then it will and does happen.

Interestingly, it is the members of the laborer caste who have risen in economic status most quickly in recent years. Jawaharlal Nehru, independent India's first Prime Minister, and the Congress Party's post-Independence land-reform legislation in the late 1950s and 1960s played a big role in this status change. Substantial amounts of land were transferred from *zamindars* (revenue-collectors and later, landowners) to laborers. Today, 20 percent of the land in Uttar Pradesh is controlled by four principal groups who constitute only 15 percent of the state's population. These groups—the *Yadavs, Kurmis, Lodhas,* and *Gujars*—are classified as Other Backward Castes (OBCs), a designation that puts them somewhere "above the Untouchables but in the lower reaches of the caste order of traditional society," according to the Backward Classes Commission of the Central Government.

Many scholars believe that the progress of some of these OBCs has been phenomenal, with many becoming primary players in North Indian politics. Ironically, several of these upper Shudra castes have been as reluctant as the upper-caste Brahmins or Kshyatrias before them to share their newly acquired power with their lower Shudra caste brethren, much less with Harijans.

Harijans, although slowly gaining political power, continue to face both subtle and tangible social discrimination. According to M. N. Srinivas, one of India's most eminent sociologists, "Concepts of purity and impurity have been seen as central to caste . . . in indicating the rank of a jati." Harijans (reminiscent to some degree of African Americans in the United States before the civil rights movement), for example, were not allowed to draw water from an upper caste person's well, to share the same utensils or even to allow their shadows to cross that of an upper caste member. In many temples untouchables were (and still are) prohibited from entering. Untouchables traditionally performed those tasks seen as polluting or dirty, such as cleaning toilets or sweeping streets.

Before going back to live in India, I had been one of those educated Indians who denied the importance of caste in modern India. I grasped at the legal outlawing of untouchability in 1955 by then–Prime Minister Nehru as my ultimate lifeline out of the pools of criticism and disgust that people often unloaded on India for this caste system.

In my defense, my parents had never been particularly interested in caste, and so, to some degree, it truly was out of the realm of my comprehension that such a discriminatory system could be thriving when I hadn't actually seen it in action. Certainly I knew it had existed; my grandmother had told me stories about how their Harijan servants would ring a bell to indicate that they had left the boundaries of the house and that it was "safe" for my grandmother's family to come outside. I had also seen firsthand the contemptuous way that lower caste servants were treated. But somehow in my desire to protect India, I had blocked the possibility that the caste system had been, and in many ways still was, India's socially acceptable form of apartheid, and that either denying it or defending it contradicted the other stands I had taken in my life on discrimination. Going to Uttar Pradesh, however, was an enormous jolt to these notions. Here, caste was alive and well, playing a part in significant and seemingly insignificant ways, weaving itself into the social, political and economic fabric of most of the state's residents.

At a tea stall in the back roads of Lucknow, I once sat next to a well-spoken older man in a rather soiled white *kurta pajama* (tunic and pants). After eyeing me unapologetically for several minutes, he asked me the standard questions about my origins and why I was in Lucknow.

Then, "What caste are you?"

"I don't believe in caste," I said, taking a deep, satisfying sip of my smoke-scented chai. (My answers to this question varied, depending on my mood. Sometimes I said I did not know, which produced disbelieving stares from my partners in conversation. Sometimes, if in possession of a little patience, I would explain that I had left India as a young child and that caste had never been an issue in my family. This also tended to meet with quizzical looks.) And then, looking directly at him, I asked, "Do you believe in caste?"

"No, no," he said, shifting his weight and moving his cane from one hand to another. "Caste is gone, *hai na?*"

Silence followed. Then, leaning toward me slightly and dropping his voice to a loud whisper, he said, "I'm a Brahmin, you know."

Another time, my landlady's house cleaner became very ill and I offered that the woman who helped clean our house would probably be happy for additional work. My landlady almost started in fear.

"No, no, she's a Harijan, you know," she said, her disapproval of the whole situation clearly apparent. "She cannot enter our house as a Harijan."

But despite what I saw over the two years I was in India, I resisted writing about caste for my largely Western fellowship audience. There were three primary issues that contributed to my reticence. First, I felt that discussing my feelings about caste would attract a single-minded focus on India as a socially backward country rather than as a multifaceted, complex, contradictory country that has as much to teach as it has to learn. I feared that criticizing caste would put me in the ranks of the multitude of writers, Indian and foreign, who write simply about the sensational and the negative. I thought that allowing myself to admit that I felt repulsed by the very existence of the caste system would somehow mean that I was not proud of my country of origin.

My feelings about caste were in line with my views that little is black or white in India. Although the system appeared indefensible for the degradation and injustice it seemed to heap on the lowest castes, there were many arguments that the old caste system was like a kinship system, offering security to lower caste members. Madhu Kishwar, one of India's leading feminists, wrote in 1989 that even though strong kinship and community loyalties can have negative effects, "the existence of strong community ties provides for relatively greater stability and dignity to the individuals than they would have as atomised individuals. This, in part, explains why the Indian poor retain a strong sense of self-respect." Other scholars, such as Mark Holmstrom, who studied the unorganized labor sector (generally migrants from the lowest castes) in Bombay, have suggested that caste plays a particularly important role for these workers because the *only* resources they have access to are their caste linkages. These are not arguments for caste in its totality, but they do give voice to some of the ambivalence many Indians feel around categorically judging a system that provided support and connection at the same time that it often discriminated.

The second factor I fell back on as a reason not to speak out against the prevalence of the caste system in India was that I felt (and still feel) that Western society also has its own caste system, although it is not necessarily called a caste system. In America, for example, the economic caste system is legitimized by the supposed equal access by all to mobility within the system. There are caste systems of race, of consumption, of technology and, fundamentally, of ecology. In these systems the ultimate fact is that the rich would never be rich without the poor. I do not mean to argue that the Indian caste system is comparable to these other more subtle discriminatory ones, but simply to explain the inevitable annoyance I would feel when Westerners would condemn the caste system without examining their own society's forms of caste. Once again, intellectually, I understood that this too did not constitute a reason to be silent about the Indian caste system.

The third factor was simply this: I was confused. In dismissing the existence of the caste system before returning to India, I had done quite a thorough job of convincing myself that it no longer existed in any meaningful way. Perhaps it existed in some villages, I had thought, but this was changing in most parts of India; that even where it did exist, perhaps it was not as oppressive as it had been in the past; perhaps the caste system was simply a remnant of the past that bore little relevance to modern India. To then recognize, admit and finally write about the existence of caste and the disgust I felt when I was asked countless times what caste I was, to witness the mistreatment of Harijans and the very acceptance they themselves had of their so-called impurities, to encounter the injustice heaped on these lowest castes and the seemingly endless cycle of misery they must face, generation after generation—this was too confronting. I retreated. I ran, not walked, through the doors of my intellectual luxury shelter. Just as some people might retreat to their five-star hotels from the dirt and grime and filth of India, I was able to do little better when it came to caste. When I started to question, I turned off the questioning. When I felt repulsed by what I saw, I either rejected those feelings or kept them completely quiet. Over my two years, I would ultimately come to understand that little in India is simple or easily categorizable, and that loving India means being able to discuss both her good and bad.

⚛

V. S. Naipaul, the prolific essayist, in his book *India: A Wounded Civilization* described India as a country in darkness, a people who had always been and would always be serfs to someone else: if not the Mughals, the British; if not the British, the rich. I had read Naipaul's book over a decade ago, and it angered me to read a description that was so wholly negative, that accorded no respect to India's achievements, that described people's ability to live in their terrible circumstances merely as a "retreat" into the unshakable certainty of their karma, and that called the poor rural-to-urban migrators "corrupters of the city."

I recently picked up the book again and found myself angered anew by the same things. Yet I also understood, for the first time, the distress Naipaul felt that caused him to make such pronouncements. Naipaul lived outside of India and yet had pieces of India within himself that he could not discard. This gave him an emotional attachment to the country that, by his own acknowledgment, he constantly fought.

The reality of living in India's midst is that there are two ways to describe, for example, the experience of walking through these slum areas where no humans should have to live. One can either move into a frenzy of despair for, even anger at, the slum dwellers and the politicians and all the other "enablers" who have allowed conditions to deteriorate to this; or one can focus on the positive changes that are happening, highlighting instead the courage of the youth group Angkur, the dedication of the school teacher who works despite the fact that the government has not paid her salary in three months, the commitment of the slum residents who sweep the streets that the government refuses to. Either view is valid and yet incomplete without the other. Together, they represent not just the complexity of India, but the murky ways individuals attempt to understand the world, the strange rationality that is used to convince oneself that the world is just when so much inequality exists, the constant desire to seek pleasure and avoid pain.

In India, I could not avoid the obvious connection that often exists between my pleasure and someone else's pain. It is easy to forget this in America, easy to believe that one's actions are independent of anyone else's, easy to trust that those who deserve a good life will get it. Here in Lucknow, however, it was much harder to swallow any of this. My conclusions, rules and beliefs seemed little more than a way of ordering the world—but not necessarily the only way or even the right way.

The Rhetoric and Reality
of Education

About a month after I arrived in Lucknow, I met Nishi Mehrotra, the director of Mahila Samakhya (Women Speaking As Equals), an organization working across Uttar Pradesh to provide alternative education to girls and women. She invited me to accompany her to the town of Karvi to attend the graduation ceremony of thirty village girls and women who had just completed a six-month "life education" course. Karvi is part of the Banda district, one of the poorest districts in the state, lying on the southern border with the neighboring state of Madhya Pradesh.

If Kerala presents one extreme of India's education picture, Uttar Pradesh (along with the Northeastern state of Bihar) exemplifies the other. Uttar Pradesh has a female literacy rate of 25 percent, but even this number is significantly elevated by the higher literacy rates in the state's hill areas (more than 40 percent). In the eastern part of the state, where my husband and I spent most of our time, the female literacy rate hovers just under 20 percent. Even more significant, although 25 percent of females between ten and fourteen attend school, by the marriageable ages of fifteen to nineteen, only 10 percent continue to attend school. By the ages of twenty to twenty-four, barely 2 percent of females attend any school or college.

There is ample evidence worldwide that educating girls and women produces benefits that stretch into a number of areas. For example, literate women are more likely to have smaller families, to educate their own children, and to use their new-found literacy for economically productive enterprises. Yet too many Indian girls are not brought up to believe that education is a basic right. Instead, they and their families believe that education will take away from the time daughters could work inside or outside the home. Because many families in rural India still believe that a girl's only role is to get married and have children, educating girls is perceived simply as a waste of money and often even detrimental to ensuring marriage.

Programs like the one I would be seeing with Nishi, then, represented a critical attempt to bring women of all ages back into the folds of education, to teach them skills that would be useful in the context of their lives and, most important, to give them a sense of self-worth. This sense of self-worth, the educators hoped, would fuel the women's desire and their ability to stand up for their basic rights in communities that may not be supportive of those rights.

ॐ

Nishi and I left Lucknow early in the morning, when the sun had yet to break through the horizon and the night's cool air still lingered. The road from Lucknow passed through the constituencies of past Prime Ministers Indira Gandhi and Jawaharlal Nehru, and its smooth, well-tarred surface reflected the special attention the areas had received over the years. Young men in white *bunyans*, tank top–like undershirts, rubbed their eyes as they made their way to the nearest handpumps to wash their faces. School girls and boys walked along, satchels slung over their heads like bandannas. The sun flashed through the trees like a gentle strobe light, casting its rays on the salt-filled land around us on which few trees, shrubs and bushes could grow.

Just before reaching Allahabad, the first small patch of water appeared, filled with purple water hyacinths. Beyond it, a kidney-shaped pond settled in sandy reclamation land. An array of trees and shrubs helped to prevent the land from flooding. Past this, the road dipped. As we rolled down and then up to the perch in the road, we caught our first glimpse of the great Ganges River. Legend has it that the Hindu gods and demons fought for twelve days over the pot (*kumbha*) that held *amrit*, the nectar of immortality. During this fight

Vishnu ran with the pot and dropped four drops of amrit on earth, making four sacred places (Allahabad, Hardwar, Ujjain and Nasik). At the junction of the Ganges and the Jamuna Rivers, Allahabad is considered the most sacred of the four places. Once every twelve years, a grand festival, the Kumbha Mela, takes place at the Allahabad *sangham* (the confluence of the Ganges, Yamuna and Saraswati rivers), drawing more than ten million people from throughout India and abroad.

The Ganga reached out like an ocean in front of us, its vast expanse of water dominating the scene. Slow cattle grazed in the fields, ambling their way to the water for a drink. A massive bridge, above which were train tracks, spanned the length of the river. To the right, the river took a bend out of sight. Reflecting the lack of rain in these hot Gangetic plains, the Ganga's water level had sunk several feet in the past few months.

We passed Allahabad and the road suddenly changed. Clearly, we had entered the area of no politico's constituency. Dug up into enormous potholes, the road narrowed and broke the dry brown earth around us into two halves. It was like entering T. S. Eliot's "Waste Land," a place "where the sun beats,/And the dead tree gives no shelter, the cricket no relief,/And the dry stone no sound of water." It was harsh, unfriendly territory. Not even bushes softened the unforgiving, unyielding land. One of the hottest places in India that summer, the Banda district had recorded temperatures of 50 degrees Celsius (122 degrees Fahrenheit).

We drove through the fields and entered stone-quarry land. Here, rich landowners hired laborers, men to dig out the stone and women to break it and extract silica sand. We stopped to meet a group of Harijan women who had organized themselves to demand that their single handpump be fixed. It had been broken for months, and they had been walking miles just to get a pot of water. They crowded around us, grabbing our arms with excitement. They pulled out two *charpoys*, rope beds, and we squeezed ourselves on to them.

For their backbreaking labor, they told us, they earned one and a half kilos of cereal (a cost of about 4 rupees, or 12 cents). If both the husband and wife were working, they could earn 10–20 rupees per day. They felt powerless to revolt, they said, because even the land they lived on belonged to their employers. If they were to lose favor with their employers, not only would they lose their earnings, they would lose their houses as well. These houses were made of small remnants of stone, uneven and often insufficient to build walls that stretched higher than a foot or two. The thatched roofs hung low over the stone, forcing the inhabitants to stay bent inside. One woman next to me in a torn blue sari put her head on my shoulder and wept, whispering that her biggest disappointment was that she would never be able to arrange a suitable marriage for her daughter.

Just then, a summer shower began. The women threw up their hands in glee and began singing. One pulled out a drum, pulled her sari over her one blind eye and beat out a deep rhythm. As she played, drops of perspiration combined with rain drops, and her nose ring glinted as she swayed back and forth. They sang with emotion about exploitation and the hardships of their lives. When it was time to go, they hugged me and vowed that they would continue to organize, to fight as hard as they could. As I embraced the last women and children, I found my cheeks wet with tears.

The short burst of rain had stopped. We continued our journey in the blazing sun. Malnourished animals took refuge from the heat under a mahua tree, one of the few trees hardy enough to survive the heat and be useful to the villagers for its flowers, which were dried and made into a local brew. The mahua seed was also used to produce oil for lanterns or cooking in remote places where other oil was not available.

We reached the small town of Karvi in the early evening. The main market strip stretched only a short way. Shops lined both sides of the street, selling the odd luxury item, but mostly essentials: rubber slippers, steel and aluminium cooking ware, school bags, medicines, lanterns and torches. Chewing paan was obviously a popular pasttime— there were four paan shops in a row in one spot. Most of the people on the streets, including the shop sellers, were men. They squatted outside the shops, their soiled, white cotton pajama pants hitched up to their knees, their hand-rolled *beedi*, clove cigarettes, hanging from their mouths, faces screwed into disturbingly vacant stares. They sat pressed against each other, fighting for an inch of the shade from the flimsy corrugated tin shop roofs. Further down, Karvi's cinema compound was filled with people who had come to escape this harshness, just for a few hours, to a world filled with heroes and heroines, wealth and glamour.

Reaching our destination, the Mahila Shikshan Kendra Center, I was welcomed warmly by the students and teachers. *"Namaste, Didi! Aapka pable bar yahan?"* (Hello, sister! This is your first time here?) Women on either side of me entwined their arms in mine and led me over to where children were making models of houses out of mud, delighting in the slimy feel under their hands as they mixed the mud with water. On the ground they had fashioned a map of India with rolled pieces of mud for boundaries.

The preparations for the next day's graduation ceremony were in full force. A big pink-and-white-striped tent had been set up to accommodate all the guests. On large sheets of plastic, black-and-white pictures of the center's activities were displayed. Nearby, women practiced a play that would be performed the next day. The play reenacted the Chipko *andolan*, a spontaneous movement in April 1973 led primarily by village women in Uttar Pradesh to save their forests from being felled. When loggers came, the villagers embraced their trees, making it impossible for the loggers to cut the trees. The movement takes its name from this action—*chipko* means to embrace. Since 1973 hundreds of thousands of villagers across India have started similar movements to save the forests from logging. I have listened to women across India emotionally tell me how important trees are to them. The preservation of trees, they say, is the preservation of a woman's life: "Trees are as precious as our babies," one woman told me. "They provide us with fuel for cooking, fodder for animals, as well as fruit and medicine."

In 1980, the original Chipko movement won a significant victory when then–Prime Minister Indira Gandhi signed a fifteen-year ban on green felling in the Himalayan forests. The movement's success sparked in women's minds the range of possibilities available if women banded together; it inspired women across the country (and the world) by proving that people *would* listen to them and their priorities if they chose to act. Today, Chipko remains an international symbol of local women's power and solidarity.

It was unbearably hot the next morning. The heat seemed to affect only me; the three to four hundred women who had come from nearby villages seemed unperturbed, their enthusiasm at full pitch. They trooped in and sat on mats under the tent, filling it with bright colors and incessant chatter. Some were mothers or family members of the girls and women in the program, some were interested in enrolling themselves, others were simply curious about this big festive *mela* (fair). In some cases, fathers, sons and brothers accompanied their wives or children, but the event remained dominated by the bright saris of the women and girls.

Ceremonies started, first with bicycle races and then various plays, testimonies from the girls, and of course, songs. Songs are an integral part of every gathering in a village; perhaps it is here that women feel they can express themselves freely, for they sing about exploitation and pain and about their hopes and dreams.

One popular song about literacy began: *"Patshallah khula do, Maharaj, mera jia pardne ko chahe."* (Open the school, Maharaj, my heart wants to learn.) A train of women picked up more and more participants as it snaked around the big tent. Girls and women danced in the tent center and on stage, expressing uninhibited joy and gracefully weaving their colorful *dupattas* (the long piece of material thrown across the shoulders on top of a salvaar kameez) through the air.

Fifteen-year-old Kavita sat down next to me. She had pulled her purple sari over her head to acknowledge her respect for her father-in-law, who attended the ceremony. Kavita had been promised in marriage at the age of nine. She would remain with her family until puberty, at which time she would be sent to her husband. Kavita's big brown eyes were bright as she leaned forward in her chair to tell me about her experiences in the program. The words spilled out of her mouth in excitement.

"When I first came, I used to cry all the time. I just wanted to run away and go back home. Now I don't want to go. I've learned so much—about trees and the forest, about food, about the reproductive tract, kidneys, lungs and organs. Did you know your heart is the size of a fist?" she asked excitedly.

Her enthusiasm was infectious. When she stopped for a breath, I asked her how this knowledge makes a difference in her life. On the surface, it could seem that knowing the size of one's heart is nice but not essential.

"*Didi*," she said, using the familiar address of "elder sister" for me, "I didn't know anything before. I was such a fool. I used to just make my dung cakes and cook food. You know, I even used to think that earthquakes were caused by snakes shaking under the ground! Now I know it's because there are big plates under the earth that move and collide with each other. See, we've even modeled it." She led me over to their earthquake model. A big pot filled with water sat on a small stove burner at the bottom of a pile. Atop it, several smaller plates were perched. On top of everything was one large plate. When the water boiled, the smaller plates started to move, colliding with each other and causing the big plate above to shake like the earth's plates during an earthquake.

Kavita and the other girls I spoke to at the graduation ceremony clearly felt empowered by their new knowledge. Chipko became a possibility for them, as did the options for family planning they discussed, or the simple understanding of how the body works.

I felt elated when I spoke to Kavita and her friends. But when I left the colorful tent and went back into the brown, dusty streets of Karvi, I felt myself coming down from the clouds. Would Kavita feel this way when she left the center's productive, supportive environment? I could not ignore the uncomfortable feeling I had in my stomach when Kavita told me that she would now return to live with her husband. She had said that even though she would have to continue to do the housework, make dung cakes and work in the fields, she would still get more education. She would not forget how to sign her name. She would learn more about how babies are born.

Kavita and I did not talk about what her mother-in-law would say if she started going to school instead of helping around the house. We did not discuss what would happen if her husband wanted to have sex and Kavita said she was still too young for children.

It seems idealistic to think that Kavita's community will believe in the worth of education when the Indian government itself shows little commitment to the issue of female literacy, let alone universal education in general. In the mid-1960s, two decades after Indian Independence, an independent federal commission issued a report concluding that universal education should be a top priority for the government. Fifteen years later, however, the literacy rate remained at only 43 percent, with the burden of illiteracy falling on women and lower castes.

In 1986 the Committee for the National Policy on Education wrote that illiterates in India would grow to five hundred million by the year 2000. The government, said the report, must decide whether "removal of illiteracy is . . . an essential precondition for the meaningful participation of the masses in the process of political decision-making and national reconstruction" in India. *Decide* whether education is essential?

The government of India continues to talk about education as one of its main priorities (the 1997–2001 plan states that "a special thrust . . . will be given to improve access to education and attain full literacy by 2005"), but I am not yet a believer. The statistics do not support their words. Today, education receives only 1.1 percent of the total central government expenditure—the same percentage that it received fifteen years ago. Even within this amount, the percentage spent on primary education in the past three decades has decreased almost 33 percent, while the percentage spent on university education, which benefits primarily the wealthy and well-connected, has increased. Although the government likes to point out that the overall literacy rate in percentages has increased over the years, it conveniently forgets to mention that the absolute number of illiterates has also increased.

The most recent Union (central government) budget specified

that "around 6 percent of gross domestic product will be earmarked for education, with 50 percent to be spent on primary education." Although this was a substantial increase from the previous plan, it translated to a per capita expenditure of only 220 rupees (about $4.50) annually in states like Uttar Pradesh where the need is greatest.

Myron Weiner, a well-known activist who has written extensively on compulsory primary education and on child labor, has scathingly called the Indian government a specialist in the "politics of doing nothing." As with many other social issues, the central government has left responsibility for education largely to individual states. The Indian National Constitution has "enabling legislation" that allows, but does not require, states to make education compulsory. Among those states that have chosen to legislate compulsory education, many have yet to enforce the legislation, leaving it completely toothless.

What I saw, visiting villages in Uttar Pradesh, reflected exactly this lack of government commitment. In one "school" in a small village in the southern part of the state, ten children squabbled over two discarded rickshaw seats, the wooden backs of which they used as chalk boards. At another school near Lucknow, children sat in the dirt in a small field and played with their tattered "school books" that were dated 1970.

In the hills, I once camped on the veranda of a locked-up school. Where was the teacher? I asked some local people.

"Oh, she's been away for weeks now. A wedding, I think. Who knows when she will return?" answered one man carelessly.

Large numbers of people in rural India do not even have access to schools. According to the government's recent Sixth All-India Educational Survey, 17 percent of the habitats surveyed did not have a primary school within one kilometer, while 24 percent did not have a middle school within three 3 kilometers. For young children with no form of motorized transport, these distances virtually guarantee their absence from school. According to the same survey, 90–95 percent of the minimal funds available are spent on teachers' salaries (miserably low), leaving virtually nothing for teaching aids, furniture, books or building maintenance or improvement.

Mothers in Uttar Pradesh's hill areas told me that they were not sure what education would do for their children anyway. "It alienates children from the land," said one mother. "We are agricultural, but my children learn in school about work in the cities. They look down on agriculture and leave us for the cities and for 'higher-class' jobs. In the end, they are unemployed and we have lost them forever. They are worse off in the cities than they would be if they stayed in the villages, but schools don't teach them this."

This was an issue throughout India. In the hills of Uttar Pradesh, a nonprofit organization working in education conducted focus-group sessions with three hundred of their youth to look at attitudes to culture, gender and other social factors. One of the exercises involved showing them an advertisement from a popular Indian magazine that depicted an Indian man and woman dressed in modern Western clothes. The participants were asked to write down their impressions of these people. Every single youth used two words, among others, to describe the models: *educated* and *civilized*. The facilitators asked the youth to further describe what it meant for someone to be educated and civilized versus uneducated or uncivilized. The former, it emerged, essentially meant progress as defined by modern, urban, global or Western ways of thinking, acting and behaving. Educated and civilized people wear Western clothes, live in modern houses, use Western medicine, speak English and have adopted aspects of Western culture and values. Uneducated and uncivilized people were considered backward for believing and following traditional systems of knowledge and behavior. Interestingly, honesty and integrity played a part in neither category.

If these are the values that India's current education system and the surrounding environment are sending to youth, how can one question a mother's reluctance to enter this system? As the youth are more separated from their traditions and from the agricultural practices, they too may end up in the slums of Lucknow or some other urban area.

Although nontraditional schools like Mahila Shiksha Kendra address some of these issues, the community at large often has yet to accept the views and lessons of the schools. Without this community support, how likely is it that young Kavita will be able to express different ideas about the role of women or that she will be able to follow some of her own dreams?

I want desperately to believe that exuberant, excited Kavita will do everything that she said she would. I want to believe that she will be able to balance her rights with the responsibilities she feels to those around her. I want to believe that she will be able to resist strong societal pressures for her to "sacrifice" herself. Even if I do not always believe this is probable, I do believe it is possible. I just wish she would not have to fight as hard against these forces as I know she will have to.

Meera and Ritu

I used to think that gray was the color of the Seattle skies nine months out of the year. Until I went to India. Here, in the middle of all the bright colors, I understood that there is a form of gray in India that is ever-present, the gray of complexity.

As much as I wanted to classify issues as black or white, I found it difficult ever to do this in India. Particularly when the issue moved from the purely intellectual realm to a specific situation that needed to be confronted, black and white suddenly took on hues of gray.

This was brought vividly home to me around the emotional issue of child labor some months later, in the winter of my first year in India, when my husband Alan and I moved to Varanasi in southeastern Uttar Pradesh.

❦

Alan and I had just settled into a house in a middle-class neighborhood in Varanasi. Our next-door neighbor, Dr. Garg, was a retired professor who had spent several years teaching in America. He often spoke to us proudly about his time in the United States and his several children who still lived there. He had offered numerous times to help us negotiate our way through life in Varanasi, so he was thrilled when I asked if he knew of anyone who could help clean the house and wash clothes. "Yes, I will bring them," he said in a comfortingly confident way.

He knocked on our door a few days later. Behind him, standing shyly, were Meera and Ritu. They came in and sat next to the wall, perched on their haunches. Meera was taller—about five feet—with dark skin and almond-shaped eyes. Ritu was a few inches shorter, her face rounder and fairer. Both girls wore a *sindhoor*, the vermilion streak on the center part of the hair that signifies marriage. Although Ritu appeared younger than Meera, Dr. Garg told me that Ritu was actually Meera's aunt and therefore senior to her in the rigid Indian family hierarchy.

"I have brought the girls for you to see," Dr. Garg said. "Meera used to work for us, and she is very sweet."

Meera and Ritu smiled, averting their eyes from me. I sat silently for several moments. "How old are you?" I asked them.

They looked at each other in surprise. "*Bhabi-ji*, we don't know!" they said, using the respectful term for an elder aunt. Knowing one's age, I found out quickly in India, is important only to the middle-class and the elite. I guessed that Ritu was about twelve and Meera about fourteen.

"They are only children," I said to Dr. Garg, who was watching us curiously.

"Yes, but they are already married. They will do good work," he said, nodding his head for emphasis.

"That is not the point. They are too young to work. Isn't this child labor?" I asked, turning to Dr. Garg. His puzzled look changed to a smile.

"Forget America! This is India. These girls have to eat. They are poor; they must work and they will do good work for you."

Meera and Ritu nodded eagerly. "Yes, *Bhabi-ji*, we will do good work. We are married already. We must work now."

This was their reality. Meera was the oldest of seven children. Her father brought in 900 rupees per month (about $25), which had to feed all nine of his family plus Ritu and her mother. Meera had already been working for six or seven years, when we met her. She brought in almost as much as her father, working as a part-time maid in three different households.

Meera and Ritu were typical of many girl children in Uttar Pradesh, who are promised in marriage by age ten, sometimes earlier.

To seal the promise, the girl will stay with her husband-to-be for one night. This is considered her first wedding, and she will begin wearing her sindhoor to show her betrothal. Then, she will return to her family to live until puberty, three or four years later. During this interim period, the girl will alternate spending three months with the husband's family, and three months at her own house. Marriage confers an ironic status to a girl: She has grown up and now must take on more responsibilities, whether at her house or at her mother-in-law's. Work is just one of these responsibilities.

The idea of hiring children threw Alan and me into tumultuous debates about ethics, morality and reality. I had arrived in India believing that child labor was one of those issues that had no "other side." I knew that approximately forty-four million Indian children ages six to fourteen work, that child labor was exploitative, serving only to deprive children and benefit the employers. Somehow, I had managed to convince myself that my absolute views were justified by their moral purity.

My natural tendency—perhaps a human one—is to try to fit the experiences and the issues I confront into pre-existing notions of right and wrong. It is a way of making sense of the world. With the issue of child labor, as with many other issues in India, I found that *right* and *wrong*—those two generals of order—no longer applied because their very definitions were formulated in a completely different context. I had had plenty of opportunities to see some Western visitors to India fall into the trap of applying their own standards to the Indian context. Quietly, I had promised myself that I would not make the same mistakes, but here I was, with Meera and Ritu, doing just that.

I was also acutely conscious of the words of Neera Burra, an Indian anti–child labor activist, who heaped scorn on "socially minded people who salve their conscience by employing children ostensibly to save them from starvation and look upon it as a social service!" At the same time, denying Meera and Ritu employment despite the harshness of their lives seemed like an inappropriate application of external standards to local issues. Ultimately, if we did not hire Meera and

Ritu, they would find work elsewhere, possibly with someone who paid them less and worked them harder.

Alan and I agonized over our decision, trying to fit it into something that would be acceptable to our personal sense of ethics. First, we offered to hire Meera and Ritu and pay for them to attend school for a few hours a day. Dr. Garg laughed when we told him our idea. "They won't go, but you can ask them," he said.

He was right; they refused. "How can I now?" Meera said. "I would be so much older than the other children. And anyway, I don't have time. I must work. I have six younger brothers and sisters at home. My mother has to stay with them. I have to bring home money or we won't eat." She was resolute, and I realized it was not just about the money. We had been naïve to think it was.

We changed our minds several times about whether or not to hire the girls. Each time, we struggled with the gap we saw between an intellectually informed decision not to compromise our ethics and the real consequences that our decision would have on these two girls' lives. When we had made what I thought was our final decision not to hire them, not to perpetuate this form of child labor, I called Meera out to the front step to explain why.

We sat next to each other but were as distant as the earth from the moon in our understanding of each other. My sentences were wisps of air floating in front of her, butterflies fluttering away before they could be caught. She was puzzled. "How can we eat if I do not work? We must earn." I tried to explain to Meera why children should be going to school, not working; I even told her that there are laws in other countries that make it illegal for children to work in any occupation. She listened but could not comprehend. As she talked about her family and her life, I found myself again questioning whether it was right to send them away hungry, while we ate good food and patted ourselves on the back for not perpetuating child labor.

After that conversation, I cried. My tears were for Ritu and Meera and their situation, for my inability to have "the answer," for all the shades of gray that were clouding my previously clear picture of right and wrong. Meera and Ritu, like so many others, were too young to work but too poor not to. If they did not work, what rights would they gain? They could not afford to go to school, much less buy books or uniforms. More important, their family could not spare them from earning a salary.

In that moment when my tears were spent and my mind was clear, I decided to hire them. We would work with them while they were in the house, try to help them as we could. Even today, I do not know if we did the "right" thing. What I did know, then and now, is that not hiring Meera and Ritu would not change their lives for the better. Ironically, it seemed to me that refusing to hire them would be the "salve to our conscience," allowing us to feel that we had upheld our principles but creating no real change in Meera and Ritu's personal situation. But with no alternative for them, it seemed unfair to punish them with our morals.

A few weeks after Meera and Ritu had started working with us, Meera invited me to go to their house and meet their mother. They lived only a ten-minute walk from me, yet worlds away. Through muddy, narrow lanes scattered with cow-dung patties, the population density increasing with each step, we walked together to their small dwelling. Tara, Meera's mother and Ritu's older sister, greeted me happily and proudly showed me their house, which they had built out of brick and concrete. Although only one tiny room, it had a courtyard and was clearly one of the better dwellings on the street. Tara looked to be only about thirty years old, but she had already had seven children, the youngest still just a baby. Tara knew next to nothing about family planning (she confided to me that she wanted to get an "operation" but did not know where to go), so she could hardly teach the girls about it. She told me that she had sent both Meera and Rajiv, Meera's younger brother, to school for some years. Both eventually had to leave, however, Meera because the family needed her to work and help with the children, and Rajiv because they did not have enough money to pay the school fees (about 30 rupees or $1).

In a strange, dark sense, Meera and Ritu probably enjoyed more privileges as breadwinners in the family than many girls their age. Throughout India a woman's biggest liability is that she is "economically unproductive." She makes up for this by being procreationally productive. If she has the misfortune to produce girls instead of boys, her in-laws, her husband and her community make her life miserable. The way the community sees it, sons earn and look after the family in old age, while daughters are only consumers of income with no returns. As income-generators in the family, Meera and Ritu were proving their value. In return, they received more food and better care than many other girls, who typically eat least and last in the family and are rarely taken to see doctors. The family needed Meera and Ritu, therefore it had an incentive to ensure that they were fed and relatively healthy

I left Meera's home that day confused and sad. What choices do children like Meera and Ritu have? What about Tara and her husband? How are they to survive? Most important, how can they be told not to send their children to work, when there are no other alternatives?

ॐ

On the surface the ethical dimensions of child labor seem obvious. But one step deeper, ethics and morality cloud over with the sediment of poverty and unemployment. The Western notions of "rights" are juxtaposed against those of "responsibilities." Society has placed limits around people like Meera and Ritu, condemning parents for sending children out to work and children for working but offering no alternative to these realities. It occurred to me several times, then and in the following months, that the gulf that separates necessity from choice yawns wide.

Most anti–child labor activists argue for an absolute ban on child labor. This would prohibit employers from hiring children and would require parents (no matter how poor) to keep their children in school until a specified age. These activists do not differentiate between children working and child labor. Working in the fields with their families, for example, is not distinguished (at least publicly) from the more obviously exploitative and abusive factory work. Particularly in rural India, where many people still believe in Mahatma Gandhi's concept of *buniyadi shiksha* (which incorporated agricultural work as an essential component of "life" education), people cannot comprehend the logic or logistics of a ban on children working in the fields.

In truth, anti–child labor activists cannot afford to weaken their position by acknowledging distinctions within the entire sphere of the child labor issue. The Indian government pays little attention to child labor and is quick to bray out any hint of a defense for its inactivity. If anti–child labor activists were to "grade" abusive factory child labor situations differently from household or agricultural child labor situations, the government would have an opening to simply announce ineffective bans on factory labor rather than working to address the entire problem at its roots for the long-term. Without a true commitment to a universal education policy that is appropriate and accessible to the rural and urban poor (and a simultaneous plan to combat the poverty in families that pushes them to value income over education), child labor remains simply a symptom of the larger issues.

Poverty becomes a convenient excuse for inactivity, with the mantra of "fix poverty first" often coming loudly from those who use child labor to their advantage. For these people they know that waiting to "fix poverty" would provide them with several more decades of a convenient and nonthreatening situation. Many of these people harbor a secret but fundamental belief that people are poor or disadvantaged because it is their karma, the result or consequences of past acts. Ultimately, like class, karma allows the poor to be blamed for their own situations.

I often found it difficult to ferret out those who want to keep child labor alive because it is in their economic or social interest to do so from those who genuinely believe that poverty is the root of all social problems and are willing to commit themselves to eradicating poverty. I saw this firsthand after I wrote an article on child labor that expressed my frustration with the tendency to portray it as a simple black-and-white issue with an easy black-and-white answer. I argued for an approach that recognized the complexity of child labor and acknowledged the position of families that sent their children into child labor. Yet, many Indian and Western friends and acquaintances (most of whom were wealthy or worked for large U.S. corporations that were fighting anti–child labor legislation) chose to take my arguments as a rationale for leaving children in child labor. "See," they would say. "Finally, someone who understands that we cannot just stop child labor. It is better for children to be working than out begging." Or "India is too overpopulated for everyone to be in school. Might as well leave the children to work."

No, I found myself repeating over and over. I was not condoning the perpetuation of child labor, simply highlighting the tremendous commitment and effort it would take to come up with a solution that did not end up penalizing the very people it was supposed to help.

❦

Some weeks after I had met Meera and Ritu, an Indian friend of mine, aware of my interest in child labor, offered to introduce me to a "master weaver" in the sari-weaving industry. The weaver, M. A. Ansari, was from the Muslim Ansari community, which accounts for 90 percent of weavers in the carpet and sari industries. Master weavers own looms that are operated by employees; they also contract work to individual weavers. Ansari's family had owned looms for eleven generations, a tradition that Ansari continued with three power looms and one hand loom. He was different from previous generations of Ansaris, however, in that he was a Ph.D. candidate, and was actively involved in India's Congress Party, dreaming of one day being part of the prime minister's Central Planning Commission.

We rode on my friend's motor scooter to Ansari's house in the heart of the Muslim weaving community on the edge of Varanasi's center. It was a long, dusty ride and I completely lost any sense of bearing after the first three *galis*—narrow, winding alleys that snake throughout Varanasi—five tea shops and six wandering cows. As two women in salvaar kameezes on a motor scooter, we drew attention in this predominantly Muslim community where few women were outside, let alone riding around. We parked outside a poorly white-washed house in a sheltered brick haven and waited for Ansari in a room decorated with a few chairs and a knobby, pea-green sofa.

Ansari was thin, of medium height. He looked older than his twenty-six years. When I asked if I could tape our conversation, he beamed. The tape recorder, to him, was the ultimate endorsement of his credibility, but his enthusiasm made me nervous. I wondered if he would say what he really felt if I was taping him.

Ansari took great pains to differentiate sari-industry workers (the "children of master weavers who are being passed on a skill and are treated well") from carpet industry workers ("poor migrants from Bihar who are exploited"). He talked for some time about his disdain for the ban on Indian carpets and his belief that the ban and the call for "child labor–free" certified carpets were part of an international conspiracy. I had heard this before. Many Indians perceived the outright condemnation of child labor by Western countries as colonial and patriarchal.

To my surprise, Ansari admitted without hesitation that hiring children in the sari- and carpet-weaving businesses was as much for economic reasons as it was for the "skill of children," the smaller fingers that allow more intricate weaving. (Many industry people argue vehemently that children's tiny fingers allowed them to perform fine work that adults could not perform and without children, there would be no fine carpets—which, they also rightly point out, have their largest markets in Western countries.) According to Ansari, children were paid about 100–150 rupees per month ($2.85–$4.25) compared to adult weavers, who could earn about 2,000 rupees per month ($57).

I asked Ansari if he thought education should be made compulsory. Without pause, he gave me the politically correct answer: "Of course, education is a must." Then he stopped and pressed his fingers together in a steeple in front of his face adding, "But what will we do with all the educated people? Anyway," he said, leaning back in his chair, "we must accept God's gift that is given to us."

"What is God's gift?" I asked curiously.

"God has made it so that some must work and some must be educated. It is God's gift if you are born into a family that has too many children and must send you to work. Education is for some, and labor is for others. We must accept this. You can't force education on the labor people," he finished definitively.

He proceeded to tell me a story about a messenger of God who asked God to make everyone equal. God complied. Then one man's roof broke so he went to the former roof repairer, who had now been made an equal. He asked the roof repairer to fix his roof, but the roof repairer snubbed him and said, "My roof too has collapsed. Why don't you fix mine? We are all equal now."

"Equality is not possible," Ansari concluded triumphantly. "That is why socialism has collapsed in all these countries. Without a social structure, there is chaos."

It was a social commentary of chilling proportion that justified poverty and apathy toward instituting social change. Like many Indians, Ansari had dismissed the importance of millions of fellow Indians' lives. In his eyes, they were where they were because of their karma. Now, they must fulfill payment for previous misdeeds; they must provide services for those who actually "deserve" to be here in some high, monarchlike position.

In India karma and its translation into caste allows the educated and wealthy to believe that they have earned the right to privilege, while the poor have earned the right to nothing.

Whose Choice Is Development?

The monsoons arrived in Lucknow at the end of August, just before I was due to leave that city. Alan was finally arriving in India from the United States. It had been five months since I had left him in Seattle for my solo adventure. I would continue to have those individual journeys, I knew, but traveling with Alan would also allow me to have access to two experiences—mine and his—that were bound to be different.

I met Alan in Delhi. We spent a long night and morning together, allowing our words to spill out as we had not been able to do on those expensive, short phone calls. We were to go immediately to Ladakh, the mountainous region within the state of Jammu and Kashmir in the northeastern corner of the country, on the borders of Tibet and Pakistan. There, we would meet two naturalist friends of ours and spend almost two months traveling around the area.

We had wanted to take a bus to Ladakh; the road was said to be spectacular. But, as was often the case, the rains had closed the road down in places. Our only option was to fly, and we were lucky enough to secure two seats on an Indian Airlines flight that day.

I had read about Ladakh. I knew about its barren beauty and majestic scenery. But still, when our little propeller plane from Delhi flew through the narrow mountain gorges and snow-tipped peaks with wisps of cloud encircling their tips, I felt unprepared to absorb the grandeur, the sense of complete remoteness, the feeling of vulnerability next to the enormity of nature.

According to the Hindu epic, the *Mahabharata*, Lord Vishnu lived on the shore of a great sea with two seagulls. Every year, no matter where the female seagull laid her eggs, the sea would come in and wash them away in its raging waters. The seagulls finally appealed to Vishnu for help. Vishnu rescued them by opening up his mouth and swallowing the sea—in its place lay Earth. Then Vishnu slept, exhausted from his feat. While he slept, the demon Hiranyankisha leapt on Mother Earth and raped her so brutally that her limbs were broken and levered up high into the clouds forming the Himalaya mountains, within whose rain shadow Ladakh is nestled.

The legend accurately reflects the intensity and barrenness of Ladakh, but it does not do justice to the absolute perfection and magnificence of the land. The arid rolling hills of Ladakh's capital city, Leh, give way to twenty-thousand-foot mountains and wide open high-altitude plains where shepherds bring their animals to graze. From the tops of passes strung with colorful prayer flags, one can see silhouettes of mountain ranges dusted with fresh snow. Although the region receives less than fifty millimeters of rain per year, glacial melt from the mountains creates rushing rivers, next to which are patches of green barley fields, well irrigated by channeled water. In the northern part of Ladakh the terrain is scattered with curved rocks, smoothed by rain into fine, ebony-colored sculptures.

From A.D. 950 to 1834, Ladakh was an independent kingdom. In the early 1800s, under attack by Mongol forces, Ladakh was forced to appeal to the Mughal governor of Kashmir for assistance, agreeing to become part of the Mughal Empire in exchange for protection from the Mongols. With the partition of India in 1947, Ladakh—like Kashmir—was divided, with part of it (called Baltistan) in Pakistan and part in India, belonging to the state of Jammu and Kashmir. Since China's 1962 war with India over disputed border territory, the Indian government has stationed hundreds of army troops in Ladakh. The region remains of great strategic importance today.

Ladakh occupies about ninety-eight thousand square kilometers (approximately the size of Ohio), an area that accounts for about half of the entire state of Jammu and Kashmir, but its population is only 160,000, less than 2 percent of the entire state's population. Ladakh remains closed for more than half of the year when its extreme weather and location allows no travel by road or plane. Ladakh was "opened" to foreigners in 1974, and planes and roads were built in the late 1970s and early 1980s to make the region accessible from other parts of India. Its beauty has made the region a national and international center of tourism since its opening.

Ladakh has attracted significant international attention in the past two decades, as it has undergone the transition from an almost completely self-reliant economy and people to an economy that depends on tourism and government subsidies for agriculture, a society that grapples with issues of urbanization and modernization.

Before this, Ladakhis—90 percent of whom are Buddhist—epitomized one of the central pinciples of Buddhism: *pratitvasamutpada*, or interconnectedness. This meant a harmony between the people and the land, a dependence on family structures and human links, an understanding that the land is the only provider and that sustainable resources are only those available from nearby. People ate primarily what they grew, used local resources like mud and bushes to build their houses and built their villages around the availability of water from glaciers. Nothing was wasted; barley, a high-altitude crop, was harvested, roasted and made into a flour called *ngamphe*. The remains of the barley were made into a local brew called *chang*. Willow trees and homemade mud bricks dried in the sun were used for housing materials. Men and women wore long robes made out of homespun, home-dyed wool, yak-skin capes and woolen shoes lined with yak or goat skin. Ladakhis used barter of goods and services, not money, as their main currency. They operated under the basic assumption that everyone was part of a community that helped each other. They shared water-powered mills to grind barley and bonded together in groups of families called *phasphuns* to provide assistance to each other during births, deaths and marriages.

When Indian Army troops flooded the area in the early 1960s, when roads opened access to the area, when twenty-five thousand tourists a year trekked through formerly isolated mountain communities and when goods and services and a monetary economic system replaced the old system, Ladakh—described by many as one of the last truly self-reliant societies in the world—collided with the modern world.

ॐ

A family friend who had spent time in Leh had recommended a charming guesthouse to us. Tucked away on the outskirts of town, it was surrounded by fields and distant hills. It took our friends and us several days to acclimate to Leh's thin air. At eleven thousand feet, Leh was at a relatively low altitude compared with the seventeen-thousand and eighteen-thousand foot passes we planned to go over. We took short walks those first few days and stayed patient with our heavy breathing and panting. Our first explorations were to Leh Palace and Tsemo Gompa above it. Built in the mid-sixteenth century, the palace stands out on the hillside with its square towers and balconies. It still belongs to the Ladakhi royal family, although they no longer live there. Tsemo Gompa, a strenuous uphill climb, is a monastery in a series of buildings made up of narrow passageways and small prayer rooms. Two monks, who had come from the state of Karnataka in southern India, kindly agreed to open the rooms for us. The smaller room was filled with the smell of incense and burning lamps, and in the middle sat an enormous two-story-high Bodhisattva image. It appeared to me that the room must have been built around the image, but the monks could not confirm this. I knelt before the image and touched my cold and sweaty forehead to the ground.

Later, Alan and I and our two friends sat on one of the wide balconies of the monastery and watched the colorful prayer flags strung across the turrets blowing in the wind. The prayer flags, the monks told us, carry the prayers and dreams of those who leave them there up to the heavens.

Our guesthouse owner, David, kindly offered to help us arrange the trek we planned to take. For eighteen days the four of us would trek through the Markha Valley with a fleet of horses and two Tibetan guides cum horsemen, forty-seven-year-old Shuzin and fifty-three-year-old Tamding. The day before we were to start our trek, however, huge dark clouds gathered over the mountains into which we would be heading. By evening, we could see that the mountains had been covered with fresh snow. David was worried: It was late in the season and we had chosen to do the trek the harder way, where we would end with our most difficult pass. But by the next morning, the sky was clear blue and the sun as strong as ever. We drove along the two-lane road from Leh to Martselang, where we would meet our guides and horses, through patches of green juxtaposed against brown hills, next to little streams channeled toward the fields by stone walls and alongside beautiful monasteries and palaces nestled in the middle of precarious hillsides.

At Martselang, Tamding and Shuzin loaded up the horses, rhythmically chanting and singing the whole time. Each morning, they would go through this process, carefully assessing which horses should carry the most weight and then distributing the burlap sacks over their backs as evenly as possible. The horses were their livelihood, and they took fine care of them.

Our first day we climbed only about a thousand feet in about two hours, understanding the need to adjust slowly to the change in altitude. Huge rock walls stood next to brown hills and craggy mountains; stone-filled paths traced the routes of rushing rivers. Our first campsite was just beyond some intricately carved *mani* walls, walls of prayer stones inscribed with religious prayers and the ever-present prayer to Lord Buddha, *Om Mani Padme Hum* (Hail to the Jewel in the Lotus). The mani walls generally signaled the entrance to a village and were often accompanied by *chortens*, domed structures that taper upward in a spire, crowned with a moon and the sun, the Buddhist symbol of everlasting unity and interconnectedness. The carvings on the mani stones, usually *chakras* (circles of the wheel of life), seemed to be alive; I imagined the deep etchings to have been done in complete faith, with love and passion. The mani walls, chortens, and gompas were constant reminders to us of how central religion had been, and for the most part continues to be, to everyday life here.

Our first campsite, just outside Sumdo village, was scenically beautiful, nestled into the V of two hillsides and looking out to the snow-tipped mountains ahead. But we could see the signs of tourism. Chocolate wrappers, empty tunafish cans and discarded plastic bags scarred the sparse and pure scenery. Some tourists had not bothered to burn or carry out their toilet paper, leaving it to mar beautiful spots near rivers, around rocky fields and even on the hilltop monastery grounds.

We began collecting this trash, much to our guides' great amusement. By the middle of the trip, we had collected a tremendous amount of garbage—ours and others—into a big polyethylene sack. Unable to bear the curiosity anymore, Tamding asked me what we would do with the garbage that we insisted on loading up on the horses every day. I replied that we were taking it back to Leh, where we could dispose of it properly. He and Shuzin roared with laughter. *"Leh tak le rahe hai?"* he asked me incredulously. Yes, all the way to Leh, I replied in Hindi, trying unsuccessfully to explain why this was important.

The next morning, we were up by 6:30, drinking coffee and *tsampa*, a local brew made of barley remains. By 8:30 we were on the road again. We followed the river up narrow canyons and gorges, alongside multicolored granite walls. We walked nervously under enormous sharp rocks perched on flimsy rock piles. The striated rock faces were jagged, like the scaly back of a dinosaur. The river water poured over rocks, flattening and smoothing them. We clung to the cool rock faces, jumped rivers and picked rosehips. It was still cold; fanciful-looking hoarfrost clung to leaves and plants along the way, completely intact despite the intense sunlight from above.

As we climbed higher and higher, my breath started coming faster and shorter. I began to get cramps in my sides from overtaxing my diaphragm. The path up the mountain to the base camp seemed to stretch on and on into nothingness. With every step there was intense pain, lessened only slightly by visual snatches of snow-covered peaks and rocky hillsides punctuated with red lichen, green rosehip bushes and gray granite. Just when we were almost to the Kongmaru La base camp at fifteen thousand feet, we spotted a herd of more than thirty blue sheep. Their distinctive large horns and the black stripes along their legs and belly stood out against the hillside. They cantered their way across the hillside, munching on the bushes and creating mini rockslides as their feet kicked down loose rocks into the canyon river below. We watched the sheep for at least half an hour before resuming our climb.

We camped in a mountain bowl that night. I could see the pass trail ahead. It did not seem that far, but I knew enough to realize that distances and heights in this grand scenery were immensely deceiving. Behind me the mountain ranges were silhouetted against each other, pink with the evening light just before sunset. I watched as the sun sank behind the Kongmaru La range, plunging our area into a dark chill.

We drank tsampa around a fire that night with another Tibetan guide who was camped with a party nearby. Tibetans, who had begun to flow into India from the time the Chinese first invaded Tibet, had become firmly entrenched in the tourist industry here, much to the Ladakhis dismay. The Tibetans were considered the best guides, surefooted and pleasant.

In Leh several Ladakhis had told me they felt resentful of Tibetans. Said one, "As refugees, they are not subject to any Indian taxes or regulations, yet they can earn substantial profits. They are richer than most of us." But Tamding and Shuzin did not seem particularly wealthy to me. They owned only two of the horses and had rented the others. They and this other Tibetan guide still considered themselves Tibetan even though they had lived in Ladakh for almost two decades.

When I asked our visitor that night if he thought he would ever be able to return to Tibet, he replied in broken Hindi, "As sure as the sun rises and sets, I will go back. It is in the Dalai Lama's teachings." He continued on: "We feel homeless here. . . . We have nowhere else to go; what can we do but stay?"

Working with tourists was clearly one of the most lucrative professions in Ladakh, and it produced an entire spectrum of unanswerable questions and issues. Our visitor, who had been a guide for almost a decade, said that tourism had definitely changed the Ladakhis.

"It is good for money," he said, "but not in other ways. Before, even if people were very poor, they would give you a little of their tsampa and chang. Now you must pay for everything."

We had heard and read much about Ladakh's changing culture. It was a controversial issue. Before we had left on our trek, I had spent some time speaking with representatives of several different nonprofit development organizations in Leh. Despite Ladakh's small size, it had a large number of development organizations working in the area. Many of these had sprouted after the well-known Swedish linguist and environmentalist Helena Norberg-Hodge had formed the Ladakh Ecological Development Group (LEDG).

Founded in 1983, LEDG had been at the forefront of protesting the rapid onslaught of Western influences through tourism and trade. LEDG's mission was to promote ecological and sustainable development that would harmonize with and build on the traditional culture. Norberg-Hodge had lived in Ladakh six months of the year for over sixteen years, initially analyzing the Ladakhi language and collecting folk stories for her studies at the School of Oriental and African Studies in London. Her time in Ladakh spanned its "opening" to tourism and afforded Norberg-Hodge a unique perspective into the changes occurring in this formerly self-sufficient culture as it modernized. In 1991, she documented many of these economic and cultural shifts in her book *Ancient Futures: Learning from Ladakh*.

"The impact of tourism," Norberg-Hodge wrote, "on the material culture has been wide-ranging and disturbing. Still more significant, however, has been its impact on people's minds." According to her, this process of change in Ladakh began in earnest in 1974 with the start of tourism. Along with the Indian government's opening up of the area came development, Western-style. This meant a focus on the monetary economy and "centralization" of services to Leh, which in turn brought about migration, a house-building boom in Leh, and a population growth. This increased dependence on outside goods and services, however, disrupted the sense of balance that had traditionally existed among people and their land. Even as we trekked through the villages, we saw that many families had converted their agricultural land into guest houses. The biggest impact, argued Norberg-Hodge, was the impact on the Ladakhis' sense of pride in their culture. She began to see young people who had previously been proud of their traditions develop a sense of cultural inferiority as they began to imitate "modern" Western ways.

Many Ladakhis, however, disagreed with Norberg-Hodge's assessment of their situation, or at least questioned her moral authority to push them in a way that they did not wish to go. One development worker, with more than a trace of resentment, said to me, "These Westerners come here and tell us we should keep our traditional clothes and eat our traditional food, while they live their Western lives and take photos of us." He was speaking specifically about LEDG's Ladakh Project, which aimed to expose Ladakhis to the negative aspects of "developed" countries and to show them that the West, having gone through industrialization and development, is now seeking the spiritual and psychological happiness that Ladakhis have traditionally had. Many Ladakhis perceived LEDG—and in particular, many Western environmentalists—as colonial figures who were expecting indigenous people to forsake precisely those things of which Westerners can take advantage.

In one development worker's words: "Before, people did not need much. They were happy to live on what the land provided. Now, people want to send their children to school. They want to have bigger houses, earn more money, buy a motorbike. The needs are greater and the land doesn't support these needs. So the young ones run away to the cities. But how can we ask them not to want these things when they see they are available in the West? How can we ask them not to want these things when these are exactly the things that the dominant forces have?"

"How stupid to expect Ladakhis to be exhibits forever," Akbar Ladakhi, one of the five Executive Councilors of the newly inaugurated Leh Autonomous Hill Development Council, had told me. "We cannot deny Ladakhis the benefits of roads, sanitation and health."

David, our guesthouse owner, was also frustrated by these attempts to keep Ladakhis in their traditional practices. "We are not the beautiful people that Helena and Andrew Harvey [author of *A Journey in Ladakh]* make us out to be. We need to survive in some of the harshest conditions in the world," he said passionately one night over chang. "We are human, like anyone else. You cannot stop change. It is here. And it is survival of the fittest. The idea that we are losing our culture is exaggerated. Just because we wear pants instead of our traditional *goucha* robes does not mean we have lost our culture."

But when I asked about the rush from villages to cities, the decline of agriculture and the changing ideas of what constituted a "good" life, David had less to say. He, like many other Ladakhis, felt naturally boxed in. The prospect of development—of roads, better houses, less physically demanding lives—was enticing, just as it had been to the West. Who was he to reject this? Yes, Ladakhis may have been self-sufficient, but life was hard. How bad could it be to avail themselves of what had dropped into their laps?

The issue was not whether Ladakhi society had changed in fundamental ways, but what to do about it. Was this change necessarily bad? Who would decide this? And even if it was leading to a road that Westerners could see from experience was full of pitfalls, did that alone give one society who had already trod that path the right to impose a different path on another society who wanted the right to its own mistakes?

Since 1942, when then–U.S. Senator Harry Truman defined huge parts of the world as "underdeveloped," people have been seeking to understand the meaning of development. Many feel that the idea of development should be abandoned all together, imbued as it is with connotations of paternalism and colonialism. Equally important, since 1969 even United Nations officials have questioned whether development, as it has been taking place, has been of benefit to societies. U.N. experts on social planning and policy in that year clearly stated: "The fact that development either leaves behind, or in some ways even creates, large areas of poverty, stagnation, marginality and actual exclusion from social and economic progress is too obvious and too urgent to be overlooked."

In the past two decades development workers and experts have looked for new approaches to development that respectfully include the communities that are being "developed": grassroots participation through nonprofit organizations, integrated development approaches and new parameters for measuring the success of development that look more at qualitative factors such as improvements in relation to gender discrimination and life satisfaction.

Alternative thinkers like Norberg-Hodge rightly point out that the conventional development paradigm has been forced on countries around the world. Technologies such as television, radio, cars and roads have made it that much easier to spread one single worldview to the remotest corners of the globe.

I have come to believe that development, as it has traditionally been defined, does no good for anyone, other than perhaps large conglomerates that line their nest eggs with a larger potential consumer market. Somehow, we have incorporated a skewed notion of progress into an equally skewed notion of development. Given this perspective, I am also a strong believer in the need to provide information and alternatives to the dominant model of development, which embraces aspects of growth and progress that are often counter to the central social constructs of traditional societies. But in the years I have worked in international development, I remain unsure of how to do this in a way that honors the changing paradigms of these societies. Whether we believe it is "better" for Ladakhis to retain their traditional ways, the choice ultimately remains with the Ladakhis themselves. Imposing an alternative paradigm of development on a society, even if it is based on experience or is "for that society's good," seems no less paternalistic than the way we impose our more traditional view of development on societies. Even Buddha was a prince in the material world before he was able to see that this world lacked spiritual satisfaction. Ultimately, whose choice is "development" anyway?

∞

The trail up to the seventeen-thousand-foot Kongmaru La pass was long and grueling (later we realized that this was the easiest pass we had climbed!). I counted my steps, stopping every hundred steps for a breath. At the top I collapsed to Tamding's smiles and congratulatory words. There, on my back, I gazed at the thousands of colorful prayer flags that had been left by all the many visitors before us. Ahead, we could see Mount Nimaling, with its rounded top and flattened sides, a glacier emerging boldly from one edge. On either side of Nimaling, mountain ranges stretched out, creating a magnificent cluster of triangles dusted with snow. Below us lay the Nimaling plains, where we were headed: flat, wide-open grasslands that contrasted completely with the narrow gorges and canyons we had just traversed. The wind was whipping by relentlessly. We quickly ate our peanut butter and jelly sandwiches and began our descent. In my excitement I began to run down the hillside. Just near the bottom, however, I was overcome by a wave of dizziness and nausea and collapsed to the ground in a faint.

I had taken the descent too quickly and had been hit with an attack of altitude sickness. The guides put me on a horse and took me, in a semiconscious state, to our campsite for the night. I remember little about that ride, except that I thought I was dying. I could not breathe, felt dizzy, could see very little around me. I had no strength to hold on to the reins or the horse, so Alan and our friends walked on either side supporting my weight. At camp a German couple near us poured a container of oral rehydration liquids down my throat, and I began to feel better.

It was my birthday that day. My gift that evening was being able to watch dozens of shepherds bring their sheep to graze, flooding the green plains with white woolen dots. We cooked dinner in Tamding and Shuzin's tent, a half of an army parachute that they had rigged up to a big wooden pole. I fell asleep that night dreaming about the words my naturalist friends had written in the birthday card they had made for me:

> We walk under soaring peaks—eroding so slowly under the spatter of a raindrop—the tiny hoof of an infant blue sheep—the heel of an old woman spinning a prayer wheel. All that we see around us is crumbling, unfixed, ephemeral. Sometimes nothing seems unwavering enough to be trusted, to be relied upon with one's whole heart except compassion, the one unchangeable which binds earth to sky to human heart.

❀

From Nimaling we walked to Hankar. We camped in a barley field on the village outskirts. This was the first larger village we had stayed in, about thirty families. On the rooftops of houses, women and children stacked fodder and dried apricots. The road we had come in on was dry and dusty, rising up and down into the valley but always by barley fields. The sound of swaying barley had become a soothing staple in our walks. In the center of the village the trail passed through a monastery and ruins.

We followed the trail out of the village alongside a rushing, clear blue river. About an hour out of Hankar, an old man came from the opposite direction and stopped in front of me. *"Kaise hai?"* I asked, somewhat tentatively. My Hindi had come in handy with some of the younger generation, who could mostly speak or understand it. The older generation, however, mostly spoke Ladakhi, a language quite different from Hindi. I need not have worried. The man gave me a big toothless grin in response to my query as to how he was. His red woolen wrap coat was ragged, his black pants dusty and worn. On his back he carried a large sack filled with something. He wore a beautiful coral and turquoise necklace. He stared fascinated at me and I at him. In that moment time seemed to stand still, two humans on the same earth, sharing without language.

Our next stop was the main village of Markha, after which the valley is named, atop a small hill. As we approached it, we saw splashes of red, green, gold and orange trees, unexpectedly luxurious color in these brown fields. We camped in the middle of a field next to a big house. It was now harvest time, and people were threshing barley all day. We rarely saw anyone walking or working alone; there was constant companionship. Just as one might imagine families in the West sitting down to dinner together, here it seemed the family got together in the fields. In one family the wife threshed the barley, the children gathered the cut barley and the father stacked and stored it.

That evening we played with the three children from the nearby house. They had five other siblings, three of whom had left the village for the city. Their mother worked in the fields and their father was a medical doctor, but most of their status and money came from renting their fields to tourists for camping.

According to Thupstan Chhewang, raising the status of agriculture again in Leh is a key priority. Chhewang is the Chief Executive Councilor of the Leh Autonomous Hill Development Council, a governmental body inaugurated in September 1995—after lengthy negotiations with the Jammu and Kashmir state government—that will be responsible for planning and implementation in the district. Residents hope that the Hill Council will be able to implement plans that address the needs of the district more appropriately than did the state planning commission. The migration of young people from villages to cities creates a labor shortage in the fields. This problem is compounded by the current education system, which does not differentiate between the knowledge needed by village youth and that needed by urban youth. Ladakhi schools use the same curricula that are used all over India, which is certainly not appropriate for this geographically isolated mountain-dwelling people.

When agriculture becomes less and less profitable, land is sold off or converted for other purposes, just like the family fields on which we had camped. As joint families split up with increased rural-urban migration, land is also split. Earlier, on the plane to Ladakh, I had a conversation with a thirty-something Ladakhi named Gyazo who had been educated in Delhi. He and his three brothers had inherited from their father a large piece of land. They had decided to carve it up and each be responsible for their own piece rather than harvesting the land as a whole. Gyazo thought that their sons would also split the land, making it even smaller and less productive. Because they did not live in Ladakh, it did not much matter to them. But even for those who lived there, agriculture was not very attractive as compared with tourism.

Finally, the increase in subsidies provided by the state government for imported grain, rice, sugar and other foods have made it less cost-effective to grow one's own food. When I had asked Chhewang about the likelihood of elminating these subsidies to encourage local agriculture again, he shook his head. "There is understandable resistance to getting rid of subsidies," he said, referring both to the Jammu and Kashmir government as well as to the new dependence Ladakhis themselves now had on those subsidies. Instead, he said, he hoped to introduce alternative crops that would make agriculture attractive again, and then to supplement incomes through the development of handicraft industries.

Pesticides and fertilizers, subsidized by large national and multinational conglomerates, had also contributed to the ultimate erosion of the land. Here, development organizations were making progress, bringing people from neighboring villages who had experienced the negative impact of pesticides and chemicals, such as hardened soil and decreased taste in barley and other crops, to speak with their neighbors. "It is tempting," said one development worker, "for villagers to use pesticides and chemical fertilizers because the government subsidizes them and because for the first year or two, yields are high. If they hear from others what happens later, it will begin to make them think twice about using these things."

Chhewang told me he believed that making agriculture a viable occupation again was possible but would be difficult. There needed to be, he felt, "a sense of dignity around manual labor that would encourage young people to go back to the fields." He wanted to see the educational system incorporate elements of improved agricultural techniques, growing methods, information about fertilizers and chemicals for agricultural purposes, and even using the harvest season (during which time there is school) as a practical training session for which children would work with their families in the fields and receive school credit.

☜☞

The next morning we walked eight hours through dry, dusty land, punctuated only by thorny bushes and the occasional apricot tree. Eventually, this gave way to river country and finally a rocky gorge whose shadows and cool walls offered much-needed shade. Then, suddenly, we saw new mountain peaks, jagged, serrated, teeth dusted with snow and holding darkening clouds in their grasp. Plain met sky, the rock around us reached up into the heavens, and we faded into our small insignificant selves. Our campsite was in a big, already-cut barley field just before the village of Skiu and next to a small irrigation canal from which we could take some water for cooking and cleaning.

It was just a short walk the next day to the small village of Khaya, or "Shangri-La" according to one of our guidebooks. We passed tiny villages of just one or two families, most of whom were out in the fields and looked up briefly to greet us merrily. And then, there was Shangri-La: barley fields, golden in color, ready for harvest with heads of soft downy pillows waving in the breeze, brushing against each other in companionship; two beautiful women with red scarves, red dresses and broad smiles deftly using their sickles to cut the grain, holding the barley close to the earth and their sickles even closer to the ground, moving rhythmically, perfectly in tune to their surroundings. I tried to cut the barley like them but was clumsy and uncoordinated. They laughed gently and told me it took time to learn. They had been doing it since they were children, and it would take them only two or three days to harvest the enormous field.

Shingo village, where we would spend the next night, consisted of only one extended family that lived in four different houses. We stayed in a room in one of the houses and drank tsampa with the family in their main quarters. The primary room was supported by four large pillars of poplar, decorated on top with small paintings of white dots and curlicues. The floor was bare mud, on top of which the family had spread blankets and mats for sitting. In the corner was a pile of blankets that they would use at night for sleeping in this same room. On the far side of the room, a variety of thick, heavy ladles from the town of Chilling decorated the wall. A wooden cabinet ran the length of the wall nearest us. In it were displayed shining copper and alum teapots. The metal stove in the center of the room had small, etched copper and aluminum panels on its sides. The back of the stove had three little doors, out of which ashes could be swept into a little pit just below. Various sized pots and a tea kettle, blackened from years of sooty use, sat on top of the stove, and in front sat our hostess, Padma.

Padma was resplendent in her charcoal-stained dress. Her hair was covered with a red scarf and her face speckled with soot. She had three children, two of whom had moved to Skiu. Everything that Padma needed to cook was within her reach, and she stayed squatting, reaching from time to time to the wooden cupboard to grab a small wooden stick to stoke the fire or to take down an aluminum container of tsampa or milk.

Padma took a liking to me. "You and me—the same," she said in broken Hindi. "Just like Ladakhi." Then she took my hand and held it in her rough, capable ones. Later, she allowed me to help her wash the cups and bowls, drenching them in hot water from a beautiful metal ladle. When she and her mother-in-law were in the front, harvesting potatoes, I crouched down next to her, sticking my hands into the earth that Padma had just pulled loose with her pick, pulling out potatoes, throwing the small ones into a basket and the bigger ones into a large burlap sack. We developed a sort of rhythm to our work, digging, pulling, throwing and, in between, smiling and laughing with each other.

Being Indian in Ladakh had made a difference. In an area where most of the tourists were Western and few spoke any Hindi, somehow I "belonged." It had been a long time since I had felt I belonged anywhere. In Lucknow, I had struggled with my Hindi, and often I could not even explain to people that Kerala really was part of India. It was a strange sense of back-and-forth, coming to a place that was supposed to be home, where in so many ways I fit in, and yet being confronted with the reality of having grown up elsewhere.

My experience in Ladakh was reaffirming to my bruised sense of Indianness. My Hindi had differentiated me from the Western tourists and connected me to Padma and her people. I felt warm, as if I belonged because of my heritage rather than in spite of it. In that sense of belonging, came a pride in being Indian, in claiming as mine the earth and the mountains and the rivers through which we walked and marveled.

☙

We had two passes left to cross in our trek. The route would take us from Shingo over Choksti La pass at 17,500 feet, to the village of Sumda Do and then finally over Stapski La pass at 16,900 feet. Even though the latter pass was lower than Choksti La, it was the most dangerous, steep and in the shadow of the mountains so that snow often blocked the route and made it impassible.

It was now the end of September, and the weather had become noticeably colder in the two weeks since we had left Leh. We were also on higher ground now, surrounded by looming, snow-covered mountains. The wind was whipping as we climbed toward Choksti La, and an hour after we started, we were bitterly disappointed to find we had somehow taken the wrong route. We backtracked, traversing across a rocky slate-filled hillside that was terrifying in its sheer impermanence. Every piece of slate that fell as we scrambled across led to not-so-mini landslides, and we would wait silently until the hillside stabilized again. We reached at least three false summits. The icy wind was blowing straight through my layers of clothes, and my fingers and nose and face felt frostbitten and dry.

But it was all worth it when we reached the summit. There at 17,500 feet, we had a panoramic view of the ridges and mountain peaks around us, including a mountain that soared above us at 21,000 feet. We ate trail mix and peanut brittle and then pushed ourselves onward through a narrow canyon gorge, walking on rock ledges cut out of the walls. It took us just under five hours to make it down the steep path that swung from left to right. As we descended, the vegetation changed and we began to see more trees, yellow in their last bursts of bloom before winter.

At the bottom of the canyon, we met some Germans who had come from the town of Lamayuru. They had wanted to go over Stapski La, they said, but they had heard it would be too difficult, so they had changed plans. This worried us. We had seen no one coming from the direction that we were heading, which probably meant the Germans were right. But we had hardly any food left and would not be able to continue the several days it would take to get to Lamayuru. After hours of discussion, tempers flaring from tiredness and nervousness, we decided that we would have to chance Stapski La. A local had told us there was a shortcut from Sumda Do to Sumda Chonoon, which would cut some of our time off and give us more time to climb up and down Stapski La.

The next morning we followed the shortcut, a narrow trail cut out of the hillsides of the cliffs that followed the river below. The trail was so narrow, the horses kept losing their footing. Tamding's worry was etched all over his face, although he did his best to reassure us that everything would be fine. When we finally made it to the Choksti La base camp, we breathed a sigh of relief. We could see the top of the pass from camp, and it and the hillside we would have to climb was completely snow-free. That night we cooked up all the food we had left. We feasted on french fries and vegetable *pakodas*, rice and stir-fried vegetables, and we laughed together until dark hit the camp.

The path up to Stapski La was grueling, following for much of the way a faint goat track that switchbacked up along the steep mountainside. When we finally reached the pass, we collapsed and enjoyed the view of the peaks and the wide, sprawling Indus River below us. Only after we had eaten our sandwiches did we venture a few hundred feet to look down the pass at the side we would have to descend. This side, shaded by the mountain, was covered in snow almost a foot deep in places. Tamding and Shuzin could not hide their fear: It would be hard for us, yes, but almost impossible for the horses. And the horses were their livelihood; if something were to happen to one of the horses Tamding and Shuzin had rented, they would have to pay back the full price of the horse. If something happened to one of their own horses, they would be close to financial ruin.

It was a terrifying descent. We sat down and slid in short stretches, bracing ourselves by digging our hands into the snow and hoping not to hit rocks on the way down. The horses refused to budge on their own, and Tamding and Shuzin had to alternately pull and coax them to take tiny steps at a time. Uncomfortable in snow to begin with (I had never taken to skiing even after being in America for so long), I burst into tears when I looked down the steep slope and realized that somehow I would have to make it down. It took interminable hours to travel the short distance of about a thousand feet. One of the horses injured its leg, but Tamding seemed thankful that it was not worse.

When we got to the village of Alchi, Tamding and Shuzin and the horses left us, with smiles and thanks. They had carried us safely for eighteen days. Like all mountain people they were strong and re-sourceful; they understood the harshness and the beauty of life in a way that we probably never could. Our trek had shown us that up here, far above the rest of the world, people still had to depend on themselves and each other; they had to bow down every day to the majestic mysteries of the mountains.

⚛

I visited many more organizations and villages in the final weeks I spent in Ladakh. I heard about and saw more instances of successful and unsuccessful development efforts. For example, the Social Worker Research Group had made solar-cell panels available to villagers, an effort that had been extremely successful because they worked with villagers from the beginning to understand and address their needs with the technologies. Similarly, LEDG worked with the Thikse monastery to install a hydraulic ram pump that used the power of gravity to lift and channel water from the stream below the monastery approximately one mile in distance and more than one hundred feet high.

Unfortunately, there were also too many examples of organizations imposing their will and ideas without listening to the villagers. The idea of using solar ovens failed because ovens themselves, used primarily to bake bread and cakes, do not serve much purpose in a Ladakhi's rice-based diet. In one instance, an organization encouraged villagers to build a canal for a ram pump out of traditional material (mud) rather than a modern one (cement). The villagers, who were building the canal, argued that the canal should be made out of cement because mud erodes too quickly. The organization insisted, the villagers agreed, and the canal was built from mud. Some months later, the canal was destroyed by rains and had to be rebuilt, this time with cement.

Development groups also often installed technologies without explaining to the villagers what they were or how to maintain them. The technologies would either not be used for their intended purpose or fall into disrepair. It reminded me of when I had worked in Thailand and saw hundreds of beautifully constructed stone latrine rooms being used as rice storage facilities! The government, it turned out, had simply arrived one day, deemed toilets as the next phase in "developing" the villages, built them and left. That was that.

Developing countries often argue that the burden of responsibility for preserving the earth always falls on them, whether in conserving the scarce remnants of rain forests, controlling pollution or checking population growth. In fact, even though the majority of population growth comes from developing countries, a baby born in America has more than ten times the environmental impact as a baby born in India. Industrialized countries take their gains and preserve their comforts at unquantifiable costs and then put the reins on their developing neighbors.

As I listened to Ladakhis discuss development, I became increasingly convinced that the most important factor in any development effort is listening to those who will live with the consequences of development. Those of us who work in the arena should continue to provide information and education about what we know and believe from our experiences, but beyond this, we have few rights to impose our will, or we will be as colonial as those before us.

Historian William H. McNeill, author of *The Rise of the West*, once defined cultural change as "much more of a process of random experiment than selective survival." Ultimately, perhaps the only lesson we can take away from Ladakh is simply that each society must learn in its own way.

Leaves and Thorns

A few months after Alan's arrival and our trek through Ladakh, I read an International Labor Organization report stating that two-thirds of the world's wage earners are women. Women workers earn only 50 percent of the world's wages, however, and own only 10 percent of the world's assets.

This report was on my mind one beautiful morning. Alan and I were driving through the small towns and villages of Rajasthan with Alan's parents, who had come for a three-week visit from New York. There, on the crowded roads, these statistics became pictures for me. They became the faces of the women I saw working, women who till the fields, attaching the ropes of a water-pulley system to buffalo to irrigate the land; women who harvest acres of mustard, onions and sugarcane; women who carry children straddled on an out-thrust hip, along with baskets of mud bricks, fodder or fresh dung on their heads.

As we drove onto the Udaipur-Jaipur Highway, we saw groups of men and women retarring the road. My husband and I counted, time after time, a ratio of women laborers to men laborers of at least two to one. The women, often with children clinging to their legs, transported mud and stones to the roadsides and dug into the road to tear up existing potholed patches. Many of the "women" were girls who could not have been more than thirteen or fourteen years old.

And while the women worked, what of the men? The men were the "supervisors," pointing a hand here or there to show where the piles should be made. The men sat under the shade of a tree and watched the women working. In one place women marched back and forth with baskets, children and shovels, while a hundred yards away, four men sat in a small circle, drinking tea and laughing, shading their eyes from the bright afternoon sun.

Private contractors in India like to hire women laborers, because they do not have to pay women as much as men. Women are also less likely to strike, protest or demand higher wages. Men, however, are always hired as supervisors. It is not that men have a wonderful life in India. Poverty is equal opportunity, striking men and women. But gender discrimination exists among the poor and among the rich too; among illiterates and educated, lower caste and upper caste.

The condition of women in India follows naturally out of the society's perspective that men are superior to women. Female infanticide, dowry deaths, poor nutrition, less education for women all stem from the perception that women are the lesser sex, to be apologized for rather than celebrated. Emotional and physical violence against women is not only accepted; sometimes it is even enjoyed. Almost always, the perception seems to be that women must have done something to deserve this violence.

❊

Just a few weeks before, I had taken an overnight "video coach" from Bombay to Aurangabad in the northern part of Maharashtra state. Video coaches are the current craze in India: buses with videos that blast out Indian films over loudspeakers scattered above passengers' heads. Luckily for those of us who cannot stand the video coaches, many of the video machines have broken down since they were introduced some years ago, and the bus owners are generally too miserly to repair them.

Unfortunately, on the particular bus I took to Aurangabad, the owner had actually maintained the video machine. It worked a little too well for comfort, going at full volume when I boarded the bus. The movie that was playing was obviously popular. The entire bus (filled with men, except for one or two other lone women) sang along to the songs, clapping their thighs with their hands and wobbling their heads around in time to the music. I watched the movie half-heartedly. The screen was in front of me and my neck felt strained looking out the window the whole time. Plus, it seemed from the light-hearted nature of the songs that the movie would be a typically inane but amusing Hindi movie.

The heroine of the movie, a "modern" woman who goes out with groups of men and wears slightly more daring sari blouses and salvaar kameez than the "traditional" heroine, was laughing loudly and constantly. As the dark of outside began to envelop the bus and we entered rural country, there were fewer lights to watch, fewer interesting roadside events to focus on. I was lulled into a semidozing state, almost forgetting about the noise blasting from the video. Out of my half-closed eyes, I watched the slightly fuzzy screen.

In one scene the heroine is at a bar with a group of men. They are all laughing and joking, gulping shots of whiskey, the heroine included. After being encouraged to drink more than even the men around her, the heroine sees the scene in front of her grow cloudy. The room spins around her, as she is dragged by four men into another room, that also contains a swimming pool. The men begin ripping her clothes off, as she screams and tries in vain to escape. The men in my bus were clapping, singing along with the music that accompanied the scene. My eyes were now fully open; I was transfixed not only by the scene I was watching, but also by the obvious enjoyment of the crowd around me.

The heroine is then thrown into a swimming pool. She cannot swim; she fights with the water to get further from her predators. They surround the pool now. As she scratches at the poolside to get out, she is grabbed by the men. They throw her down onto the floor, and the four men, standing like vultures around a fresh kill, unzip their pants, still laughing. The screen blacks out.

The bus was full of energy by this time. They wanted to see the next scene. It came in the form of a court case. The woman and her sister have brought the four men to trial. The woman is made to recount the entire story to a disbelieving judge and group of jurors who look as though they may get their kicks out of hearing the story recounted in graphic detail. The cases are made in short order and the jury produces its verdict: not guilty. The men in the movie cheer, and their cheers are echoed by the men on the bus. The heroine and her sister cry.

The next scene shows the four men breaking into the heroine's house to exact their revenge on her for taking them to court. They beat her up and then rape her again. They leave laughing and zipping their pants.

I could not watch anymore. I wanted to run to the front of the bus and turn off the video, scream at the men on the bus to think about what they were laughing at. Disgust bubbled up. I was too afraid to turn the video off in a bus full of men on a dark road in the middle of India. I felt helpless, helpless to voice what I saw as blatant discrimination, helpless to do anything to stop it. I struggled with the battle that had become constant: to determine for myself what an isolated incident says about the attitude toward women in this country, but at the same time to avoid generalizing unfairly.

⚙️

There is a Malayalam movie based on the true story of two girls in a Kerala village who ended up committing suicide. They were strong, independent girls who made choices to work outside the home and did not tolerate the everyday harrassment of the men around their village. They fought back at a system that they perceived as unfair, where the injustice was because of their gender. In the end, however, they could not beat the system. Not only were they demeaned publicly, their families were as well. The only bearable way out they saw was death. So they threw themselves into the swirling, foaming ocean they used to play in. The ocean was their friend; it promised a place where they would be freed from the injustices of being women.

Along with their families, the only person who mourned their deaths was a wise boatman who had begged them not to rebel, just to accept the system and their lot in life. "Whether a leaf falls on a thorn or a thorn falls on the leaf, it is always the leaf that is damaged," he said.

I cannot accept the boatman's words. Injustice is to be fought not accepted. But how? Some of the efforts undertaken today serve only to widen the abyss of judgment and blame, not to unite. I am not looking for women to triumph over men, just for both genders to be treated with dignity and respect.

৯৹৹

It is hard to express how I feel as a woman in India. I am often asked this question, and I am always torn in my response. First, I qualify, I cannot answer for the typical Indian woman, because my life has been so different. No, my questioners say. We mean how do you, an independent, strong-willed woman, feel in a country where women are treated so unjustly?

Should I tell them that I am angry that Indian women must go through so much injustice? That my skin breaks out in goosebumps when I hear that a woman is made to stay a hundred feet from her house after giving birth because she is considered dirty—for bearing a child? That a big lump forms in my throat when I ask someone how many children they have, and they respond by telling me how many boys they have, discounting the lives of the girls before they have even been given a chance at life? That sometimes I just do not want to see or acknowledge the injustice anymore, because my brain hurts from thinking about it, and I just want to feel good and comfortable and safe about all the privileges I have in my independent, strong-willed world?

But, if I say all this, I will simply reinforce the many stereotypes that people already have of Indian bride burnings and girls in prostitution. And so, I stop. I work to fight injustice in my own ways, but I check myself from talking too much about the injustice itself. Often I feel I cannot win, because both in my silence and in my words I am betraying my Indian women friends.

Perhaps, I think, I should instead talk about the strength I derive from so many of the Indian women I have met. Perhaps I should talk about those women with whom I connected, not just emotionally but physically—a grasp of hands, a leaning on my shoulder as our bus jolted from side to side, or the brushing of our saris as we walked.

Perhaps I should talk about the fisherwomen I traveled with on a long, narrow boat from Cochin to Vypeen Island in Kerala; how I huddled among masses of women in bright saris gracefully balancing baskets of fish on their heads as we bobbed dangerously across the waters; the complete delight I felt when the boat took an unexpected bump, and the woman next to me grabbed my hand and grinned, white crooked pearls in a sun-darkened face, her touch and smile all-inclusive, generous, open.

Perhaps I should describe my time with Padma in Shingo village, describe how even after our hard work picking potatoes for hours, Padma seemed vigorous, ready to prepare another full meal for the dozen people who needed to be fed, while I collapsed, exhausted, my soft urban muscles aching. Like so many Indian women, Padma was tireless, adept at managing life without identifying its hardships, as those of us brought up in physically unchallenging urban lives tend to do.

Our concept of burden, like any concept, is completely defined by our environment. To a working, independent Western woman, a village woman's life may be the ultimate burden: hauling heavy buckets of water on her head, incessant cooking and cleaning of the house, tending the fields in the hot summer. And yet, when I leave India and return to America, I see men and women carrying equal burdens of a different nature. We work twelve-hour days, spend an hour or two with our children, replace human connections with efficient but alienating technology, and rush from place to place on concrete highways at such a pace that our hearts rattle from nervousness. Would village women really want to exchange their lives for ours?

⚙

Ultimately, I answer the question about Indian women's status with a little of both sides, because there, in the shades of gray, lies the only truth I have found about women in India. Yes, the average Indian woman lacks access to many basic rights and freedoms. We must continue to fight these injustices, to change the perception of woman, to allow choices where there have been none. But simply to pity the Indian woman who is the victim of these wrongs is incomplete and unfair. If we can teach her about our perception of freedom, she too can teach us about strength, about living in the present instead of constantly thinking about what lies ahead.

Through women like Padma, I understand that we, in a more technological, modern world, forget to nurture our innate strength and endurance. We depend on outside sources to replenish us. We lose appreciation for the simplest pleasures: the contact of hands to earth, the holding of a child, the appreciation of the rains. And in our effort to be supermen and superwomen, perhaps we also forget the power of our touch on other human beings. We just are not pushed to develop our own strength.

Padma fought for women's issues by living her life with compassion and dignity. Not involved in theoretical discussions that take place a comforting distance from reality, she was engrossed in survival, in maintaining equanimity no matter the situation she was handed. Women with strength like Padma's began the famous Chipko movement; women like Padma banded together to force local liquor shops to close down because they had become tired of suffering abuse from their drunken husbands.

In their own ways and according to their own agendas, Indian women are taking up fights that make sense in the contexts of their lives. In joining their fights, I learn to appreciate the freedoms I have come to take for granted. In fighting with them, I acknowledge both the injustice and the strength that dominate Indian women's lives. And in the end, I bow my head in respect, because they understand life as it really is so much more than many of us do.

PART II

Spirit and Soul

Life and Death in Varanasi

Varanasi. Alan and I arrived on a cold January day. A cape of morning fog settled around our shoulders, spraying our faces and arms with a light mist. Squeezed in the back of a rickshaw with our backpacks on our laps, we rode from the city's pastoral outskirts into Gowdolia, its teeming, pulsing center where cycle-rickshaws packed the streets, wheel to wheel. Cars struggled to maneuver their large metal frames through the rickshaws, crowds and ambling cows.

There, in the city center, we paid our rickshaw driver and descended into the mass of humanity surrounding us. Gods and goddesses peered out from unexpected places: small roadside shrines, heavily garlanded frames just inside the iron window bars of old houses, faded posters on the walls of small phone booths, and blue and pink drawings in chalk on dirty white-washed walls.

Tiny sidewalk shops, housed in innocuous storefronts, sold everything from lanterns to bicycle tires. People thronged the streets, treading their way gingerly through mud and puddles left over from yesterday's rains, between rickshaws and buffalo, past young children sweeping the streets. Fruit and vegetable sellers sang out the names of their offerings as they wheeled their wooden carts through the masses: *"Alu, phul-gobi, tomater, pyaz,"* (potatoes, cauliflower, tomatoes, onions) echoed with a competitor's offer for bananas, oranges and limes, *"Kele, santare, nimbu."*

As we walked, we moved through a microcosm of India, little countries enclosed in brick and mortar boundaries, defined by the faithfuls who honored their origins in these sections: Bengali Tola, filled with Bengali sweets and saris; and the South Indian quarter where, seated on a small stone bench and kept company by a prepossessing bull with a red and yellow flower garland around its neck and a dozen homesick Tamilians and Malayalees, we enjoyed the South Indian specialities—hot *idli* and *dosa*, steamed rice cakes and fermented rice pancakes served with a soupy lentil mixture called *sambar*.

And finally, down to the river—the famous Ganga Ma, the Ganges—the life-giving water that is the center of Varanasi's core of spiritual renewal and salvation. That day was Saraswati-puja, when Saraswati, the goddess of knowledge and learning, is honored. Devotees had made elaborate idols of Saraswati from straw, clay and wood, which were then paraded down the streets on palanquin-type structures. The processions made their way down to the Ganges, where the idols were then thrown into the water. For at least a week afterward, I could see Saraswati idols all along the river banks that had washed up on shore, soaked and drowned wet straw that served little resemblance to their original forms.

At the river thousands of *yatris* (pilgrims) from around the country bathed in what Hindus consider the holiest river in India. As the sun moved out of the fog, old women, *sadhus* (holy men), children and men greeted the rising, brilliant red circle of light. Waist-deep, they outstretched their arms, raised their palms to the sky and chanted the names of gods: "Ram, Krishna, Shiva, Devi." They worshipped the water, scooped it up in their cupped hands and trickled it over their heads, or held their noses and plunged their heads into it.

Around them toothless old boatmen rowed their passengers down the river, reciting the stories of each *ghat*, literally the steps leading down to the river: How Parvati's earring dropped into the Ganga and formed Marnikarnika, how the fallen temple at Scindia Ghat housed a yogi in an underground cavern; or how the great poet Kabir, unable to receive a mantra from his guru because he was a lowly Muslim weaver's son, lay on the steps of Panchganga Ghat until the guru tripped over him and shouted God's name in surprise, which Kabir took to be the blessing he would not have otherwise received. The boatmen spun their tales like gold, seamless, glittering, evocative pictures of a city bathed in the light of the most powerful gods.

This was Varanasi at its most beautiful; the Varanasi we had heard about, the spiritual center of Hindu India, which is centered around the holy Ganges. Over and over again, in the months Alan and I lived in Varanasi, I went to the river to absorb it. And every time, as I watched the sun rise and set, I understood, for a few seconds, the eternal, the inevitable, the wondrous in life.

We went to Varanasi because we wanted to see it; we stayed because we wanted to experience it. Indians, in particular, often asked us how we could possibly enjoy being in Varanasi, a city where little functions effectively, where entire thoroughfares have been immobilized for years by potholes that are "being worked on" in perpetuity, where one must walk amid cow dung and red spittle from paan chewers, where one must smell the burning of bodies being cremated nearby, where one must see some of the poorest (and the richest) bathing in the river in a final effort to achieve a better life.

But for me, Varanasi was life illuminated with all its contrasts: beautiful, ugly, loud, serene, a public place where I could be completely private. In Varanasi, like no other place we had lived in India, I felt I had a space that had waited for me, embraced me, stimulated my every sense so that I could journey inward with that much more awareness. It still seems strange to me that such a crowded and in many ways intrusive place would allow for such inner exploration, but that is part of Varanasi's fundamental contradiction.

Varanasi, the city's official name, comes from its location between the Varana River, which flows into the Ganges on the north, and the Asi River, which joins the Ganges on the south. Panchganga Ghat, the northernmost ghat, is the place where five rivers are said to come together: four that are (or were) running rivers, and the fifth, the invisible but ever-present river of life and spirituality.

Even more descriptive of the city is its oldest (and still most popular) name, Kashi: shining one, luminous one, illumining one. This was the name used nearly three thousand years ago to refer to the kingdom of the ancient king Kasha, for which it served as the capital.

For Shaivites, those who worship the Lord Shiva, Kashi is their link to Shiva. In the Hindu trinity, Shiva is known as the Auspicious one, the Destroyer and the Creator. In eulogistic literature about Kashi, it is written: "Because that light, which is the unspeakable Shiva, shines here, let its other name be called Kashi." Indeed, Kashi is known as Shiva's city (just as the city of Vrindavan is known to belong to Krishna, an incarnation of Vishnu but honored and loved in his own right as the cowherd god) and abounds with sacred sites that Shiva or his consorts are said to have graced with their presence. Although Shiva is said to be omnipresent, Kashi is his permanent home, the place where his brilliance is most visible and accessible.

Some of the most intense experiences I had in Varanasi were being jostled amid hundreds of pilgrims, men and women seeking spiritual truths, perhaps following the path of holy men by renouncing their homes or simply coming to bathe in the holy river. Varanasi is said to have a floating population of about half a million people: men, women and children who have traveled hundreds of miles on foot or by bus with minimal possessions, simply to have *darshan*, a viewing of holy places and deities.

I never tired of watching these pilgrims. A hardy crowd, they carried cloth sacks on their heads that contained their bedding. Often with no money to spare, they used their life savings for the trip and then to give to priests in gratitude for darshan, or for a special prayer or blessing. They bathed in the Ganges and often did the entire Panch Kroshi pilgrimage, circumambulating the city and its 108 sacred shrines with bare feet in five days. For many of them Varanasi was the only place they had ever seen other than the village in which they were born and had lived their entire life.

What did the pilgrims think as they worshipped? Why did they come to Varanasi, to these temples, to these gods? They came because they believed in the power of the place, in the *shakti*, the power, of Kashi to end all sadness, all *dukhi*, to cleanse away one's sins. They came to thank God for answering their prayers. Others came because they believed that the more prayers they offered, the better their lives would be. They came to die in Kashi and attain *moksha*, salvation and liberation. Kashi held the promise of absolving mortals of their sins, if they merely bathed in the river. Dying in Varanasi is said to be an automatic guarantee of salvation. Indeed, many of the rulers of the princely states subscribed to this belief. They built enormous, intricate palaces on the banks of the Ganges in which they could retire when it came time to die.

One old swami, known simply as Swami-ji, lives in a beautiful, simple, serene shelter on the riverbanks. He tells a story of being very sick and coming to Varanasi to die more than twenty-five years ago. But when he arrived in the city, his health improved. Finally, he decided he would simply stay in Varanasi until his death. No one knows Swami-ji's age, but he is still alive, carrying out his daily baths in the Ganges and waiting to die in Varanasi.

Every pilgrim I spoke to believed fervently that Ganga water is holy, pure. Sensing any shred of disbelief, they would counter, "Haven't you tried to put Ganga water in a jar? It will stay fresh with no odor for years." Perhaps the real miracle is that every day, cows and bulls defecate in the river, dead bodies are dumped in, piles of refuse and sewage are thrown in, and yet there were hundreds of people I met who had bathed in the river their entire lives without ill effect.

To date, the efforts at publicizing the polluted state of the Ganga have failed. The enormous concrete water pillars that were built in a multimillion dollar project to purify the river in the 1980s during Rajiv Gandhi's tenure as Prime Minister are generally out of order. Moreover, all the facts in the world about the state of the river cannot take away its magic and healing power for the millions of Indians who bathe in the water. The *New Yorker* recently highlighted this contradiction when it described the practices of V. B. Mishra, the founder of Varanasi's famous Sankat Mochan temple. Mishra, an engineer by training and a revered Hindu *mahant* (priest) by birth, is leading the renewed fight to clean the Ganga. Although he has studied the contaminants in the river, every morning he bathes in that scientifically contaminated but spiritually life-giving water, immersing his head and drinking in the millions of microbes against which he fights.

I could never bring myself to bathe in the Ganga. I suppose

ultimately I am still a product of my Western upbringing, with a particularly keen sense of public health, given my previous career in that field. And yet, in testament to the contradictions that plague my being, Ganga Ma remained the well for my outpourings, the supreme spirit to which I directed my queries and cogitations, and eventually, the source that blessed and cleansed me.

When Alan and I celebrated our fifth wedding anniversary in Varanasi, we took silver rings made by a local silversmith and, in the dull shimmer of moonlight, dipped them in the river and splashed Ganga water over our heads. Then one year after we left Varanasi for America, I returned to the river and floated three *diyas*, oil-soaked lamps, down her waters in thanks for the child that had been born to us.

Was my relationship to the great river characteristic of my split persona? On the one hand, my refusal to bathe in the Ganga may have been an expression of my resistance to simple faith, a symbol of my ambivalence to religion. On the other hand, my ultimate belief in her power, my eventual return to her, could just as easily have been an expression of my inherent tendency to believe in a greater presence.

ॐ

Varanasi was bathed in music. All around us, we heard music of all kinds: spiritual songs, melodic prayers, Hindi film music and, of course, inspiring classical music. Our initial contact with Indian music was mundane. Every morning, we would wake up at 5 a.m. to taped music, blared through loudspeakers tied to telephone poles around the neighborhood. Many songs mixed and clashed, each one drowning out the melody of the other. The music continued until 7 a.m., when the neighborhood would retreat back into relative quiet, and we could hear the creaking of the cart that belonged to the man who distributed gas cylinders, the twittering of the crows outside and the sharp giggles of the young girls on their way to school.

We asked Sheila, our landlady, about it one day. "The music . . . where is it from?"

Her face lit up. "Isn't it wonderful?" Her beady eyes sparkled

under her glasses. "This is a very special place we are in. We are surrounded by temples. Each one plays its own devotional songs, *bhajans*
and *kirtans*. I love it. Very good for meditation, don't you think?"

I decided I needed to learn more about Indian music. I found a
teacher from the local university who was from South India and was
delighted to teach another South Indian. I went to her house two or
three times a week at 8 a.m. She would serve me a steaming cup of tea,
and then we would go into her music room. We would each sit on a
mat on the floor, facing each other. Behind her towered a statue of the
goddess Saraswati, who was always depicted carrying a *tanpura*, a four-
stringed instrument with a rounded pumpkin gourd bottom. The design of the tanpura provides the constant drone sound in Indian music
that serves as a music reference point for the artist and the listener.
Saraswati always had a fresh garland of flowers around her neck and a
lit stick of incense in front of her. Before our lesson started, my teacher
would touch her hands to her own tanpura and then to Saraswati, to
thank both for the gift of music.

There were no music scores, no notes, no words. My teacher
would sing and I would follow, trying to repeat the tune and sounds as
best as I could. She probably thought I knew more than I did about
Indian music, because she never explained to me the basic concepts of
raags, the backbone of Indian music. I did not know what scale I was
using, what I was singing, nor what constituted the song and what was
merely exercise for the voice. They all blended together and made me
too confused to even formulate proper questions.

The lessons were in the classical tradition of *guru-shiksha*, teacher
and disciple. As a center of classical Indian music, Varanasi has birthed
many of the most famous Indian artists. Many, like Ravi Shankar, Pandit
Jasraj and Zakir Hussain, make at least one annual pilgrimage to play
in Varanasi. Concerts remain, as traditionally has been the case, free
to the public and extremely well-attended. Many are several-day festivals and feature various forms of Indian music.

Young and old musicians talk about how different music is today. The traditions are dying, they say, and little is done to preserve
and further Indian classical music. Audiences no longer appreciate music

in its purest form; everything has become "fast" to keep up with today's fast-paced life.

Chote Lal Misra, a tabla guru of international repute, said to me that in the guru-shiksha tradition "the guru is like God. A student worships his guru as God, and through that guru-God, the disciple gets inspiration. Only if you give yourself completely to your guru can your music be inspired." Chote Lal showed me his puja room, where the walls were filled with black-and-white pictures of his guru as a young boy, playing the tabla, teaching, posing with students. Interspersed with these pictures were a few framed pictures of some of the common divinities.

"He is still my guru," said Chote Lal reflectively. "I lived with him for twelve years, from the age of six to eighteen, until he died in 1958. I was his son in every way. I did everything for him, not just studying music. I took care of him and his family, which I treated as my own. I went to every concert with him and learned the art of music by watching everything he did. Even after his death, I continue to do everything for his family. His wife is still alive and I look after her, financially and otherwise. Same with his children, who are like my brothers and sisters."

"And today?" I asked. "How is it different?"

"Today? There are few real gurus or shikshas left. Most of the gurus are just interested in money, not in teaching. And most of the shikshas just feel that they are paying money and deserve to get a service for that money. These people will never be able to progress properly on the path. They may learn some things, but they will not be truly great performers."

"What about the Westerners who come to learn?" I asked, knowing that Chote Lal had many Western students.

"Many Westerners come here just for a few weeks, in between their tourist activities. They are not committed to it. They do not come to me. They go to those people who claim to be teachers but who can barely play themselves. But even among those who are serious about music, there are only a few who are truly devoted to music and understand the need to follow the guru-shiksha tradition. But," he said leaning forward, "if they do understand this, then these Western-ers are often better disciples and progress further than the Indian stu-dents. Westerners have no tradition like this in their culture, so when they begin to understand this tradition, they are understanding with their intellect. When they believe in it and its benefits, their faith is so strong, it cannot be broken. Indian disciples often only believe in the tradition because they have heard about it, not because they truly understand it and its implications."

Like Chote Lal, most great Indian musicians believe that truly inspired music comes from the gods and is dedicated back to them. They speak about instruments in terms of the gods—Krishna's flute or the coming together of Lord Shiva and his consort Parvati in the sound of the drum. The greatest of performers say that they perform for the gods. The musicians draw inspiration from the divine and transform it into magical music for ordinary mortals.

Those who know Indian classical music well talk of both the physical sound and the spiritual sound. Physical sound provides im-mediate pleasure and is audible for the simplest person to enjoy. Spiri-tual sound, however, is produced from the ether of the soul and is more difficult to hear. Those lucky enough to hear it, it is said, are liberated by it forever.

৯

Varanasi loves celebrations and festivals. For every festival the city is decorated with glittering lights, the streets are adorned with bountiful flowers and garlands, special ceremonies take place and loud music blares. In the winter, especially, Varanasi becomes one enormous wed-ding ground. Wedding bands playing the latest Hindi pop songs en-tertain raucous dancing processions. The turbaned groom, decked out in gold and white garb, sits atop a horse—or nowadays, in a signal of modernization and display of wealth, in a shiny new red Maruti car. The live band, in red and gold uniform, precedes him, and the wed-ding party (consisting mostly of young men) surrounds him. The young men gyrate unabashedly to the music in an odd cross between the limbo and John Travolta. A train of paid laborers, young girls and women, connected by the wires of the large electric lamps they carry on their heads, encloses the crowd. The lamps are attached to a generator that follows the whole crowd on a big platform. The generator's deafening noise competes with the band, but few seem to be bothered.

Although important festivals occur almost every other week in Varanasi, each is celebrated as if it were the last. The compounds around important temples undergo massive transformations. Roads normally filled with cars and auto-rickshaws turn into veritable flower markets: Smart entrepreneurs expertly erect makeshift shops selling garlands of jasmine and marigolds, carnations and roses, on either side of the temple entrance. Others sell various offerings to be given as food to the gods—condensed milk sweets, small packets of white sugar balls and coconuts. Long lines often form for men who want to take darshan. A separate, much shorter line usually exists for women who want to take darshan, so that men and women will not be pushed against each other in the mad crush of devotion. One can often see water and milk trickle out of the temple onto the road, evidence of the thousands who have taken *prasad*, offerings that have been blessed by the priests, or have had holy water or milk poured onto their heads by a priest.

During Holi, the festival of colors that signals the entrance of spring and the new year (generally held in March, just before the harvests), all that is bad from the previous year is symbolically released through the burning of straw statues of the demoness Holika. For weeks before Holi, the streets are lined with shops displaying pyramids of colored powder. Holi morning is called "Wet Holi" for the gallons of water mixed with colored powders that are thrown over friends, families and passersby. In the midafternoon everyone returns home to bathe and put on their new white clothes. This begins "Dry Holi" and visiting hours. Families and groups of people walk around together visiting relatives and friends, dry colors are smeared on foreheads as a sign of welcome and Varanasi hospitality is at its finest.

We visited several households during dry Holi and came home with our stomachs stuffed with *dahi-vada*—fried balls of ground lentils and rice, covered with yoghurt—and salty snacks of *namkeen*. Our foreheads and faces were smeared with red, pink, yellow and green. By nighttime, bonfires blazed and straw images of the demoness Holika were thrown in and burned. By midnight, a smoke-filled city slept again, exhausted by the day's activities.

There are countless other festivals throughout the year: Shivratri (the greatest Shiva festival, which celebrates the marriage of Lord Shiva to Parvati), Navratra (the nine-day festival honoring different forms of Goddess Devi), Ram Navami (which celebrates the birth of Lord Rama, the warrior king incarnation of Vishnu) and Burhwa Mangal (the river festival of music). But Varanasi does not only wait for festivals to celebrate its gods and goddesses. Individual days of the week belong to a different god or goddess: Monday is Shiva's day, Tuesdays and Saturdays belong to the goddess Durga and the monkey god Hanuman, Fridays are for Santoshi Mata and Sankata Devi. Each day the temples that honor that day's particular god or goddess are flooded with devotees. Devotees know their gods, know their eating habits, know their good days and bad ones. Hanuman, for example, must be given *ladoos* (sweet fried balls made of besan flour and sugar), while Lakshmi, the goddess of auspiciousness, wealth and fortune, must be honored with specific grains and flowers. Certain days are good for weddings, while others are better for travel. Tuesdays and Saturdays, in particular, are the days during which the deities deal with the world's problems. These are days to be feared, while Wednesdays and Thursdays are generally auspicious days.

Bringing meaning to each season, festival, day and even specific time of day internalizes the existence of the divine. Without compartmentalization, the god or divine spirit that is celebrated in each of these occasions is allowed to run free, to exist at the forefront of consciousness rather than in the folds of its deep interior where it is brought out once a week like a prize object at show-and-tell. Ultimately, it is this omnipresence of the divine—in language and in thought—that encircles Varanasi in spiritual light.

ॐ

"Death may be the opposite of birth," wrote Diana Eck, a well-known Western authority on Varanasi, "but it is not the opposite of life."

Certainly not in Varanasi. In many parts of the Western world, people fear death. Perhaps this is because death in a Western context often signifies the end of an individual persona, the end of ego. In the West, people turn their faces from dead bodies, plan tombstones that will remember them in that individual form after death and distance themselves from the entire process of death and dying by stashing the old and the dying in hospitals and retirement homes where no one will have to witness the natural process of aging and death.

Across the oceans, however, Indians welcome death as the ultimate goal of life, the possibility of moving onward and upward, of achieving moksha. Indeed, in Hindi the accepted way of saying a person has died is to say *"Moksha mila,"* literally, he or she has received salvation.

In Varanasi, once termed the world's largest cremation grounds, wooden stretchers carrying dead bodies are transported by family members to the river. In wandering the streets of Varanasi, I became accustomed to seeing bodies, wrapped in magnificent bright pinks and blue, lying in the middle of crowded roads. Once, I witnessed a body surrounded by a group of seven or eight men chatting, unconcerned about the traffic or the body. Like those around me, when a dead body crossed my path, I would raise my hands in a traditional *namaste*, the common greeting which means "the divine in me greets the divine in you." The greeting acknowledged the dead for the possibility that they may have achieved their final fulfillment.

⚮

I am standing on the balcony of an old building just above Marnikarnika Ghat, the most auspicious place in Varanasi, "the place of earth's creation as well as its destruction." Every day, in the patch of riverbank below me, 150–200 bodies are cremated. In their destruction comes the creation of a new life; and, it is hoped, a better life.

Today five fires burn vigorously underneath me, each one managed by a couple of *Doms*, the untouchable caste of people responsible for cremation. The Doms retain exclusive authority for all goings-on at cremations, from buying and selling wood, to tending the fires, to collecting fees for the burning of each corpse.

No one seems particularly concerned with my presence here, but I feel odd, out of place, to be looking in on someone else's passing out of this world, someone I do not even know. "Can you imagine," Alan whispers to me, "if a couple of strangers showed up at a funeral in America? It would certainly not be acceptable!"

A hundred feet away from the funeral pyres, children play cricket. Hundreds of people, some possibly family but most simply laborers, stall owners and passerbys, stand and watch, talking and laughing as if at a social gathering. Lines of men carry loads of wood to and from the ghat. Boats take families into the middle of the river to sprinkle the ashes of their recently cremated ones. As the smell of burning flesh wafts through the air, I gag reflexively.

To the right of the cremation site, I notice a massive weighing scale that measures the wood for each cremation.

"It takes two quintals of wood to burn a body," says an Indian man next to me, noticing my gaze.

"What kind of wood do they use?"

"Depends on how rich the family is. If they are very wealthy, they use sandalwood. If they are very poor, they use whatever they can find." And then, matter-of-factly, as if he is describing a movie he recently saw, he reports, "It takes three hours for a male body to burn, and three and a half if it's a female body, because of the hip bones."

My hands instinctively travel to my hips, caressing them as if to assure myself of their presence on my own body. As he talks, I marvel at the macabre art of cremation. First, the body is blessed and dipped in the Ganga. Then it is wrapped in a very specific way, with pieces of wood inserted here and there between folds of cloth to ensure that all the right parts will catch on fire. Once placed on the fire, the Dom again blesses it, circling it three times in the air with a lit stick of wood. Now the cremation begins. The Doms move, turn and flip the body as deftly as the greatest of chefs. As the edges burn, the body begins to shrink. And as the body turns into a simple blaze of fire, I understand that I am witnessing the disintegration of the physical into its metaphysical soul. I am seeing the ultimate commonality of this physical life, which no matter what caste, what class, what country, always disintegrates.

⚛

The Festival of the Gods, Dev Diwali or Diwali of the Gods, follows Diwali, the Festival of Lights. It signals the end of the auspicious autumn month of Karthik. The last night of the month is Karthik Purnima, the night of the full moon when sun, moon and earth are lined up perfectly, when hundreds of thousands of bathers flood to the Ganges for a bath and puja. Along the river for days, *akash deeps*—sky lamps— have been planted in the ground, thin tall reeds of bamboo that have at their tops clay lamps to guide the trapped spirits of ancestors from earth to heaven.

Dev Diwali, fitting to its name, turned Varanasi into its most ethereal self. The ghats were decorated with thousands of diyas. These lamps were placed in rows along the steps of the ghats, along balconies and rooftops and around the outlines of drawings of a map of India and representations of the goddess Lakshmi.

We took out a wooden boat that night. As we floated down the river, I watched the Ganges shoreline sparkle in a necklace of shimmering lights. On our right, the moon—Chandra Amma, as she is called—rose regally, first just a red shadow where the setting sun had just disappeared, and then a ball of fire that metamorphosed into radiant gold, rising higher and higher into the sky until she assumed her rightful place high above humans in the sacred skies. Firecrackers burst and noisy rockets were launched from the riverbanks that exploded in reds and greens somewhere above our heads. People sent diyas floating down the river, and their flames shimmered even in the reflection they cast on the black glittering water.

We floated down the river until there were no more firecrackers and some of the diyas had burned through their short, oil-soaked cotton wicks. Then, unwilling to leave what felt sacred, we sat for hours more on the ghats and waited until all of Varanasi around us had settled into a quiet darkness.

Sitting in Silence

It is four a.m. From far away, a bell sounds. As my conscious mind stirs, the gongs get closer. I open my eyes slowly, stare at the dark room, pull the quilts higher over my body. At this vulnerable moment of awakening, light seems too harsh, so Mrs. Goel, my roommate, and I dress in darkness and silence. Once dressed, the light goes on in an attempt to jar the senses into alertness. Cold water splashed on the face, teeth brushed, we hear the gong sounding its five-minute signal. The gate creaks as we unlock it and go outside.

It is still dark, except for a faint silvery glow to the sky signaling that in a few hours, day will break. The path up to the *dhamma* hall (named for the universal law of nature in Buddhism) is marked by the gleam of the painted white bark of the trees. This is the sacred place where the divine is said to live. I feel the rocks and stones of the mud path through the soles of my rubber sandals and wool socks. It is cold, but the air feels good against my cheeks. A big shawl, neck warmer and hat keep my body heat locked in. We take our shoes off outside the hall, and take our "seats"—cushions on the floor—for the day's first meditation session.

For ten days our mornings would begin like this. We lived like monks and nuns, meditating for ten hours daily, taking a vow of silence (except to ask the teacher questions about the meditation technique), and refraining from reading, writing and even making eye contact with others. During this period we were to undergo what was termed a "surgical operation of our minds," a physically and mentally exhausting process to penetrate the unconscious levels of our minds.

Alan and I had left Varanasi to spend a few months working with a development organization in the hills of Uttar Pradesh when we first heard about the Vipassana meditation technique. The organization believed strongly that spirituality needed to be incorporated into "development," that this would help in bringing about a sense of balance and community that was needed for traditional development efforts to be successful. A new Vipassana center had just opened in the foothills of the Himalayas, and we decided to attend a meditation retreat there.

Although I was raised a Hindu, I have often felt more connected to the tenets of Buddhism. Meditation as a means for exploring one's inner self was the path that made the most sense to me. Best of all, it did not require priests to let others in the door. It was just about the self. Vipassana, one of India's oldest meditation techniques, was rediscovered by Gautama the Buddha twenty-five centuries ago. It became the basis of Buddha's teachings and was practiced by large numbers of people across northern India and later Burma (now Myanmar), Sri Lanka and Thailand.

Five centuries after the Buddha, Vipassana again disappeared from India. This time, however, the teachings were preserved by a chain of teachers in Burma. The technique was more widely popularized in recent times by S. N. Goenka, a seventy-four-year-old Burmese native. Today, there are more than twenty Vipassana centers worldwide, half in India and the rest in America, Australia, France, Japan, Nepal and the United Kingdom.

Vipassana, we would learn through our nightly discourses, is an experiential journey along Buddha's Eightfold Noble Path to enlightenment. This path, also known as the Noble Path of Truth or the Middle Way, has three main components: *shila* (moral living), *samadhi* (mental concentration) and *panne* (wisdom). To uphold the concept of shila, each Vipassana student is required to undertake five moral precepts: abstention from killing, stealing, lying, sexual misconduct and the use of intoxicants. Vipassana develops samadhi in each student through the initial practice, during the first three days of the camp, of *anapana* meditation, which focuses on observing one's own respiration. Only on the fourth day are students introduced to the actual practice of Vipassana meditation, the beginning of *panne*, or wisdom.

Vipassana courses are a minimum of ten days (although there are now variations of Vipassana that offer shorter courses). No fees are accepted for the course, board or lodging; past students donate the funds to sustain the centers and the courses. Donations are completely voluntary, a way of giving thanks for the wisdom one has received. Vipassana's growing popularity over the past two decades is just one indication that increasing numbers of people seek "meaning" in their lives, and are searching for an intangible sense of inner peace and purpose. Silent meditation is social change that starts and ends with the individual.

⚭

The Vipassana center was set next to a protected forest reserve. Within the compound a wide dirt path separated the men's and women's residences. The residences comprised several rooms set around a central open courtyard. The rooms, concrete rectangles that measured about ten feet by eight feet, were simply furnished with two single beds on beige-painted steel frames. Above the beds were a few shelves for our belongings. Some rooms had attached toilets, but hot water could only be obtained from the large common bath area tucked in one corner of the courtyard. We took our meals in a simple dining hall where, again, men and women were separated. We sat on thin, straw floor mats, feeling the cold concrete beneath the mats seep through our warm layers of clothes and into our bodies, only to be warmed temporarily with simple but hearty vegetarian food.

Separate paths for men and women led to the dhamma hall, where all the meditations occurred. About thirty feet by sixty feet, the room had high pointed ceilings and a tin roof that magnified the outside noises of leaves falling, langurs playing and the gentle patter of rain. The hall was lit with two bare bulbs, one in the front, one in the back. We took the same seats each day, with men and women segregated on different sides of the room.

Each course was staffed by an assistant teacher, who sat at the front of the room. With the rapid increase in the number of Vipassana camps across India, Goenka no longer leads every camp as he used to. However, he is stilled called The Teacher and, to preserve consistency in the teachings, all instructions on meditation technique as well as the ninety-minute nightly discourse are taped recordings of his voice. Our assistant teacher was a radiologist by profession from the neighboring district of Tehri. He had a round face, usually the only part of his body not covered by the enormous shawl he wrapped around himself. He would sit perfectly still, cross-legged and straight-backed, for hours on end, his face serene.

Because the course we attended was only the third to be given in the new center, we were two of only seven students and the only ones who were "new," meaning we had never participated in a Vipassana course before. Not surprisingly, Alan was the only foreigner. Our fellow students were Dr. and Mrs. Goel—he a surgeon—probably in their fifties; Ravi, a young pediatrician from Ludhiana; Mr. Mehta, a limber, yoga-practicing retired engineer in his seventies; and another small woman who was a college professor and always sat as straight-backed and still as the assistant teacher.

Our daily schedule was tightly regulated: wake at 4 a.m., meditate for two hours, a ninety-minute break for breakfast and rest followed by a two-hour meditation session and then a two-hour break for lunch and rest. The afternoon consisted of four hours of meditation, followed by a one-hour tea break. The evenings started with another hour of meditation, a ninety-minute taped discourse and a final half-hour of meditation. Because we were not allowed to read or write in our rooms (and we were exhausted after a full day of meditation anyway), sleep came quickly and completely.

I found it hard to be silent, in language and thought. Most human beings allow so little time to practice this. Meditation is at its core about this practice: about creating balance and strengthening the ability to look inward and rely on ourselves to generate the water that fills our wells of emotion, stability and, ultimately, ability.

⚜

We spent the first three days of the camp practicing anapana meditation, a meditation that requires simply observing one's own breathing. Unlike some yoga practice, which regulates breath, anapana asks simply that one notice the breath and become familiar with it.

This felt impossible at times. Not only were we to observe our breath for a seemingly never-ending ten and a half hours a day for three days, we were to observe it only in one small space, "the small triangular space including the inside and outside of our nostrils." The second day we were allowed to expand this area of observation to include the area above the upper lip and below the nostrils. And finally, on the third night, to prepare our minds for the extreme concentration and alertness needed to practice Vipassana, we were asked to again narrow the focus to the small area below the nostrils and above the upper lip.

It seems almost too simple to think that we could actually understand the undisciplined, transient nature of our minds by becoming aware of which nostril our breath enters and leaves; or where, on this small area the size of my forefinger, we feel our breath touching. But the ultimate lesson is not the actual sensation but simply the observation: observation that must be without judgment or anger; observation that focuses on the undisciplined mind calmly and persistently; observation that allows us to, without frustration, bring the mind back each time, like a parent with a straying child. Developing equanimity is the real lesson to take from meditation practice into real life.

On the fourth day we were introduced to the actual technique of Vipassana meditation. Instead of observing breath, Vipassana involves observing the sensations on one's body. To do this, one divides one's body into small pieces about three inches wide and then moves one's attention from top to bottom, noting the sensations taking place in every three-inch piece of one's body. These sensations are obviously different for every student. I experienced a range of sensations, from gross pain and stiffness to itching and tickling, to an awareness of bodily heat or cold.

The theory behind observing sensations, according to the Buddha, is that mind and matter are interrelated. As thoughts arise in the mind, they manifest themselves as sensations on the body. Observing the mind directly is almost impossible, because it is abstract and invisible. The next best thing is to observe the manifestations of the thoughts that arise in the mind as they appear in bodily sensations.

If one were to categorize sensations, they would fit into two distinct categories: pleasant (perhaps a relaxed, gentle throbbing) or unpleasant (pain, heat or cold). According to the Buddha's teachings, one generally reacts to these sensations either with craving or aversion. If it is a pleasant sensation or experience, one craves more of that pleasantness. If it is an unpleasant experience, one tries desperately to avert and avoid that unpleasantness. These reactions are based on habitual patterns of reacting that have been established in the unconscious mind from past reactions. For example, when one feels an itchy sensation, one might automatically respond by scratching, because one is conditioned to avert an unpleasant sensation like itchiness. Vipassana teaches that if one would instead simply observe the itchiness objectively, one would see that it, like everything in nature, is impermanent, passing. In not reacting to sensations in the patterned way, one starts to rid the unconscious mind of its habitual patterns.

The understanding of impermanence, *anicha*, was fundamental to the Buddha's enlightenment. According to dhamma, everything is impermanent. The world, composed of infinite subatomic particles of matter, is constantly changing. The physical and mental structures of the body and mind are also changing. Yet, humans react to these impermanent sensations as if they either can be made permanent or are permanent. It is these reactions of desire and hatred, of craving and aversion, that are the root causes of suffering, said the Buddha. If one can develop equanimity—centeredness in the face of change, of ups and downs—with the understanding of impermanence, one would be liberated from miseries.

The idea that one should maintain equanimity in one's life was difficult for me initially. I imagined this path leading to a world full of dispassionate, equanimous robots that have no strong beliefs moving them to action. Certainly in my life I felt that much of my work for social justice had been motivated by a strong emotional conviction about how the world should be. How could this emotional conviction be reconciled with equanimity and a seeming lack of passion?

I asked the assistant teacher this question. "You are confusing passion with compassion," he said. "The human mind is naturally full of compassion. Harnessing this compassion, rather than giving way to our passions, actually conserves energy and allows us to work efficiently, effectively and with full commitment to our beliefs. There is nothing that can be achieved with passion that cannot be achieved with compassion. As Goenka-ji says, 'Vipassana will make life full of action but free from reaction.'"

Remaining equanimous is only the first difficult step of the extremely long process of enlightenment. Remaining equanimous to sensations during meditation, similarly, is the first step to becoming aware of how one responds on a daily basis to the vicissitudes of life.

During the first three days of the camp, we had been allowed to change postures during meditations. However, on beginning Vipassana, we were instructed that we should use *adithana*, or strong determination, to maintain the same position during the three daily one-hour group meditation sessions. This instruction is primarily to facilitate the observation of sensations, such as pain, and to understand the power of mind over matter. In the beginning, it seemed impossible. My knees screamed with pain after about fifteen minutes, my feet felt as if they would fall off from numbness, and I developed searing pain in the muscles between my shoulder blades from trying to keep my back straight. Yet I found that as I watched, the pain in my knees lessened and eventually disappeared. The pain in my back too disappeared. And on the seventh day I was able to move away from using the wall as support, despite a long-standing problem with a missing disk in my lower spine that has caused me severe pain in the past.

Even more difficult than maintaining the single posture, however, was controlling my innate desire to "succeed" at meditation, a desire which is completely antithetical to the very nature of meditation. This was where I saw the lessons of maintaining equanimity most starkly. Despite warnings from the Assistant Teacher, I found myself elated when I was able to focus my mind, able to observe my sensations. When I actually reached the point at which I felt my entire body pulsing as if energy was flowing through my body, I found myself craving that feeling again and then being upset when I was not able to achieve it. As I sat there, experiencing these ups and downs, I realized that this represented my life. Filled with desires to succeed and achieve, I was focused on the future and rarely on observing the present, on simply accepting the vicissitudes of life. Ultimately, the degree to which I could develop this equanimity in daily life would be the measure of my progress on the path to enlightenment. In Buddhism this stage in which one is without craving or attachment is nirvana, literally, *ni* (no) *vana* (craving).

The Buddha's teachings discourage individuals from blaming others for their discontent and instead place complete responsibility for individual happiness in that individual's hands. One choose's one's own state of mind. Goenka offers the example of someone who has been wronged and chooses to take the case to court. It takes seven years and many appeals courts before the case finally reaches the Supreme Court. The court rules in favor of the individual, but has it taken away the unrest of the mind over the past seven years?

Another story of the Buddha describes a man who verbally abused the Buddha in anger. The Buddha simply smiled. The old man became more furious.

"Why are you smiling? Did you not hear what I said?"

"Old man," replied the Buddha, "if someone gives you a gift and you refuse to accept it, where does the gift go?"

"What a stupid question! Of course, if you do not accept the gift, the bearer of the gift will have to take it back and keep it."

"Exactly," said Buddha. "If you come bearing this gift of insults, and I refuse to accept it, you will have to keep it. You will be miserable, not I."

Mahatma Gandhi, though he did not practice Vipassana per se, shared much in common with its teachings. He too, in his search for truth, had seen the value in making the mind equanimous. In his autobiography, *The Story of My Experiments with Truth*, Gandhi wrote about the difficulty of this task:

> But the path of self-purification is hard and steep. To attain to perfect purity one has to become absolutely passion-free in thought, speech and action; to rise above the opposing currents of love and hatred, attachment and repulsion. I know that I have not in me as yet that triple purity, in spite of constant ceaseless striving for it. . . . To conquer the subtle passions seems to me to be far harder than the physical conquest of the world by the force of arms. . . . I know that I have still before me a difficult path to traverse.

ॐ

In one sense, the Vipassana meditation technique is more scientific than spiritual. It is a logical, rational process in which one is asked to believe only that which one experiences. There is no place for imagination in Vipassana. Unlike many other meditation techniques that focus on visualization of objects or idols, or the chanting of mantras to concentrate the mind, Vipassana focuses on observing only breath and sensations. Vipassana teachings ultimately hold that mantras and visualization, although effectively concentrating the mind, take away from observing one's own fundamental and tangible truths.

The logical nature of Vipassana makes it easy for those of us used to intellectualizing everything to embrace the theory without maintaining the practice. Goenka himself warns that simply playing "intellectual games" provides no benefit. The practice must include daily meditation as well as bringing the principles of equanimity into daily situations. The Buddha's teachings, including the technique of Vipassana, are entirely centered around individuals developing their own wisdom through personal experience.

Our final morning at the Vipassana center the sky was filled with tufts of clouds, their edges tinged with the pink of daybreak. I stood for a few minutes in the peace of outer and inner quiet. A crow, its blackness accentuated by the blue and white sky, sailed away in the distance. The time had come to leave this safe cocoon, to integrate theory and practice into everyday life. I knew it would not be easy to maintain an awareness of the present moment given the forceful rush of life. But I also knew that somehow it would be essential, the basis of the ultimate journey to self-discovery and enlightenment.

I struggle with this now, as I did then. The world, in its tangible busy form, can be destructively powerful. The brief flashes of awareness from concentrated meditation provide glimpses of what is possible, but those glimpses are so terribly fragile, shattered by the slightest happening or thought. If ten hours of sitting meditation seemed intolerable during the retreat, after the retreat it seemed unimaginable. "Did we really sit for that long?" my husband and I asked each other back in our house in the hills as we disengaged our creaky legs from their cross-legged stance after a mere thirty minutes.

I began giving myself all kinds of excuses, eventually reducing the required meditation time from its original two hours to "as long as I can." My biggest problem in continuing the practice was that I had reentered the world. There were things I needed to do after meditation, things I had done before meditation that my mind kept drifting back to. There were fights I had with my husband, new anger that had built up and began occupying any empty spaces I had managed to create through meditation. There were newspaper reports of injustice, books I had read that got me thinking about all kinds of interesting, valid, completely absorbing issues. I now understand why monks-in-training have to shut themselves off in a cavelike situation for some time, or, like me, they would be distracted by the world.

I am not monk material. But I believe that the only answer I am going to find leading to my personal search for truth and meaning will be through journeying inward. I also know that a search that difficult will be impossible for me to sustain if I do not catch a glimpse of where I am going. Perhaps maintaining that sustenance from my own desire to move inward is actually my test.

When I do manage to meditate now, it provides for me a sense of grounding. It is time with me—not *me*, as in the physical self that sits on the ground and closes its eyes, but *me*, the collection of physical atoms that comprise the body, that are part of and one with the surrounding world. But there is another type of meditation different from sitting meditation that develops as I become more aware. This meditation is mindfulness, part of the ongoing cycle of life that tells us to be present to our surroundings, feelings and emotions as we go about our days. Both kinds are essential; they are linked to each other and they link me to an inner self and an outer world.

Because I am in a physical reality that I can see and touch, continuing meditation in its many forms often seems like a huge leap of faith. Because I also have a persistent sense that there is another reality than this physical one, I see meditation as my only means for exploring this nebulous, unsettling unreality. It is this very unsettled feeling that ultimately pushes me to look deeper, to question. Ultimately, it *is* a leap of faith.

Religion: The Faith and the Business

T emples are one of the best investments you can make," a friend once commented to me dryly. Not far from where Alan and I lived in Varanasi, a new temple was being built. The owners were in stiff competition with the owners of Varanasi's popular Sankat Mochan temple. To raise money and popularize the temple even before it was completed, they stationed the primary Shiva *lingam*—the phallic and iconic stone shaft that is Lord Shiva's sacred symbol—in the back of a brand new, richly garlanded van. Brahmin priests gathered around the van's back door to do *aarti*, the lighting of lamps before the divine image, complete with bells and chanting. A rope was tied at the beginning of the street where the van was parked, indicating the entrance of the temple, where we were to remove our shoes. The van was a "touring temple van," making its way through the country and stopping for months at a time in different places. The big money, after all, comes from the ongoing spate of funerals, births, exorcisms and illnesses.

The longer I stayed in Varanasi, the more I saw the exploitation of faith and religion, the abuse of honest belief and devotion. The corruption of religion in Varanasi was spurred on initially by its *thugs*. Although now a common word in the English language, thugs were the original band of professional assassins and cheats active in North India. Many of these thugs worked with or were directly employed by powerful *pundit* families, religious priest families, who controlled the masses through religion. A well-known movie made in the 1960s called

Sangarsh detailed the hypocrisies of these so-called religious families. There is a scene in the movie where the pundit tells an unsuspecting couple that they must "offer" their daughter to him, then they can buy her back with several thousand rupees and the wife's string of pearls.

I have been told by many in Varanasi that these incidents actually did (and do still) happen. There continues to be an elaborate system of "trapping" unsuspecting visiting pilgrims by getting them locked into a particular pundit family, in the same way that unsuspecting tourists might be lured to a particular hotel or shop. On the train several stops before Varanasi, a man working for a thug will board the train and begin to gain the confidence of the pilgrims he meets. True con artists, these men are well trained to recognize where people are from, to mention names of known families from the same villages, to endear themselves to the pilgrims. Upon reaching Varanasi, the pilgrims are taken to the pundits, who advise them to perform several rituals, including large donations of money and jewelry, to please the gods.

The former mahant, head priest, of the famous Kashi-Vishwanath Temple was put in jail in the early 1970s for stealing from the temple hundreds of thousands of rupees in silver and gold. His son continues to call himself mahant, even though the government has since taken over the temple and installed its own mahant. It was clear just from the hourlong conversation I had with the younger mahant that the power, status and wealth gained as a powerful religious leader was hard to give up. Given that absolute power corrupts absolutely in other arenas of life, it should be no surprise that it might do the same in the spiritual arena.

Like in other parts of the world and in other religions, many religious leaders are determined to keep the masses in their clutches, and the best way to do that is to keep religion mystical and unfathomable, distant and therefore accessible only through one of God's chosen interpreters. After all, if people actually began to feel empowered to talk to God themselves, what use would they have for the priests?

According to popular legend in India, there are sixty-four ways for ghosts and *pishachas* (goblins) to be created. The most common way is during an accidental death of an individual. Other ways include dying at the hands of thieves, dying from tuberculosis or infection, dying while seeking wealth or dying as the prey of wild animals. In all of these ways the human being has not lived out her life and the ghost of her spirit is trapped. Once trapped, ghosts can be unleashed on people by others or can occupy bodies of their own accord. They manifest their presence through the body they have occupied in the form of illness, insanity or general mischief.

To get rid of these ghosts, and also to bless the spirits of their dead ancestors (the latter done especially during the festival of Pitri Paksha, the fortnight of the ancestors), people visit *ojhas*—traditional village or witch doctors. Largely found in villages, though also in fewer numbers in cities, ojhas can perform rites that are said to rid the inhabited of their ghosts. The ojha, frequently in conjunction with a temple pundit, will take on the wrath of the ghosts, and often, the illnesses that have manifested themselves in the inhabited individual. For recompense the fees to both ojhas and pundits run high, often into tens of thousands of rupees, depending on the wealth of the client, and the number and type of ghosts.

I have heard and witnessed many testimonials to the healing power of ojhas and other traditional healers. I have read and seen enough to know that spiritual power is not only plausible but real. What disturbs me, however, are the stories of how this same spiritual power can be so easily abused. An Indian friend of mine named Vidhu had served as the translator for a foreigner doing dissertation research on ojhas. I asked him about what he had found along these lines. "Some are good," Vidhu said, "but most are . . . " he stopped. "Never mind. I will take you and you can see."

According to Vidhu, the best place to see ojhas in action in Varanasi was at the Pishachas Mochan temple on the outskirts of the city. This spot, a forty-five minute rickshaw ride away, was the place where "pishachas are liberated." Vidhu and I were dropped in the middle of a crowded market and then walked five minutes through smaller lanes, where bicycles and pedestrians going in opposite directions gave way to each other. The few shops along the way were closed in deference to the afternoon sun. The narrow lanes eventually led to a thoroughfare. As we walked, Vidhu explained that there were five ghats on this particular strip, all built alongside an enormous temple tank and known for getting rid of ghosts.

The main temple was bigger than the others but without the imposing structure I had imagined. It was painted peachy-red and the inner sanctum was surrounded by a wide, cool, shaded area. On the veranda outside was a large round stone head of Pishacha himself, a goblin who was caught sneaking into Kashi by the god Bhairava, then decapitated and allowed to remain in the temple to liberate other goblins from their painful condition.

Whatever his powers, the statue of Pishacha was not particularly pleasing. The head was big, round and neckless, emerging spontaneously from the ground where the rest of his body appeared appropriately trapped. A bushy mustache followed his upper lip and his teeth were pulled into an odd, mocking grimace.

Vidhu and I settled ourselves in a squat behind the temple priest on the shady covered stone temple porch. The priest had a belly that protruded almost to the ground in his cross-legged position, and between the folds of flab on his bare tummy, sweat collected and glistened. He grunted in our direction when Vidhu touched his feet and introduced me, seeming quite content to have us watch the proceedings. In front of the priest sat an ojha, a woman in her fifties who lived in a nearby village. Around her, the family who had hired her sat on their haunches. Apparently they had been plagued with a series of bad events, from dying crops to inexplicable noises in their house. The ojha had told them they had seven trapped ghosts to deal with. Because there were so many ghosts, she had advised seeking the help of a pundit at this temple.

The ojha and the priest conducted several rituals, chanting around a small fire lamp, that culminated in trapping the ghosts in a dark brown pasty lump about two inches long and shaped like a mini teepee. The ojha took the lump and, holding it away from her body, opened the metal door of a large pit next to her and dumped the lump in with a loud yell. The family, slightly dazed, raised their hands to their heads in a namaste greeting. Without allowing for much recovery time, the large pundit had rolled off his haunches to demand payment. Whatever the family gave was not sufficient, because he began excoriating them, threatening that the ghosts would come back if they did not produce more rupees to reward him. The ojha motioned to the priest to step aside; she talked with the family in low tones until they fished in their pockets and pooled together their last rupees.

As they stood to leave, the pundit handed over what looked like a certificate.

"What's that?" I asked Vidhu.

"That's a guarantee that their ghosts are gone," he said, smiling wryly.

"But how can they guarantee that? What if bad things keep happening? Can the family come back and get another service done at no charge?"

Vidhu laughed cynically. "Of course not. When they come back, the priest will just tell them that these are different ghosts. Most of the time the people will believe him, they'll pay more money for another ceremony and the cycle will continue. Eventually, their bad luck will end, and they will attribute it to these priests and ojhas. Maybe they will then come to give him more money in thanks. Why do you think these priests are all so wealthy?"

We turned to thank the priest. As we walked away, I am almost certain I saw him wink at us, as if to let us in on his game, a lucrative one that unfortunately preyed on those simply trying to follow their faith.

֍

I met Amarnath Yadav, a pilgrim from the rural area outside Varanasi, on the riverbanks during the nine-day festival of Navratan. He had come to have darshan with the goddess Shitala Devi. His first visit had been some years ago when he had prayed to Shitala Devi for sons. His wife had since had two boys, and Yadav had come back to perform a *mundan*, a ceremony when a child's first full head of hair is shaved off and offered to the goddess in thanks.

The long steps down to the river at Dasashvamedh Ghat lead toward scores of small wooden platforms covered with bamboo umbrellas. From the river it looks almost as if it is a beach resort. From the shore one can see that the platforms are occupied by various pujaris who will perform the necessary rites and prayers and (for a small fee) watch one's clothes while bathing in the Ganga. Dozens of barbers had joined the pujaris to perform mundans.

Yadav's son's mundan took place about a hundred yards from the Shitala Devi temple. Yadav's wife, a slim woman with a lustrous black braid of hair down her back, held their six-month-old son on her lap. His eyes were lined with the typical thick, black kohl, his forehead marked with vermilion and ash. The barber, along with many others, had set up shop under a big paper and bamboo umbrella. He squatted next to the child, sharpened the blade of his razor on a rock and then went to work on the baby, shaving long lines from the nape of the child's neck, up and over to the top of his forehead. The child cried, long pitiful wails, while the mother reassuringly patted his thigh. When the hair had all been shaved, it was wrapped in a piece of newspaper and handed to the family to make as an offering inside the temple.

Like many others, Yadav had learned about Hinduism and its rituals from his ancestors. He used to work for a corporate firm but left when the computer and other technologies were introduced. "I did not believe in the machinery, and there was no need for me anymore," he told me. "I went back to working in the fields. I am sure God will take care of me and instruct me to do his will. I come to the Ganges to bathe because it gives me peace of soul. My wishes will be fulfilled here, because it is the place where the gods also bathe. If you bathe on the special days, you can cleanse yourself of all sins. I get peace when I come here."

Inside Shitala Devi temple it was dark and smoky. An extended family of about twenty was performing a *hawan*, lighting a fire that was believed to rid the family of evil spirits and cleanse the souls of their sins. They made room for my husband and me to sit among them, but we felt too uncomfortable intruding (a common occurrence for us in India, when our Western notion of privacy seemed to be the only real intruder). Instead, we watched from behind the circle as they chanted and clapped their hands rhythmically. As they poured oil onto the fire, it sizzled and flared. The pujari was supervising half-heartedly. In between his prayers, he looked off to the side, shouted an order to someone, talked to another who had come up to slip him money for a prayer. He wore a brown shirt with a white lungi around his waist; three long strings of green, brown and clear beads hung incongruously around his shirt.

"People are always coming for sons," the pujari said, the silver filling on the right side of his mouth glinting in the firelight. "Daughters are heavy. Whatever you accumulate goes with them. Just to give one daughter in marriage, you have to give away a thousand cows. It is a sad gift of *Kali-Yug* (the Dark Age) that women are treated badly. This is not how it used to be, you know. My father, who was the head pujari of this temple, got only one coin of silver when he got married."

"So you believe in the equality of women?" I asked.

"No, no," he said impatiently. "Women must stay within the boundary of honor. It is funny, no, that Westerners are adapting to our traditions (gesturing to my husband in his kurta-pajamas), and we are adapting to theirs?"

He turned away to talk to someone else. When he turned back, he wanted to talk about money and religion, not about women. "The population is going up, but our devotees are going down. They give more importance now to making money rather than to religion. Of course, it is true that offerings have become so expensive that people can only make them in small amounts." The pujari said this with no remorse, unaware or uncaring that he was so much a part of a structure that made money so important, even in religion.

࿐

One afternoon, I stationed myself on the long flight of stairs below Kedara Temple. The temple is not particularly appealing from the outside, a flat-roofed box decorated with vertical red-and-white stripes.

The main doorway is an incongruous pink, its frame inscribed with Tamil characters. Several plaques in Tamil and Hindi line the front wall.

Attractive or not, the temple is one of the most important Shiva temples in Varanasi. It contains a particularly sacred Shiva lingam. According to scholar Diana L. Eck, in her book *Banaras: City of Light*, the legendary ancient Indian king Mandhatri was a particularly devoted Shiva follower. He gave up his kingdom and went to Kedara, Shiva's home in the Himalayas, hoping that he would be granted Shiva's darshan, the manifestation of god in some form that is said to give liberation to those who witness it. After spending years in the cold mountains, worshipping Shiva and waiting for his darshan, Mandhatri received a message from Shiva that the only place he would ever receive Shiva's darshan was in Kashi (Varanasi). The king went to Kashi to live. Every day before eating, however, he would return to the Himalayas, traveling with the "swiftness of thought by virtue of his yogic powers." In this way, the king was able to continue his devoted worship in both of Shiva's favorite abodes.

As the king grew old, it became difficult for him to make this daily pilgrimage. Again Shiva spoke to Mandhatri and told him he should eat his meal first each day and then commence the journey, strengthened with food. The king, following Shiva's instructions, prepared some *khichari*, a simple dish of lentils and rice. But when he went out to find a guest with whom to share his food, as was proper, Mandhatri could find no one. Unwilling to eat without serving a guest first, he worried that he would be unable to make his pilgrimage that day.

At last, Shiva appeared, disguised as a mendicant, and was invited to be Mandhatri's guest. The king happily cut the khichari in two, but when he offered half to his guest, the whole plate had turned to stone. Shiva appeared to him, right out of the khichari, and revealed his lingam form. It is this lingam that Kedara Temple houses today.

As I sat on the long bank of stairs, I watched an old woman above me pray. Dressed in a soiled white sari, she clasped her knees near her body. Her eyes were tightly closed, concentrating on her prayer, perhaps for her family's good health, or for peace, or for a good husband for her daughter.

Below me, at the river's edge, a man straightened from his squat and readied himself to enter the water. He whipped off his *dhoti*, the simple piece of cloth worn by men, revealing surprisingly skimpy, brightly printed Calvin Klein–like briefs underneath. Next to him an old sadhu also prepared himself for the river, first pouring water on his long white hair, brushing his long whiskers and then carefully draping a baby-pink cloth around his upper half.

Next to me a wizened, stooped man brushed by. In one hand he carried a blue plastic basket filled with flowers; in the other, a shiny brass water pitcher. As he walked up the steps, he chanted "*Om Namah Shiva Lingam,*" carefully pouring water over the lingams that lined the sides of the temple steps. He stopped at a small green-and-white-tiled shrine that housed statues of a seated Shiva and his consort Parvati and was graced from above with a tile of Ganesh, the elephant god and provider of good fortune. The old man smeared vermilion on the foreheads of the idols, then placed a burning stick of incense in the shrine. He continued up to the temple and disappeared inside the pink doorway.

To my left a group of Bengali women had miraculously changed from wet petticoats and blouses into dry ones. Somehow, they had pulled beautifully starched, elegant saris from plastic baskets, donning them gracefully with a minimum display of bare skin. They ran combs through their long black tresses and whipped them expertly into knots. Dressing now complete, they skipped quickly down to their husbands who waited for them in a boat on the river.

It was time to enter the temple. I looked up at the doorway strung with yellow flowers and at the orange glinting eyes of the equally orange Ganesh that adorned it. As I entered, temple bells clanged loudly: time for darshan.

The main lingam sat on a small platform inside a little room. I stood in line to view it, bells and chants ringing in my ears. Darshan was not momentous for me, but around me I heard gasps and sighs as the lingam was unveiled and showered with milk and flowers. I walked around the temple clockwise, stopping at each lingam, each statue. At Mata Devi's platform, a priest covered the goddess with cloth like a sari and decorated her with flowers and vermilion streaks. He beckoned me closer and streaked my forehead with vermilion. I thanked him and was about to walk on when he put his hand out for a donation. I bristled to be asked so openly for a donation in a temple, but I had become used to it. It seemed that this was normal practice in most temples these days. I fished in my pocket and pulled out a 5 rupee note. He looked at it, then at me, and in a wheedling voice, he asked for more. I shook my head, annoyed, and walked by. He followed me, obliquely threatening that it would bode badly for me if I did not give. I found myself turning to angrily tell him that he should not ask for money in a temple. He was still cursing me as I walked out.

I stopped outside to breathe. I was angry—at him, at myself, at the moment. The practices and rituals of the worshippers had been simple, sincere, moving. But the greed of the priest had cheapened and commercialized even faith. I silently apologized to the gods and goddesses of the temple. "I mean no disrespect to you," I explained in my mind, amusing myself with this need to explain anything to anyone, "but people should not be harassed for money in the temple. And priests should not be threatening devotees who may not have anything but their faith to offer in a temple."

At the top of Dhobi Ghat, where scores of *dhobis*, washermen and washerwomen, whirled clothes in the air and then slapped them against big stone slabs smooth from years of pounding, I stood and rested. The white soap lather from the clothes floated on top of the river, and then dissipated. The ghats were beginning to empty out as the mid-morning sun blistered down. The water in front of me was comfortingly peaceful. As I stared at it, I felt my anger flow out of me, down the stairs, into that water and away with the river. I settled myself against a big stone pillar and lulled myself to sleep with the sounds of the water and the rhythmic slapping of clothes.

Pilgrimage

A ten-day trek in the Garwhal Himalaya took Alan and me up and down mountain ranges, over lush, high meadows, among shepherds and their hundreds of grazing sheep and finally to the amphitheater of majestic Kuari Pass, where the rising sun threw a circle of red and pink across the top of dozens of Himalayan peaks.

We walked on broad paths made of inset rocks, paths similar to those in the garden of a landscape architect, perfectly sculpted but created by natural hands. Our feet crunched on pine needles, releasing nature's pure fresh fragrance.

Rhododendrons and kharsu trees lined the sides of the paths. The kharsu tree, part of the oak family, fascinated me. It was a gnarled tree with sturdy branches that curled outward in unnatural twists. Its leaves were spiky, clumped and dark green. But it was the kharsu's roots that mesmerized me. Dozens of long talons pushed apart by wind, rain and erosion, the roots clung to the hillsides. The tree trunks bent permanently over the plunging valley below but stayed attached to the hillsides because of their roots. Without them, the kharsus would have fallen headfirst, and all their branches and spiky clumpy leaves would have splintered into countless shards on the green fertile ground below.

❀

It was June. We had just come from a conference in the small town of Kausani in the Kumaon region of Uttar Pradesh. After the conference we drove to Gwaldam, just a few hours away. It was pre-monsoon weather in the hills now, and at night we could watch huge storms brewing outside, hear the wind blowing fiercely and the metal roof of our tourist bungalow rattling. Gwaldam was a friendly village, where we would walk along and smile at everyone. During one walk some teenagers offered us handfuls of *kaphal*, delicious, local wild berries. In a tiny teahouse shack we met two local guides, Tularam and Madan, who agreed to take us on the ten-day trek from Gwaldam to Joshimath.

From Joshimath we took a two-hour bus ride up to the Hindu pilgrimage town of Badrinath, at an altitude of 10,300 feet. The bus had originated the day before in the plains at a town called Hardwar and was filled with yatris from all over India. Most of them had traveled between eighteen and seventy-two hours to come to Badrinath. Many of them were doing the *char dham yatra*, a pilgrimage to Badrinath, Kedarnath, Gangotri and Yamunotri, the four pilgrimage sites in Uttarkhand (the hill region of Uttar Pradesh).

We hopped on the bus at the last minute. I was squashed in the front "cab" of the bus next to the driver, sitting on the hot engine plate, my back against a big burlap sack the driver had kindly pulled out for me. When I did not have to concentrate on making sure the driver's hands avoided contact with my body every time he switched gears, I could marvel at the scenery. It was truly the valley of the gods, a sacred place, pristine in its beauty. The narrow road wound up through giant fissures of rain-stained granite slabs, below the blinding snowy summit of 19,500-foot Neelkanth Peak, and past rivers that had turned to ice on the way down and now lay on the rock like the fanned tresses of a woman's hair.

When the bus pulled into the carpark, there was a sense of excitement as the pilgrims raised a cry of *"Jai Shri Badrinath!"* (Hail Shri Badrinath!) They piled out of the bus toward shelters for travelers— *dharmshalas, ashrams* and rest houses. No matter how old or young, they carried their own possessions effortlessly in bundles on their heads or over their shoulders.

According to the Hindu *shastras* (texts or treatises considered to be of divine origin), no pilgrimage is complete without a visit to

Badrinath, one of Lord Vishnu's four abodes: "There are many shrines on earth, heaven and hell, but none has been, nor will be, like Badrinath." *Badri* is the wild fruit that Vishnu is said to have existed on while doing penance in the area; in fact, Vishnu is often referred to as Badri Vishal. Badrinath is a place of significance: It is where Lord Krishna, an incarnation of Vishnu, commanded his disciple Uddhava to go and meditate on him; it is one of four centers of God established by the great South Indian monist philosopher, Shankaracharaya, in the four cardinal directions of India (the other three being Puri in the East, Dwarka in the West, and Shringeri in the South). Most encompassing, it is *tapobhumi*, the ultimate place for meditation and penance.

Despite Badrinath's importance, I was reluctant to enter the Badrinath temple. Those we met could not understand this. Most pilgrims go immediately to the temple; unless one enters the temple, there is no purpose to a visit. After taking darshan, they often turn around the following day and head for the next destination on their pilgrimage.

It took me three days to set foot inside the temple. Instead, I would walk toward the temple and stand outside. The road from Badrinath town led down a small hill through a narrow alley lined with prasad shops and stalls selling devotional videos, books and other trinkets. Jostled between all the holy men and women—yatris, sadhus and sanyasis—clad in faded orange clutching their alms canisters, I would make my way to the bridge. The bridge crossed the Alaknanda River to the east bank, where Shri Badri Vishal resided in his brightly painted temple. To the east of the temple rose Neelkanth Peak, said to hold the face of Lord Shiva in the changing light of sunrise. To the west, toward the Indo-Tibetan border, other pointed peaks guarded the temple and its valley.

The temple stood out clearly among its immediate surroundings: hastily constructed buildings with low roofs of red corrugated metal, crumbling blocks of cement and black plastic sheets stretched tight against rain and snow. From the far bank of the bridge, just below the temple, were the *Tapt Kund*, hot springs where pilgrims bathed before entering the temple. Men and women purified what could be cleansed with water and left the rest to be cleansed through worship and darshan with Badri Vishal himself. Twisted white spires of heat rose from the springs into the cold morning air. Water gushed down onto moss-covered tall rocks and then ricocheted into the river below.

I would walk across the bridge, sandwiched between the hundreds of young, old, decrepit, cane-leaning bodies. Halfway across the bridge, I would slip to the side, standing among a few squatting, alms-seeking sadhus, and look down into the river, the brown swirling waters that disappeared into fast-turning eddies and then were swallowed in the next rushes of rapids. I would turn back to watch people set foot on the bridge, getting their first unfettered view of the temple. *"Jai Badri Vishal!"* The cry went up and was echoed by hundreds, as they touched their hands to the bridge's cold, stony surface and to their foreheads, then raised their hands in a high namaste.

They would continue, the pilgrims, up the steps past more alms-seekers, past the men who give coin change for rupee notes so that temple-goers can have access to easy change for distribution, to the end of the long queue of people waiting to enter the temple. I would follow them, but only to the small square in front of the temple, where photographers lingered with impressive cameras hung around their necks and photo albums in their hands to demonstrate the quality of their work. For 15 rupees (50 cents) they would take photos of pilgrims in front of the temple, even loaning stainless-steel *thali* plates of offerings to those pilgrims who could not afford to buy them. Mailing addresses would then be given to the photographer, usually with some concern on the customer's part that the photo would reach them, and the standard reply would return from the photographer: *"Pukka, saab, phikre mat karo."* (Sure, sir, do not worry.)

From this vantage point in the small square, I could watch the variety of people who had come to worship: the young woman in a hunter-green, raw silk salvaar kameez with a black L. A. Raiders cap; the group of fragile, tiny-boned grandmothers squatting, petticoats hitched up to their knees, the long tail of their saris pulled over their heads; the brightly turbaned men who balanced thalis of offerings on their turbans. The two silver-painted lions on either side of the temple entranceway gleamed in the sun, and the green-uniformed guard at the top blended into the temple's green-, blue- and red-painted windows. The best thing about my chosen spot was that it was outside the temple. From there I could lose myself in watching and analyzing others. I could avoid confronting my own reluctance to enter. I could simply create stories and draw conclusions about those I watched, yet remain detached myself, removed from the confusing onslaught of feelings that rushed out every time I entered a temple.

Inside temples, I often felt like a kharsu tree whose roots had let go. Inside temples, I felt as if I had fallen and splintered into a thousand pieces because I could not feel the same devotion as do the millions of people who come to Badrinath, the devotion that I thought every "true" Hindu Indian should feel.

❀

I was raised as a Hindu, whatever that means. I say that because it seemed to me that Hinduism was a loose, fluid religion—more a way of life than a religion. There were a few rules but not many, and even those, it seemed, were simply guidelines that one could choose to follow or not. I knew, for example, that Hindus were not supposed to eat beef, yet my parents did. There were no temples that we visited weekly or even monthly. We celebrated our special holidays, like Onam (the most important festival in Kerala, which falls at the close of the southwest monsoon and celebrates the annual return of the exiled emperor Mahabali—in actuality, a demon—to his people), at home with no priests. At my wedding our simple Malayalee ceremony had no officiant; our consecrator was the fire, around which we walked seven times, one round for each of the seven principles of married life: ideals, strength and power, wealth and fortune, happiness, progeny, lovelife and spiritual comradeship. We worshipped the goddess Devi, while other Hindus worshipped Shiva or Rama. Basically, it seemed to me, Hindus were left to decide how, who and when to worship.

As children, the one ritual my sister and I observed without fail was the lighting of the lamps, once in the morning and once at night. In the mornings, when our eyes were still blurry with sleep, my mother would lead my sister and me to a small room at the corner of our veranda. Inside, we would stand in darkness as she lit the twisted, oil-soaked cotton wicks on two Kerala-style lamps. The lamps were of bell metal, a brass alloy, each about a foot tall, like fully bloomed lotus flowers emerging out of their round bases.

After lighting the lamps, my mother would set aflame one or two small camphor squares in the middle of a brass tray. In that flickering light, we stood in front of the lamps and a picture of our goddess Devi, and recited the prayers we had been taught by my grandmother: *"Om Namah Shivaya, Narayanaya namah, Achuthaya namah, Anandaya namah, Govindaya namah, Gopalaya namah . . . "*

We did not know much about these gods and goddesses whose names we recited, but we knew these prayers were important. At the end of the prayers, my mother would take the brass tray and circle the picture of Devi with it three times. Then she would hold it in front of us, and we would cup our hands over the flame and bring them up to our face, spreading the aura over ourselves like rain water. We dipped our middle finger in the camphor ash and marked our throats with it. My mother would then wave her hands in front of the lamps to put out the fire—"never blow it out"—and we would leave, putting the ritual and its meaning behind us as we went about our day.

Nostalgia says those morning and evening rituals grounded me. At the time, though, I did not particularly want to be marked by ash or by rituals. In fact, I probably did not even feel the need to be protected. Religion was just a hand-me-down, perfected by the ages, honed by the wise and passed down through prayers; but it was not *mine*, not a personal part of my life or belief system.

It was not that I did not enjoy the rituals as an observer. When we visited my grandparents in India, for example, I loved watching my grandmother Ammamma pray. Early in the morning, I would go out onto the cool veranda before the sun began baking the earth. My grandmother would be in a curved wicker easy chair, a basket of jasmines in her lap. She showed me how to thread together the jasmines into a thick garland, head of one to the stem of the other so that there would be no holes in the garland. "Never smell the flowers before giving them to Devi," she would admonish me kindly. "They must be fresh for the goddess, no smell taken out."

After making the garland, Ammamma would take her bath. She would emerge from the bathroom in a petticoat and blouse, her long hair wrapped into a cheesecloth towel. Inhaling the small of sandal-wood soap, coconut hair oil and sweet talcum powder, I would lie on the bed and watch her dress. After donning a crisply ironed sari, she would open the wood doors on one side of the bed to reveal a small cupboard that housed framed pictures of various gods and goddesses and a shelf with a set of Kerala lamps and trays like we had in our puja room. She would string the garlands around the frames and then settle into a surprisingly nimble cross-legged stance to recite her prayers. As Ammamma sat chanting on the ground, she would toss loose jasmines at the gods and goddesses. I believed she had a hotline to God, be-cause anything she prayed for seemed to come true.

Only at the very end, when she would motion for me to sit next to her, would I quickly recite my prayers. Just like in Badrinath, I much preferred to observe others practicing their religion than to practice it myself. Perhaps that is because I simply had no idea what I believed.

ॐ

The Honorable N. Vishnu Namboodiri was the thirty-third *Rawal* (head priest) of Badrinath Temple. All the Rawals of Badrinath were the same sect of Namboodiri Kerala Brahmins from which the famous sage Shankaracharaya hailed.

Steps led down from the temple to the Rawal's unpretentious entranceway. The main room in which he saw people was dominated by a platform on which stood two beautiful statues, one statue of Badrinath in pure ivory and the other a silver idol, so heavily gar-landed and dressed that I could barely see the face. The platform was covered with an intricately woven golden cloth. Incense, flowers and eternally burning lamps filled the rest of the platform. The room felt cozy, infused with the warmth of the thick, red woolen rugs that cov-ered the floor, a sense of peace and serenity and the aroma of incense.

The Rawal entered, greeted us and went to sit on the floor next to the window, leaving empty the quilted cushion in the middle of the room that was his formal "seat." He seemed to love that place next to the window; he would lean his head against the baby-blue painted shutters and gaze out at the mountains, into the valley or at the hundreds of people scurrying across the bridge. As Rawal, he was allowed only to be in the temple or in his house. He could never go outside; perhaps this was what created that wistful look, that desire to fill his head with what he could see, but not touch or feel, of the outside. In many ways he was an observer of life in the same way that I was an observer of religion.

I had written out a list of questions to ask the Rawal, questions about the history of Badrinath, the differences between various types of pujas, the apparent commercialization of religion and the connection between religion and development. Yet within half an hour of being with him, I realized that I was not yet ready to hear the answers to my questions. What I would hear at that time would be filtered through the biased armor that shielded my own doubts and confusion about religion and its role in my life. As I sat there, I felt my years of experiences with religion—my own personal convictions, resentment, anger with what I saw as today's masquerade of religion—wash over me. I did not realize, until that day with the Rawal, that it was my own aborted religious journey I returned to each time I watched or spoke to someone about their journey. In talking to people about Hinduism and its meaning to them, I was not really listening to what they were saying. I was unable to rid myself of my own stained notions of the corruption of religion; through these lenses, no matter what people said, my vision was tainted by the disdain I felt for today's version of Hinduism.

My list of questions for the Rawal suddenly became irrelevant. Until I understood my own pilgrimage, I realized, I could never hope to understand the pilgrimages of others.

ॐ

The Rawal was probably in his late thirties. Unlike some other so-called religious teachers I had met in Varanasi, the Rawal seemed uninterested in power or in emphasizing his own enlightened status. He wanted us close to him, where he could watch us intently as we spoke. He forbade us to take notes, wanting us to simply concentrate on our words. The Rawal alternated between intimidating and humorous, sagelike and childlike. He displayed his humility in various ways, often leaning forward to bow before those who touched his feet in respect, once even touching the feet of a child who folded his hands in namaste. He downplayed his own knowledge and talked about his weaknesses. He was approachable and human, something I had never expected from someone of his stature.

Over the next few days, the Rawal spent many hours each day with my husband and me, letting us sit with him as he received people who had come to pay their respects. He periodically left us to conduct pujas at the temple next door, instructing us when to come back. At the following session, he remembered exactly where he had left off and began by asking us to summarize our understanding of the past session. He often clicked his tongue impatiently if we did not give the answer he was looking for, once even cutting me off midstream when I was getting long-winded. But always, regardless of how long it took, the Rawal made sure that we understood his concepts.

Nothing I said went unquestioned, and for the first time I found myself trying (rather unsuccessfully) to define such words as *man, service, religion* and *Hinduism.* Though it might sound like a philosophic discussion, it was not. The Rawal was interested in placing people on the practical path of the ancient Indian belief of *sanatan dharma,* or "right living."

The Rawal spoke limited English, and I could not always grasp in Hindi the complex ideas being discussed. For some of these discussions, a visitor named Krishnan would sit in and translate. Krishnan, a scientist originally from Madras, had settled in America but had returned to India on his own inner search. Having taken a one-year sabbatical from his teaching post and his distinguished service on the National Science Commission, Krishnan was living in India, talking, watching and inquiring. When Krishnan was not there, the Rawal spoke with us in Hindi, interspersing several clever examples to illustrate points.

If the Rawal sensed that we did not fully understand his words, he would look around, his eyes scanning the room for something he could use to illustrate his ideas. One of our first lessons was devoted to the idea of the essence of humankind. He had brushed away my simplistic explanations of the physical being of humankind. Humankind is *nash*, he said, except for the service one renders to others. We could not understand the meaning of *nash* and *anash* (its opposite), so he gave us several examples. You eat food, and it is *nash*. Ah, we said: gone, finished. Not quite. A few more examples and then he thought of something, leaping up excitedly and pulling out from a cupboard near the puja platform a box of incense sticks. He lit them and told us to ponder the burning incense. Then he dipped his finger in the fallen ash and smeared it on his forehead and waved his hands to indicate the sweet fragrance of incense floating through the room. Incense is *anash*, he explained, after taking us as far as we could go ourselves. It gives pleasure through its sweet smell and service through its fallen ash used to bless those who come to do puja. This is its significance in the puja rituals. It is eternal. *Nash* and *anash*: transient and eternal. Humankind, the physical being, is transient, but the service one does is eternal.

The Rawal refused to comment on Hinduism, saying it was just a name. Instead, he distinguished religion as the path of sanatan dharma. "This is the way of our ancestors, of this country, what is written about in the Puranas (the mythical histories of gods and kings recorded mostly in the first millennium of our era). The essential elements of right dharma are truth, good intention and nonviolence. If we carry out all our actions based on these three principles, we will be on the path of true dharma."

It is difficult to find a translation for sanatan dharma that does it justice. *Sanatan* has the broad meaning of "eternal," while *dharma* (although often translated as "religion") is the law of truth, the law of nature that guides the cosmos, the idea that each object in the universe has its own intrinsic nature. In his book *Travels through Sacred India*, Roger Housden speaks about it this way: "[Sanatan dharma] is in essence defined by no outer ritual or even religion: it represents a natural way of living in harmony with life. At the very heart of its ethos is the principle of sacred relationship. Everything in the universe is related, and the divine, rather than being somewhere above and beyond life, is right here in the middle of it."

The Rawal liked to emphasize the similarities between different religions, often referring to Christianity (probably for my husband's benefit, although Alan had probably read far less of the Bible than the Rawal had). In these comparisons the Rawal wanted simply to show that all religions seek oneness with a universal power, and the path toward that oneness is essentially the same.

"There are many 'isms,'" he said, "but underneath them all, there is only one dharma, one universal truth. Think of electricity: In one form it lights a bulb, in another it activates a refrigerator, and yet in another it makes a radio work. Three different manifestations of electricity, but underneath it is only one power driving them all. Dharma is the underlying power of all religions; it does not belong only to Hindus; it is for everyone." Motioning to Alan as a representation of foreigners, he said, "They do not know less about dharma or *sewa* (service) than Hindus." Rising to his knees in front of me with a twinkling challenge in his eyes and referring to a particularly eloquent comment Alan had just made, the Rawal said, "In fact, he knows a little more about sewa than you do."

The Rawal's conviction about the similarity between religions helped take away some of the sour taste left in my mouth by the discrimination and fanaticism propagated by so-called religious people. I was also reminded of how my own nondenominational views of religion were formed, how my distaste for religious single-mindedness was born through a series of experiences early in my life.

❊

The school I attended as a child in Jakarta had a large contingent of Southern Baptist missionary kids—Baptist MKs, we called them. Their parents had been stationed by the Baptist Church in various remote parts of Indonesia to actively convert Indonesians to Christianity. The children were schooled at home by their parents until the seventh grade, after which they were sent to Jakarta to live in a Baptist missionary hostel near the school.

They were a talented group of children, accomplished in sports, music and academics. Most of all, though, they had each other. Their large, close-knit community seemed to have a tremendous amount of fun at Baptist parties and dances, movies and dinners, competitions and contests. The Baptist MKs took their meals together in a big, noisy dining room at the hostel. After dinner and homework they would linger in the common room talking.

To them I was a perfect target for conversion. Hinduism, as a religion, remained abstract to me. Nor did it hold out any special offerings of community as did Christianity. Because I was not particularly attached to my own religion at the time, conversion did not seem too high a price to pay for a ready-made set of friends. I was serious enough about converting that (around the same time I was chosen to play Jesus in a church choir musical) I announced my intention to my mother. She was horrified—perhaps as much by my announcement as by watching her little brown Indian child wrapped in a white sheet, crown on head, singing "Kill the fatted calf!"

Needless to say, my conversion did not come to pass. Even then, I recognized that I was attracted to the community aspect but not necessarily to the form of religion and worship. Christianity, as it was practiced by the Baptists I knew, was terribly structured compared with Hinduism. One had to go to church on Sunday mornings and youth group on Sunday evenings. One had to sing, kneel and pray along with the hundred other people in the church. And, if a convert, one had to declare in front of everyone exactly when and how Jesus came into one's life. It felt too confining. And besides, Jesus had not appeared to me as yet, and I had no confidence that He would any time soon.

Ultimately, the turning point came with Eric's betrayal. Eric was a Baptist MK, a few years older but in the same grade. One day, he righteously told me that if I did not convert to Christianity, I would burn in hell. I was twelve years old. Eric's words conjured up pictures of red demons with horns and pitchforks, of flames that would devour me limb by limb, hair by hair. I have never responded well to pressure and even then, scared as I was, I could not believe that my Devi would not have mentioned this small necessity of conversion to me. Nevertheless, Eric had succeeded in hurting and confusing me, singling me out and making me wonder what religion and God were all about if, in the end, one would be condemned simply for praying to a different form. Could it be that arbitrary?

It was another friend's father (a pastor, ironically, although of different faith) who finally consoled me. The pastor viewed religion, he said, as a big mountain with God at the top. Depending on where you stood at the base, the mountaintop and the paths leading to it looked different. "Different religions take different paths," he said, "but ultimately they all lead to the same place." Since then, I have substituted God with the idea of a universal power or spirit, but the analogy of the mountain has stayed with me.

ॐ

The Rawal's description of the concept of sanatan dharma as true religion allowed me to see that by scorning today's version of Hinduism, I had also denied myself the wisdom of traditional Indian thought, the all-inclusive, tolerant, practical notion of sanatan dharma. Sanatan dharma was not the radical, exclusive, phobia-ridden fanaticism ravaging the world in the name of religion. It was simply a kind of selfless focus, of interdependence among individuals, of a belief that we are simply part of a larger cosmic universe.

The Rawal was careful to emphasize the need for understanding one's actions. He believed in thinking and questioning those things that are done just because "they always have been." We were discussing this topic when a large family entered the room. They had just had darshan at the temple and had come to pay their respects to the Rawal. They were obviously quite wealthy, the mother (perhaps in her mid-thirties) wearing a beautifully embroidered salvaar kameez and heavy gold bangles, the father and brother-in-law in starched homespun *khadi kurtas*, their hair slicked back with copious amounts of Brillcreme. Several of the children were dressed in the Indian equivalent of designer clothes: jeans, tennis shoes and T-shirts with English slogans emblazoned on the front.

The Rawal went around the room asking each one individually how they had felt about their darshan. One by one, they replied, most with *"bahut accha"* (very good) and one with *"bahut sunder"* (very beautiful). After they had all answered, the Rawal looked around at them and repeated, almost musingly, "Very good, very beautiful." He became stern. "Food is very good; a flower is very beautiful. How can you use these words to describe your experience in darshan? The purpose of darshan is to find joy, true joy in yourself through being with God. If you do not get this from darshan, there is no benefit. You have walked away from the temple empty-handed."

The Rawal then fixed his gaze on the mother, who was clutching a *mala*, a string of brown wood Rudranath beads.

"What is that?" he asked.

"A mala."

"What do you do with it?"

"I chant." And then getting no response, she quickly continued, *"Hare Ram, Hare Krishna*, like that. I do three rounds."

"Tell him the whole thing you chant," piped her husband, a little anxiously.

She complied, repeating a string of prayers. The family waited expectantly. The Rawal was still not speaking. He looked into the distance.

"But why do you do it?" he asked the woman.

She looked at him, almost resentfully. I could tell she was nervous and thought I even saw tears forming in her eyes. She had probably never been questioned like this before.

"It makes me feel good," she finally said.

He moved his head slightly. "You need to know why you do things, where it comes from, what it means. Everything has a meaning, comes from somewhere. Without this understanding, the action is nothing. Do you understand?" The group nodded, uncertain of what to do. The father broke the awkward silence that followed by rising and offering several fifty-rupee notes to the Rawal. The Rawal tossed them unceremoniously, almost angrily, into the small silver dish sitting on the platform next to the silver idol.

After they left the Rawal turned to us and said, "Did you understand?" We said we did. "What did you understand?" he asked in his usual penetrating manner. We talked about how meaningful actions become meaningless rituals when not accompanied by understanding, and about the lack of willingness to question why. I could certainly relate: This was the story of the first twenty-five years of my life we were talking about, all those years of lighting lamps for puja, saying prayers, asking God for whatever I wanted, as if this were the main reason that this great power existed.

The Rawal was satisfied with the answer. "I did that questioning of them for you. They did not understand anything. So many people—they come here, talk, ask. Many never understand." He sounded almost wistful. He leaned his head against the shutter and looked outside. "I often find that Westerners are more willing to question than Indians." He fixed me with his piercing gaze. "Even you, you are not as open as he is." The Rawal pointed to Alan. "He speaks freely. You still have Indian in you. You sit too quietly. What will I do to you if you speak?"

His frankness caught me off-guard, his prescience amazed me, but more than anything, his words stung. I had always prided myself on my frankness, my ability to talk to anyone courageously, and this made me sound like a timid wallflower.

I stewed over his words all that day and that night. Even in my anger, my unwillingness to believe him, I recognized that he was right. In India I was far more timid than I was in America. For the first time I understood that for all that India gives me, it also takes away some of my freedom to be, to ask questions of anyone, especially those who are "above" me in the traditional social hierarchy. Constructed in complex fashion, like a jigsaw puzzle with pieces from different cultures, I was not so easily deconstructed into simply "Indian" or "American." Yes, I belonged in India, but I also retreated back into the old rigidities of social hierarchies passed down from my parents and grandparents, of norms, of ideas, of individual rights that depended on others' perceptions of appropriate rights and roles. In America I naturally grasped at the freedom from hierarchy. Students in America are supposed to question their teachers; children, rudely and respectfully, challenge their parents. Everything is up for skepticism and doubt; little is sacred.

Despite my seeming irreverence for the reverent, he was right that I was unable to fully speak my mind to him, to question and argue the way I might otherwise. If I with my Western "logical" training still felt bound by certain structures, why should anything different be expected of those devotees who believed in religion in a way that I did not? What was it in Indian society that created this dynamic of acceptance, of unwillingness to push the limits of understanding? And what was it in me that allowed, in India, suppression of my otherwise fiery, almost combative attitude to structure and hierarchy?

❃

I began questioning the existence of God years ago, in my mid-twenties. For the first time I stopped saying my prayers before I went to sleep. Who were these gods whose names I was chanting? I saw no logic, no reason for praying. Every once in a while, however, I found myself secretly saying my prayers, usually when I was scared or lonely. I would pull my bedcovers over my head and start reciting. The prayers slid off my tongue, an invisible ferris wheel spinning effortlessly. With the prayers I recreated the smells of safety and companionship, of my grandmother, of jasmine and of Devi's protective aura. This felt right while praying, but afterward I felt only guilt, as if I had done something I knew I should not do.

I remember asking my mother and grandmother to explain Hinduism to me, to draw out in clear strokes the religion's basic tenets and rules. They were quite flummoxed. Hinduism, my mother explained, is a way of life.

Hinduism, the "religion" of over eighty-five percent of Indians, has evolved into its contemporary framework over the last several thousand years. Its origins can be traced back to the second millennium BC when the semi-nomadic Aryans entered northwest India, bringing with them a belief in gods associated with the elements of fire and sun, among others. These Aryan beliefs were transmitted orally for centuries and finally written in Sanskrit in the scriptures of the *Vedas* between 1000 BC and 500 AD. The Vedas include the lyrical Rig Veda, a collection of hymns to the deities; the Brahmanas, which detail correct ritual performance; the Aranyakas, which focused on the cosmic power source known as Brahma; and the Upanishads, which describe in poetic verse the union of soul (*atman*) with Brahma, achieved through meditation, renunciation of worldly values and asceticism. The Upanishads detail most specifically the concept of *samsara*, the cycle of death and rebirth, of suffering and desire from which one must try to liberate oneself and achieve *moksha*, salvation.

These scriptures, however, while providing the basis of early Hinduism, do not provide the kind of rigid structure that exists in many other religions. Hinduism has no founder nor prophet; its creeds are many and its forms of practice varied. Although the philosophies of Hinduism are explained in such books as the Upanishads, they are themselves esoteric. *Tat Tvam Asi*, say the Upanishads. *I am That.* How does a young mind capture this? The written texts hold concepts that are simple yet so broad that they become lofty, which makes it easy for people to discard the concepts and attach themselves to the rituals instead.

The most popular texts quoted by the average Hindu are not the scriptures but rather the popular epics, the *Ramayana* and the *Mahabharata*, thought to have been completed by the fourth century AD. When discussing appropriate moral and ethical behavior, Hindus will often refer to the Bhagavad Gita (literally "Song of the Lord"), the sixth book of the *Mahabharata* in which Lord Krishna and Arjuna (one of the five Pandava brothers in the epic) engage in a philosophical discussion about Arjuna's duty, dharma, as a warrior. Krishna explains to Arjuna that to uphold his duty, even if it means killing his cousins in battle, will both display his devotion to God and guarantee him salvation. The *Ramayana* has been turned into a television series that has swept India with its popularity. Every Sunday morning, millions across India in villages and cities gather around television sets to watch the young, handsome Rama as he undertakes new trials and battles, conveying in each episode a new moral platform.

For me, not understanding (in a rational, logical sense) Hinduism gradually progressed into a distancing from it, a disdain for religion itself. Moving from the private sector to the nonprofit world years ago had opened another channel of thought for me. The shift itself was not about spirituality per se but rather about fulfillment (which, at the time, seemed quite separate). This understanding that I needed to work at something that was in line with my own personal values and beliefs was the beginning of looking at the accepted goals of life differently. If making money was not the end goal of life, what was? These thoughts were jumbled, as vague to me in some ways as Hinduism. But they were the beginning of a small spark of spiritual awareness that eventually would take me, many years later, back to India. I had begun some sort of profound shift.

And yet, now back in India after so long, not having religion occupy an irreplaceable space in my being as it does for many Indians made me feel incomplete, unsteady and insufficient.

ॐ

Perhaps it was the Rawal's critical words that prompted me to ask him a question the next day that would have been, for many people, unthinkable to ask a holy man of his stature. Yet this question was at the core of my reluctance to go into the temple and had to be asked: Is full acceptance of the path of sanatan dharma contingent on some form of worship and prayer? I could not rid myself of the pictures in my mind of men and women blindly praying, the idea that rituals were simply meaningless acts repeated over and over again.

The Rawal clearly did not expect the question. He looked down and thought for a minute. His answer, when it came, was distinctly distant. "Yes. Definitely. They are important disciplines that must be maintained." There was silence. I do not know what I had expected him to say, but somehow I felt deflated. Once again, it seemed, religion had been equated to ritual.

The Rawal did not say much more. He excused himself to go to the temple for his nightly service. Krishnan, who had been there with us, Alan and I sat quietly. Krishnan, sensing that the conversation was far from over, gave us his own interpretation: that the Rawal knew we were not at a stage where he could just tell us to stop performing puja, that there were certain techniques of worship, like mantras, that were known to invoke the sense of oneness, of respect for that universal power within one's soul.

"It may not be for you to go to the temple and pray," Krishnan said to me later. "I go, but only with appreciation for its history, its significance in the lives of so many of our enlightened sages. You may find your own way, your own acts that create meaning for you, your own methods of discipline. Go to the temple, take what you can and then create something for you."

ॐ

It was after that last conversation with the Rawal that I finally went to the temple. It was drizzling, so the line that normally stretches up to half a kilometer long was relatively short. I wound my way around the iron bars, looking expectantly up at the tiny covered rectangle where people peered in to get a glimpse of the black stone Badri Vishal in the inner sanctum. I was pushed with the crowd to the front. There I saw the Rawal inside, conducting the puja, plucking and throwing flower petals on the idol. It flashed through my mind that by questioning the need for rituals, I was in essence challenging what he did, what he stood for.

The temple and the pilgrims looked different to me that day. Had I missed, all this time, the from-the-bottom-of-the-soul emotion, tears, overwhelming happiness that these devotees felt in front of their gods? How could any process that produced that kind of feeling be wrong? With more than a little envy, perhaps I wished that I too could feel that way. Seeing this emotion for what it was broke through my academic limitations, my endless negative analysis of rituals, of one-dimensional definitions of Hinduism.

Rituals are rituals only when they become habits, actions that are not accompanied by meaning or understanding. To me, all that I saw—pouring milk on a Shiva lingam, giving offerings to an idol, saying prayers—were rituals because I did not understand them, because they had no meaning for me. I had forgotten that the key person who needed to understand the rituals was not I—it was the person who was performing the actions. To that individual, those actions that I called rituals might have produced the kind of joy that the Rawal had been talking about; it might have been accompanied, at least for some, by the actual practice of sanatan dharma.

৩ঞ্চ

I did not see the Rawal again. We left suddenly, without even thanking him. I was as reluctant to see him again as I had been to go into the temple, but for completely different reasons. I did not know how I would thank him, what I would say. He had given me a new way to look at what religion means not just to others, but to me; an insight into the kind of effusive joy that can fill a devotee who comes in the presence of something that reminds him of that universal power. He showed me that the essence of Hinduism—indeed, of religion—is the path of sanatan dharma, a dharma that embodies concepts I believe in, concepts that I can feel proud to have passed on from my heritage, my ancestors, those wise men and women who spoke not of Hinduism but of what were the seeds of Indian spirituality.

In many senses the Rawal gave me back my roots, the beginnings of a sense of connection to Indian spiritual traditions. His words challenged me to look differently at the actions of those who worship and to understand that the role of religion in people's lives is intensely personal. He opened a pathway for me to create actions for myself that complement my own belief in spirituality, actions that are a genuine part of acknowledgment, respect and self-expression.

I no longer felt like a kharsu tree about to fall. My roots had dug themselves in and were holding me—however tenuously—to the hillside.

A Path of Inquiry

Alan and I arrived at Ramana Ashram in the middle of a hot August afternoon. Most of the visitors had retreated indoors from the strong afternoon sun, leaving the ashram compound silent. We took off our shoes just inside the gate and walked across the gravelly, red sand courtyard. In front of us was the temple and the main hall and to the right, a series of small rooms. One had a small wooden sign that said Office. We waited inside the room, the cool floor pleasant against our hot feet. A man clad just in a dhoti, his upper chest bare, sat behind the desk. He took our names and assigned us a room in a building just across the street from the main ashram.

The room was simple but comfortable, with its own bathroom. A framed portrait of Ramana Maharshi adorned one wall. I went to sleep looking at the portrait and dreamed about Ramana.

In my dream I was standing at the foot of Arunachala, a mountain that Ramana described as "the physical embodiment of Shiva, God himself." As I stood and looked at the mountain, it took on its own human, physical form, metamorphosing from inanimate to animate, from distant vision to personal guide. I began to climb, but the path up the mountain kept fading in and out of view. Several times I stumbled around looking for it, until suddenly it would appear again. About halfway up the mountain the path disappeared, and no amount of searching produced it again. Just then, Ramana's face appeared in front of me, its proximity intensely uncomfortable. Then it too began fading, and when I called the image to come back, it seemed to pause its movement just long enough so that I could hear three words: "Who am I?"

∞

Ramana Maharshi, considered one of the greatest spiritual masters of the twentieth century, experienced his first glimpse of self-realization at age sixteen. He was sitting alone when he was suddenly overcome by a "violent fear of death." The fear pushed him inward, striving to understand in that split second what it meant to die. In *The Teachings of Bhagavan Sri Ramana Maharshi In His Own Words* (edited by Arthur Osborne), Ramana describes the experience:

> The body dies but the Spirit that transcends it cannot be touched by death. That means I am the deathless Spirit. All this was not dull thought; it flashed through me vividly as living truth which I perceived directly, almost without thought-process. "I" was something very real, the only real thing about my present state, and all the conscious activity connected with my body was centred on that "I". From that moment onwards the "I" or Self focussed attention on itself by a powerful fascination. Fear of death had vanished once and for all. Absorption in the Self continued unbroken from that time on.

Soon after this experience, Ramana left his home as a sadhu, a holy man. He traveled to the foot of Arunachala mountain, to the town of Tiruvannamalai, where his ashram is housed today. There he withdrew from the physical world, barely eating until he became skin and bones, a testament to his conviction that his body was simply a physical trapping for the real spirit. People came from all over India and from many foreign countries to seek his counsel on the process of self-realization, of spiritual enlightenment. For the most part his answers centered on the seemingly simple but intensely complex exercise of answering the question, "Who am I?"—the same question he was forced to answer when he confronted his fear of death.

∞

I sit cross-legged on a cold marble floor in the New Hall at Ramana Ashram. The sounds of chanting Brahmins wash over me, entering my body and filling me like water in an empty well. On my right an enormous floor-to-ceiling photograph of Ramana Maharshi hangs on the wall. His warm, liquid-brown eyes have followed me to my spot here in the back of the room; somehow, it comforts me that he seems to be watching me.

The Brahmins' chanting has continued for almost an hour, a melodious soothing orchestra with different parts, choruses, melodies and harmonies. I am brought back from my distracted meditation by a bell, the signal that *Maha Abishek*, the grand puja, is about to begin. During Maha Abishek, Lord Shiva's sacred symbol, the lingam, will be stripped of all its finery and put in plain sight of the devotees.

Toward the front of the room, four pillars of gray stone surround the shrine where the deity is to be washed and readied for the audience. In between the front two pillars is a garlanded black stone Nandi bull, Shiva's revered companion and mode of transport. The chanting Brahmins stretch themselves out in front of Nandi, knee to knee, like a protective fence.

I circle the shrine along with the other devotees and end up in front of Nandi's serene face as we wait for Maha Abishek to begin. One of the older Brahmins performs the puja. The string that Brahmins wear tied diagonally across their upper bodies lies loosely across his chest. His worn white dhoti is pulled through his legs in traditional fashion. He and a young assistant take off the old garland and pour water over the black stone lingam. He runs his hands over the lingam tenderly, scrubbing and stroking it until it shines so intensely that the reflection of the overhead lights is liquid fire in its blackness. Next, the old Brahmin initiates a series of washings, pouring different liquids over the lingam; first, several dousings with milk and water, then curds. The curds stick to the lingam like thin layers of icing, but only briefly before they are washed away again with water. Then tender coconut water and a final water cleansing. The Brahmin dries the lingam, places the golden naga snake on top and drapes the lingam with multiple strands of jasmine. It is barely visible. More and more flowers and petals are thrown on top, until only the tiny golden gleam of the naga head is visible. The entire creation is dressed with a skirt and pink garland on top. It is ready again for worship.

Bells begin clanging and we file into the old temple next door for darshan. I stand in a line of women in front of the sanctum; across the aisle from us is a line of men. Big golden curtains shield the deity from our eyes. In front of the curtains, in sharp contrast to the gold, is another gleaming black Nandi, garlanded in white and pink flowers. Two young Brahmins come out and wave camphor and incense in front of Nandi. The bells get frantic. The curtains are whisked open with a flair of finality to reveal a heavily garlanded figure inside. When the tray of camphor and incense comes to me, I wave some of the smoke toward my head and smear *vibhuti* (ash) and red powder on my forehead. We retreat back into the temple to receive our prasad from the Brahmins—hot milk, then sticky-sweet sesame seed balls. I cup my hands to take the milk, sip it and drizzle the rest over my head. The sesame seed ball, which I have received with my right hand, goes into my mouth whole. It is delicious. I file outside with the rest of the line to the stone island around which are several water faucets. We wash our hands and go back into the New Hall for evening songs.

We sit cross-legged in the middle of the New Hall, men on one side and women on the other. The songs are almost like a question and answer session between the lines, and there is a palpable joy in the singing. The singing is in Tamil, so I cannot understand the words, but I belt out the tune anyway. I love to sing, and I feel completely included by the smiles of the women around me. We sing for a good hour; around us, against the walls, people meditate and enjoy our music.

We stop about half an hour before dinner for silent meditation. At 7:30 the dinner bell rings, and we move ourselves to the dining hall. We sit in rows on the floor, in front of beautiful placemats made of sewn-together leaves from the banana trees outside. I have seen them being made, and it is incredible to me that we will use these beautiful mats only once and then throw them away. Not as incredible, I remind myself, as how Americans use nondecomposing items like plastic bags only once and throw them into piles of landfill. The ashram workers, all men, serve us from huge stainless-steel containers—rice, *dal* (lentils), *idlis* (steamed fermented rice cakes) and vegetables. It is delicious and simple food. When we are finished, we fold our mats in half and leave the dining hall.

Our first day has ended. I feel a little lost, like I do not know quite what to *do* to begin the self-inquiry process Ramana advocated. My search for meaning, for my life's work, has sometimes seemed frustratingly slow, spurred on by the writings of some great spiritual leaders: Krishnamurti, Gandhi or the teachings of the Buddha. Perhaps because of this, Ramana's process amazes me even more. Ramana relied on no individual, no book, no accounts of others' enlightenment. He described his experiences of nonduality and enlightenment in much the same way as many of the great philosophers and sages, but without ever having read their accounts. Indeed, he has written that he did not even know the words *Brahman* (the essence of life, the supreme, transcendent One, the reality that is the source of all being and knowing) or *samsara* (the world of change, the ceaseless rounds of birth, death and rebirth) or even nonduality. When he eventually read the various sacred books and accounts, Ramana found that "the books were analysing and naming what I had felt intuitively without analysis or name."

Somehow, the fact that Ramana never read any books until years after he had his glimpse of self-realization makes him purer to me, even more real, and ultimately, this makes the achievement of that self-realization seem within my reach.

ॐ

My favorite room at the ashram is the room where Ramana lived. It is now a small meditation room, fitting perhaps twenty people at most. One corner holds a small platform with a tiger-skin rug, statues and lit lamps. This is where Ramana would sit and meditate and answer the seekers' many questions. The room feels far more comfortable, more appropriate to me than the New Hall. For me, there is a dissonance between the rituals I see taking place in the New Hall and in Ramana's essential teaching, which is so sparse, so unadorned, so completely focused on going within rather than out.

I have read Ramana's essential teachings in the slim, almost newsletter-like pamphlet *Who am I?* These were the questions and answers that transpired in 1902 between Ramana and a devotee, Sri M. Sivaprakasam Pillai. Intellectually, I can understand that the real "I" is not composed of organs or senses or breath or even mind. Taking away these things leaves only awareness—the real "I." I even believe the possibility that the world as one sees it is only a product of one's thoughts; that there is no world at all, just *maya*, illusion. Ramana teaches that when the mind is completely quiet, when there are no more thoughts, the world will disappear, and then one shall see the true self as awareness: existence, consciousness, bliss. Constantly quiet your thoughts and ask yourself, "Who am I?" for every thought that occurs, says Ramana. This is the path.

I feel I am ready, or so I think. And yet how do I control my thoughts rather than allow them to control me? One of the most difficult lessons of meditation for overachieving individuals who are used to filling up their lives with clutter—be it thoughts, books or events— is the challenge of doing something that holds absolutely no markers of "success." The judgment one has toward oneself, so completely intertwined with ego, becomes starkly clear in meditation. How badly I have wanted to "succeed" in my meditations! And how silly it is to see enlightenment as a goal. As I have become more and more aware of the nature of consciousness, I realize it is just as Ramana said in a discourse with a devotee on the nature of man (from *The Teachings of Bhagavan Sri Ramana Maharshi In His Own Words*): "Pure Consciousness has no ego-sense about it. The ego-sense or 'I' notion . . . flourishes as an indiviudal being. [It] is at the root of all that is futile and undesirable in life. . . . This is Liberation or Enlightenment of Self-Realisation."

I sit and gaze at the tiger-skin rug, then close my eyes and meditate. My body seems to want to move away from the earth, but I am unable to let it go. I realize I am afraid to believe that the physical "I" may not exist. What, then, will take its place?

❧

I sit again in the New Hall for morning prayer. Next to me, an old woman with shaky fingers strings together a garland of frangipanis. When she sees me looking at her, her face breaks into a wide smile.

"Malayalee, aren't you?" she asks.

I nod, smiling back.

"I knew it from your face!" she says triumphantly. We exchange information about where in Kerala each of us is from and then sit in companionable silence.

I have just finished reading Paul Brunton's book about Ramana Maharshi and Brunton's own spiritual quest in India. It has made me wonder if I am destined to find a teacher of some sort to help in my inner search. I have been feeling lost here at the ashram, a place with no structure to follow, no teachers to tell me what to do. As a seeker, I am expected to know what I need and then to take (or find) it. I am here at Ramana Ashram because I am drawn to Ramana's teachings, but I can call neither him nor anyone else, alive or dead, my guru.

I rise and pad softly to the shrine. I circumambulate it again, this time walking with my eyes half-closed, focusing simply on my each step. As I walk, buried in thought, I begin to feel my body vibrating ever so slightly in response to the chanting around me. I have been told that some of Ramana's most powerful vibrations come from this very place around the shrine.

Something unique happens to me in ashrams. Perhaps it is the music, perhaps the energy of hundreds of seekers coming together in one place, or perhaps simply changes that occur within me. It is impossible not to feel touched by a certain sense of calmness, of concentration, of desire—if not ability—to move inward rather than outward. Being in an environment that supports spiritual growth cannot help but push one along, however gently, towards that same kind of growth. Natalie Goldberg, a Buddhist writer, put it best when she wrote: "If the culture you live in has no money and does not value it, it gives you the freedom not to have it too." Most ashrams give individuals like me the freedom not to subscribe to the values that are so common in the Western world today. Perhaps that is why some Westerners flock to ashrams in droves, searching for a supportive environment to needle them along to search for what really matters.

During my fifteen months in India I have had a growing sense that social change is best achieved through individual transformation. This is a conversation I have had with myself many times, and each time it raises questions that I cannot answer. When I left the business world years ago, it seemed clear to me that the best thing I could do with my life was to dedicate it to work that tried to improve conditions for the less fortunate in "developing" countries. As I endeavored in that arena, however, I began to see that "helping people" could be just as much of a business, as much of an ego-journey, as working in the private sector. As I watched a litany of failed development efforts parade before my eyes, I have wondered if real change must start first with the individual. But it is often difficult for me to reconcile this growing sense with my desire to "make a difference in the world."

In traditional Indian spirituality, there are three *yogas* (practices or ways) to progress on the spiritual path: *jnana, bhakti* and *karma.* Each way leads to the same ultimate goal of oneness with God and self but through different methods. In *jnana yoga* self-realization comes completely through meditation or inquiry, through a complete focus on concentration of the mind that does not use outside stimulus. In *bhakti yoga*, realization comes through the enactment of one's devotion to God, through chanting of God's name, through prayers, through pujas and rituals. In bhakti yoga individuals begin with a clear sense of God being separate from the individual, but eventually, through constantly praising God's name and worshipping the Divine, the individual becomes one with God, recognizes the godly presence and spirit within herself or himself and within everyone around them. Similarly, in *karma yoga*, the individual worships God through acts of selfless service. Eventually, through this way, it becomes one's nature to act with godliness to those around one, and in the process, to manifest God within the individual person. There are, of course, many overlaps. To practice only one of these three yogas is unusual. In each path, the ultimate lesson is to rid actions of ego, of any sense of individual attainment and achievement.

In *The Teachings of Bhagavan Sri Ramana Maharshi In His Own Words*, a conversation is recorded between a disciple and Ramana Maharshi. The disciple asks Ramana about social reform. Ramana replies, "Self-reform automatically results in social reform. Attend to self-reform and social reform will take care of itself. . . . Without understanding yourself, what is the use of trying to understand the world?"

ॐ

Almost immediately upon my arrival at Ramana Ashram I find the spirit there powerful. But additional confirmation of this comes just after the morning prayers when, still thinking about my need for guidance, I walk through the courtyard and see a beautiful peacock about to spread his feathers. A group of older men sits on the stoop to the right of the peacock. We all watch in wonder as the feathers open, exposing greens and blues, reds and purples, a display of royalty and grace. *So that's what it means to say a preening peacock*, I think to myself as the peacock struts around, clearly enjoying showing off his finery.

Just then, one of the men says to me, "Yes, that's what it means to say a preening peacock!" I startle to have someone else express my thoughts so accurately. I smile at the man, who puts his hands together in namaste and says, "I am supposed to meet you here. That is why I have come." I look at him in puzzlement. "You do not know this," he laughs. "But I knew we should meet. Come, let's talk."

I sit on the stoop next to him and we talk. His name is Natesan, and he has lived in the small rooms on the back side of the ashram for the past decade and a half since his retirement. We talk about Ramana, about the difficulty of meditating on this single, complex, sometimes seemingly meaningless question. I ask him if he feels he has ever achieved that sense of complete oneness. He smiles and shakes his head.

"Never for very long. But I have had glimpses. I know it can happen. But most of all, I trust Ramana. He is my guru. Perhaps it will not happen in this life for me, but it is my duty to continue trying."

"Don't you get frustrated?" I ask, embarrassed by the naïveté of my question, but needing to ask it nonetheless.

"Frustrated? Yes, sometimes. But I know this is the most important thing I can do in my life, to go inward, to search for the truth of existence."

Natesan invites Alan and me to visit him in his room later, and we talk for another hour. He pulls out worn books from his bookshelf and flips through them, reading to us Ramana's answers to various questions posed by disciples. I am drawn to this old man, feel as if he has come to me in direct reply to the questions I have posed in my mind regarding a guide and a teacher.

When it is time for us to leave, we tell Natesan regretfully that we are leaving the ashram the next day. He nods.

"Physically, yes. Don't worry, it will stay with you, and you will return one day."

He looks at me with a twinkle in his eyes. "The next time," he says, "you will have a child. A boy."

I smile. I am not unused to hearing this. Many Indians feel somehow compelled to tell me in their own way that I should already have children. "Maybe," I say, not wanting to tell him that just the week before, my husband and I had begun actively trying to get pregnant.

"No, you have one inside now," says Natesan to me confidently. Then he laughs when he sees that I have mentally dismissed his prediction. "You don't believe me now, but you'll see. Write to me and tell me if I am correct."

We raise our hands in namaste to him. I feel a sudden urge to bend down and touch his feet in gratitude, but I do not because the gesture feels too foreign. Natesan pats my head, puts his hands on my shoulders and says, "Bless you child. Search with strength." He blesses my husband, and we take our leave.

Three weeks later, I learn I am pregnant with my first child. Tracing the date back, I find our son was conceived one week before we met Natesan.

ॐ

We are crossing fault lines, fields recently watered by monsoon rains, dark human figures behind grey, hulking buffalo, bedraggled dogs, children clad in tattered clothes, rain running down their hair and faces in rivulets. Our train from Madras to Varanasi speeds through mountains of refuse piled on the banks of what may have been, at one time, a clear blue lake. Today it is black, black with sludge, with harmful chemical by-products of nearby factories, of decomposed waste and piles of garbage. A lone fishing boat tries to find something that can survive these waters. Behind it, the sun sinks into the earth, turning the sky's gray into melting red and pink and purple. God's work, this beautiful sun and sky.

And whose work is the horrifying refuse, the suffering children? How can beauty exist so closely juxtaposed with horror?

I have stretched my feet across the narrow bunk, pressed my body up against the window so that I can watch every drop of rain as it hits the window and slithers down to crawl across the cold metal of the train body. And then, for a brief moment, I understand what it would mean to be free of the physical world and our physical bodies, free of craving, of aversion, of the constant searching and striving. Just for a glimpse, I see the possibilities inherent in renouncing attachment, in embracing complete detachment. The feeling is so overwhelming, I shudder and then start crying. It is involuntary, this crying, as if the tears are being willed from somewhere else. They roll down my face, caressing it before dropping off and melting away.

"What is it?" my husband asks worriedly. His voice is far away, and I cannot bring his face into focus. Nor can I tell him what I have just felt, although I try in broken words. He nods and holds me close. He does not know what I am saying, but he does know that I have been touched for a brief second by something so powerful that I can neither understand nor explain it.

PART III

❧

The Gift of India

Swadhyaya: Toward a New World Order

On a bus ride up to the small town of Mount Abu in Rajasthan, I read the 1996 *United Nations Human Development Report*. The worldwide gap between rich and poor, it said, has widened faster than ever before. Today the richest 20 percent of the world's population earn 85 percent of the world's income. The net worth of the world's 358 billionaires (in dollar terms) is equivalent to the combined assets of 2.3 billion of the world's poorest people, who account for almost half of the world's total population. As the poorest get poorer, Western countries spend more on cosmetics, ice cream and pet food than would be necessary to provide basic education, clean water, basic health and nutrition for everyone in the world. Ironically, all of this consumption seems to do little for inner peace. In these same consumptive societies, happiness seems elusive. Depression, violence and hatred wrack wealthy nations, destroy communities and skew the sense of balance.

Too few people are aware that economic structural adjustment programs promoted by "developed" countries to help "developing" countries actually contributed to a regression of per capita incomes in most of these countries, down to their levels of the 1960s and 1970s. From 1950 to 1980, for example, the South (or the "Third World") had an economic growth rate higher than the North's during the same period, higher even than the rate for those same "developed" countries during their early states of development. Poverty and destitution (in economic terms) were actually declining in the

1960s and 1970s in many "third world" countries, without any structural adjustment programs.

Equally important, the focus on economic development subordinates the wealth of culture, tradition and spirituality that exists in countries such as India. In making material development the ultimate apex toward which to ascend, inner development is sidelined. Too often, the emphasis on outer development goes hand in hand with a loss of self-respect, interconnectedness with others or reverence for that which cannot be controlled by humans.

It had now been sixteen months since arriving in India, and my thinking on development had undergone a transformation. I had moved from believing that nongovernmental organizations (NGOs) offer the "solution," to the realization that the solutions offered by most development efforts treat only the symptoms rather than the real issue at stake: a global society that creates and encourages poverty and inequality, which ultimately results in the myriad social problems evident today.

The current system, the model on which many development programs are based, encourages accumulation of wealth by a small percentage of the world's population, while a large majority continues on a desperate struggle to eat one decent meal a day. Even the best-intentioned efforts often focus on "fixing" problems or on "helping the poor"—both reflections of an implied social hierarchy and a largely materialistic definition of poverty.

What we need, I had begun to believe, was nothing short of a new social paradigm, a world order that emphasizes spiritual over material development, community over individual relationship, collaboration over competition. This world order, as a by-product of its inherent connectedness, would allocate wealth more equitably, conserve rather than consume essential resources and focus on the fundamental sameness of human beings.

It sounded good, but the daunting fact was that no institution—government, donor or social-service organization—had yet offered an acceptable large-scale alternative development model to the current one. Many had tried and some had been successful on a microlevel but more often than not, the inextricable links between various aspects of a society's development and the sheer dominance of the existing model overwhelm most groups. In the end, even the most well-intentioned groups end up cutting off dead branches or trying to bring some back to life, rather than observing and attacking the agents of decay and rot.

Many NGOs, the original renegades that pushed for change in the government's "standard operating procedures," have been thwarted by questions of ego, national scale versus local effect and the still ill-defined concept of sustainability. Recently, several NGOs have also been co-opted into accepting government money and taking on government responsibilities. In the process they become part of the very system they are trying to change.

These thoughts left me depressed, uncertain about how to be successful in any community development effort when what was needed was an entire shift in consciousness. Then I encountered Swadhyaya.

"A silent but singing revolution," as one author has termed it, Swadhyaya was named one of the most exciting and powerful movements in the world by the United Nations in 1997. It has spread to a phenomenal one hundred thousand villages and twenty million people across India. Despite this, Swadhyaya has maintained a low national and international profile for the many decades since it first took flight in the mid-1950s. The movement takes pride in its lack of interest in quick results or publicity, and in its total independence from donors and religious or political forces. Swadhyaya is neither a membership organization nor a political movement; Swadhyayees describe it simply as a stream of thought and consciousness.

The underlying concepts of Swadhyaya are simple but powerful. Swadhyaya, meaning knowledge or discovery of the self, is based on the ancient Upanishadic concept that the highest stage of spiritual development is the stage at which God is not merely *within* each individual, but the point at which there is no difference *between* God and individual. The Upanishads detail three stages of realization in a human being's spiritual development: *Tana Ivam Asi* (You exist because of Him); *Tasya Ivam Asi* (You belong to Him); and *Tat Ivam Asi* (You are

Him). In this third and highest stage God does not reside in a temple or church, but within me, within you, and within every living creature. By virtue of our creation, we are related, part of a world community, connected to each other and to nature.

The respect that develops out of this perspective is the essential underpinning of a healthy society. In this view, the work that people do to take care of each other and the earth simply becomes a manifestation of bhakti, devotion to God, as described in the Bhagavad Gita. In the process of individual transformation, then, societal transformation occurs as a by-product.

Although the ethos of Swadhyaya is Hindu, Swadhyayees emphasize that it is not just for Hindus. While resistance to certain concepts of the movement still exists, Swadhyaya has gradually gained acceptance among groups of Buddhists, Christians and Muslims. "Religion is a spiritual order to go to God. There may be different kinds of orders, therefore different religions," says Pandurang Shastri Athavale, Swadhyaya's founder, "but bhakti is present in all of them and, in this sense, is universal."

I had first heard of Swadhyaya at a conference in 1996 in the hill town of Kausani. The conference, titled "Re-Thinking the Current Economic Order: Gandhi and Beyond," was about the focus on the current dominant economic paradigm: Is it appropriate? If not, what should be in its place? How is such a change to be brought about? The articulate and passionate voices of longtime socialists, the convictions of Gandhians for a world imagined by the Mahatma but never realized, and the urgency of those working in the field who are frustrated with merely providing "band-aid" solutions—all crescendoed into a single realization: that a basic sense of reverence for something other than ourselves needs to be restored.

One of the conference participants was an eminent professor from the Center for the Study of Developing Societies in Delhi. He brought up Swadhyaya as an example of a movement that focused on individual spiritual development and ultimately sought to change the paradigm within which the world operated. In August 1996, soon after the conference, the Gandhi Peace Foundation invited my husband

and me to participate in a tour of Swadhyaya communities and projects across Gujarat state in Western India. The tour would culminate in a meeting with the movement's founder, Shastri, or Dada (meaning elder brother) as he is affectionately called by all Swadhyayees.

"Dada-ji is the first person since Indian independence that I would put in the same category as Mahatma Gandhi," said Rajiv Vora of the Gandhi Peace Foundation to me before the tour. A few months earlier, Shastri had been granted the prestigious Ramon Magasay Award for his vision and service; in 1997 he would be granted the equally prestigious Templeton Prize for Religion, a prize given twenty-five years ago to Mother Teresa. These prizes are simply one acknowledgment of the change Shastri has brought to the communities with which he works. The more compelling acknowledgment comes from those communities themselves and the changes they have seen since embracing Swadhyaya.

⚛

As a young boy, Dada was schooled for twelve years in the Indian shastras, logic and philosophy at a Sanskrit school started by his grandfather. When he finished this at age twenty-five, Dada enrolled himself for another twelve years in the study of Western philosophy.

In 1954, Dada attended the Second World Religious Congress in Japan. There he presented a paper that rejected the material track he felt the world was moving on and instead advocated the spiritual way described in the Bhagavad Gita. This path, he said, stressed bhakti, devotion to God. A person's responsibility is only to do one's duty to the best of one's capability for God and without attachment to the fruits of the labor. In performing duty as an expression of love for God, the concept of the individual as "doer" disappears. The individual is simply a pathway for actions to be carried out; God is the "doer."

Dada impressed his audience enough that they clamored to know where in India they could go to see these principles in action. At that moment, Dada, lost for an answer, realized that much of what he believed was the answer to the world's problems was quickly being lost to the monoculture of modernism. He vowed to devote his life to reviving an interest in the critical messages of the old and wise Indian texts and teachings, a vow that resulted in the beginning of Swadhyaya.

Dada's early group of followers was small, a handful of primarily liberal, urban intellectuals. Even this devoted group found it difficult to always accept Dada's teachings, so different were these teachings from the world in which they lived. Dada's central message was to do God's work, work that ultimately meant recreating the "brotherhood of man." To do this, Dada said, these urban intellectuals needed to go to the villages and reconnect with the people there. These were their real brothers and sisters, related by virtue of a common creator.

Dada's message was simple but the implications were tremendous. These intellectuals, generally from within the upper two castes of the Hindu caste system, were extremely well-educated and relatively wealthy. Often, they held high status in their communities. Their "brothers and sisters," on the other hand, were in many cases from the lowest and middle castes, agricultural people with little formal education and, far too often, living in economic poverty. The lives of these groups would rarely have crossed except for these visits.

Hemraj Ashar, one of Dada's early followers who is now a respected attorney in Bombay, remembered the doubts and trials of those early days. "Dada told us we should go to the villages, find out how these people, our brothers and sisters, lived. We should get to know them, he said. At first, we didn't want to go! What would we say to them? What would they say to us? But Dada insisted that we should just tell them the truth: that we were their relatives in the family of the Creator, and that we wanted to get to know them."

In 1957 a group of seventeen people went to villages in what was to be the first of the Swadhyaya *bhakti pheris*, or devotional visits. Their mission was simply to reestablish this lost connection; it was important that villagers understood that no motive other than this existed. Although many of these urban intellectuals had their own vehicles, Dada instructed them to take a bus to a central point and then to walk, carrying their own supplies of food, stoves, blankets and lamps. Fancy cars or motorcycles would focus attention on the differences between these city people and the villagers, creating a hierarchy of wealth before a meeting even occurred. Perhaps Dada also wanted the city people to go back to the simplicity of years past, when walking, talking and seeing the countryside were part of building a relationship with fellow travelers, with nature, with God.

Today, the bhakti pheri is the driving force behind the growth of Swadhyaya. These devotional visits are now carried out by thousands of people across India and, to a lesser extent, abroad in America, England and various African countries. Many Swadhyayees devote half of their yearly vacations to going on bhakti pheris. The basis of the visits continues to be building a relationship of trust and bringing people to the realization that each individual, each living thing is divine. Swadhyayees visit the same people over a long period of time; Swadhyaya is not about visiting one family one week and another the next. There is no underlying motive of conversion to a particular religion, no intent even to "change" someone, simply the desire to meet and to know. It is precisely because of this lack of ulterior motive that Swadhyaya has been so successful. Many Swadhyayees also say that continually explaining the concepts of Swadhyaya to others helps them to internalize the concepts and develop a true understanding of the principles espoused.

"At first, when people started coming, we thought they were coming either for votes or money or some other motive. Nobody ever comes without a selfish reason," said Harshan Behn from Kajali village in Gujarat. "Why would they want to get to know us? But then, when they kept coming back time and time again for years, taking nothing from us but just wanting to get to know us, we began to believe them." Hemraj Ashar is still in touch with the original families he met on his first bhakti pheri. They are part of his community. The key purpose of the bhakti pheri—to stimulate informal dialogue with people, over time and with the complete commitment to form and maintain individual bonds—allows real trust to develop and to be sustained.

🕉

About a month before we embarked on the tour of Swadhyaya communities and projects throughout Gujarat, Alan and I attended one of Dada's Sunday discourses at a temple in Bombay. It was a rainy morning. We reached the temple and followed the streams of people (an estimated ten thousand) who were walking into a big mud-floored, thatched-roof area. Rain poured through the roof and saturated the floor, the excess bubbling up into dirty puddles. To the right of the entrance, men and women left their shoes and then hitched up their saris, pants and dhotis to wade barefoot through the mud. Like a choreographed dance, they split at the end of the room near the stairs, men to the right and women to the left. The room upstairs was already packed full of people sitting cross-legged.

I sat next to an elderly woman with a peaceful smile, wearing a simple white sari. She had become involved with Swadhyaya through her sister-in-law, who was one of Dada's first listeners. My companion, who was from Gujarat and had been a close follower of Mahatma Gandhi, told me that Dada had once stayed with them, and they had known immediately that this was someone very special, someone who could one day lead the world—not in a political sense, but in a spiritual one. Dada's simplicity and genuineness had touched her, even then.

"He did not call himself a saint or an enlightened person, but that was one of the first thoughts in my mind—this is what a saint is like," she said. Years later, she had been among the first group to go to England on a bhakti pheri. It was not until after I met her that I found out that this simple woman was also a millionaire, involved in running a very successful family business.

As we were talking, a murmur went through the crowd. Dada had entered the room. Dressed in a simple white kurta and dhoti, he had his hands folded in a namaste and was walking slowly down the huge room toward us. Despite the large number of people in the room, his eyes and body seemed to be greeting each one individually, acknowledging the divine in each soul.

His lecture that day was brief. He was recovering from a recent illness and still seemed a little weak. In his gentle voice, he told his followers that he had come to have darshan of the people. *Darshan* is a term typically used to describe a "viewing" or audience with God; Dada was pointing out that his own community of human beings was his God. He joked several times, laughed, coughed; he was human, connecting in the most personal of ways with every individual in the room. Dada talked about an understanding, awareness and respect for a spiritual power greater than humankind and greater than religion. The path to that power was questioning, learning and only then, believing. He inspired not just with his words, but with his very way of being.

As he often did in his discourses, Dada warned that day against "blind faith." Like the Rawal in Badrinath, Dada was frustrated that religion is often accepted without questioning, becoming then a hierarchy that can abuse power. Dada urged his followers to question everything he said, and never to accept a message from an authority figure if they did not believe in it themselves.

Dada's pleas for reason and against blind faith softened some of my own discomfort around Swadhyaya's constant references to God and devotion. Later, through talking with countless Swadhyayees I would also understand that "God" could mean a universal force or a guiding spirit. The tenets of Swadhyaya simply placed creations in a greater context, made each one responsible to the other.

After Dada's discourse, I stood at the window on the upper floor and looked out at the sea of people gathered in one of the muddy rooms below. They had congregated in small groups, laughing, talking and enjoying the aura of peace and companionship that permeated the room. I understood then that one of the most important manifestations of the individual and societal transformations that occurred through Swadhyaya was the re-creation of a family of individuals, a family that extended beyond blood, religion, caste or community.

வ௷௺

The tour of Swadhyaya villages took place primarily in Gujarat, one of the areas where Swadhyaya had flourished and, not coincidentally, the site of Mahatma Gandhi's birthplace. Our group of twenty shared a common concern for the direction in which the world was going, a path that seemed to neglect spiritual development of the individual and ultimately of communities. But the group was tremendously diverse in a variety of ways.

One of the tour members was a *maulana*, a revered Muslim leader known throughout India for his work for religious tolerance and his intense love for the country. At age seventy, the maulana made a striking figure with his long white beard, beautifully lined face and white robe. He took notes copiously and would ask people to write in his small book their prognosis for India's future. There was also a *rinpoche*, a high Buddhist monk, who had worked closely with the Dalai Lama for Tibet's freedom. There were people from extremes of the political continuum—from the fundamentalist Hindu Rashtriya Swayan Sewak party to India's Socialist party—as well as professors from well-known universities, journalists, social scientists, environmental activists and social reformers.

The tour's first stop was a *chawl* just outside the city limits of Ahmedabad, Gujarat's largest city. Chawls, common sights in most urban areas, are economically poor slum areas often made up largely of lower caste people. The road to the chawl was merely clumps of reddish-orange mud interrupted by puddles of cloudy water with sewage floating on top. Inside, the small narrow lanes were populated with buffalo, people and children. A sudden spurt of heavy monsoon rain beat down on the tin roofs of the shacks that lined the roads. Dada has said that Swadhyaya should reach "unto the last"—how much further can one go in terms of social oppression than the Harijans? Since 1984, Swadhyaya has touched more than one-fourth of all the chawls in Ahmedabad. At a recent meeting of Swadhyayees in the city, four hundred thousand Harijans were present. Dada's display of love for these individuals allows people to reflect on their own prejudices and blocks to building relationships with their brothers and sisters.

According to one of the chawl residents, "[Dada] welcomed us, held us. It made us cry to be loved in a way that we had never experienced before. Because of him, people who used to throw us out of their houses and throw vessels and stones at us also began to see that we were their brothers, divine representatives of God."

We made our way into a concrete room. The walls were peppered with small shrines with pictures and statues of deities. These were strung with fresh garlands of flowers and marked with wet red paste, indicating a recent puja. The room was filled with men, women and children who lived in the area, mostly of the sweeper caste and widely considered "untouchables." They greeted us with roses, streaked our foreheads with the same red paste to bless us in welcome. *"Jai Yogeshwar,"* people murmured around us. This Swadhyaya greeting means "victory to Yogeshwar," the name Swadhyayees use for God. Dada selected this name because it is universal across Hinduism and does not connote sectarianism as some of the more common names of deities might.

A well-dressed man stood up and began speaking. The manager of the local State Bank of India, he lived only one kilometer away, but for thirty years he had never bothered to visit this area. "I used to think that this caste was too low for me. Dada's words changed me. I began to think if I won't go there, who will?"

A stream of shared experiences followed. There was Pushpa Behn, a strong, stout woman who used to get furious with the disparity between the way her Harijan caste was insulted and the way rich people were honored. "Because of my caste, I was not even allowed to carry the [Bhagavad] Gita! Now, not only have I learned the Gita, I feel I have a head full of thoughts." There was Narayan Bhai, a reformed alcoholic who said he gave up drink with the realization that God was within him. "If we leave our shoes outside the temple before going to see God, shouldn't we keep our bodies pure if God is within us?"

The accounts followed one after another, a stream of testimonies to personal change that had formerly been unthinkable, a periscope into the troubled lives of before that had now opened to hope. These visits, from people who did not know the chawl residents and who asked for nothing except friendship, seemed to rebuild a basic trust in humanity and in self. "Change," said another Swadhyayee, "is a process that starts to move inward and then spreads. It is a continuous process that takes time. We follow Dada's words that we must listen, practice and think. Swadhyaya affects our thoughts, makes us begin questioning things we have never questioned before."

We left the chawl to a line of singing people holding small wick lamps in their hands. As showers of red rose petals landed on my head and flitted down past my nose, I smelled their wonderful sweet fragrance. It was raining but no one seemed to notice. How could Swadhyaya be so based on the traditional texts and yet create a social revolution? Dada explains that such issues as discrimination are inventions of the modern world, not the traditional one. The so-called revolution, then, is merely an entire reorientation to some of the best pieces of Indian traditional thought.

⚙

Perhaps the most remarkable thing about Swadhyaya is the way in which individual transformation has led to societal transformation. The concepts are completely logical, but yet so alien to the way in which the development world thinks about "development" and societal transformation. It is used to seeing small changes, which usually occur as part of a project designed to create those changes. But Swadhyaya achieves social and economic change—both of which have been elusive to social service organizations and governments for so long—as an extension of creating healthy individuals and communities.

But what does this mean in practical terms? The notion is that once Swadhyayees truly believe that God is within them and all living creatures, their duty in the world becomes simply to express their devotion to God by offering their time and talent to contribute to their larger community through various community "experiments." In this manner, social activism reinforces faith and faith reinforces social activism.

These community experiments generally take place in villages where 90 percent or more of the villagers are committed to Swadhyaya's ideals. They have ranged from soak pits constructed by villagers that reduce the amount of exposed human excrement and stagnating water (and consequently, the incidence of malaria and tuberculosis), to addressing caste discrimination, to establishing the Swadhyaya Vidyapeeth, a children's school that teaches about agricultural practices along with the spiritual thought that Swadhyayees hope will eventually combat the dominant economic model. Swadhyaya Vidyapeeth aims to create from the base an entirely new type of individual. Many of these experiments have produced remarkable and visible results.

In the fishing villages along the coast of Gujarat, one fisherman's lucky day may be another's day of shortage. Mother Water is not always kind and those fishermen who do not have their own boats usually work as laborers on another's boat. On a good day, they earn enough to feed themselves. Life is hard. Inequality of income is often great, and alcohol a warm retreat from the harsh realities. But in Veraval village and many others like it, Swadhyayees have built a *matsyaganda*, a fishing boat that is for the entire village (*matsya* is the fish incarnation of Vishnu, *ganda* means boat). Swadhyayees built the boat using their own tools and building materials, and they now donate their labor, their "efficiency," to the matsyaganda. Every day, five different fishermen contribute their time to fish on the community boat. Their catch is sold in the market, and the proceeds are distributed to those in need. The distributions are considered prasad, offerings blessed by God.

This concept of impersonal wealth—wealth that belongs to God to which no individual has a claim to—is also from the Upanishads and is fundamental to many of Swadhyaya's socioeconomic experiments. The fishermen's catch on the matsyaganda does not belong to them as individuals but instead is the result of their contributing time and talent to God. The money made from the catch also belongs to God, and the ultimate distribution to the community is from God. Impersonal wealth takes away the notion of the "helpers" and the "helped." In fact, the identities of those who receive monetary help are only known by those who distribute the prasad.

In another village we entered a *loknath amritalayam*, "eternal abode of the Lord of the people." It was a small, thatched structure with (appropriately) no walls. A young woman and her husband were the pujaris for the day. The young woman sat confidently in front of large brass lamps, flicking flower petals toward statues of deities in front of her, sonorously chanting prayers. Her husband was at her side, his turn would be next. It was extraordinary, this sight, because the young woman was a Harijan. Traditionally, Harijans have not been allowed to enter temples or to recite verses from the holy books. Women harijans have two strikes against them, since women are never allowed to be pujaris.

But in the loknath amritalayam, the rules are rewritten. It is the people's temple, built by the villagers from locally available materials. It serves as a cohesive and inclusive force to draw people together and to foster respect and even as a place to informally discuss individual and collective problems. In this temple, the role of pujari rotates among villagers. Anyone who thinks and acts in accordance with ideas of respect for God, self and others can be a pujari. Through discussion, philosophical and religious constructs that may have been previously inaccessible because of caste or illiteracy become relevant, important and inspiring.

Another strong example of a Swadhyaya experiment that has changed the notion of community and individual relationships is the *shri darshanam*. Inspired from a visit Dada made to Israel, where he visited a kibbutz, shri darshanams are experiments in community farming. A shri darshanam is a piece of land that has been purchased by the Swadhyaya trust for tending by a group of twenty proximately located villages. (Only when 90 percent of all twenty villages are Swadhyayees is a shri darshanam started, and only if the villagers request it themselves.) A different person, who is called a pujari, from each village is assigned to work on the land on specific days of the month, so that on any given day there are a minimum of twenty people working. Pujaris themselves provide the tools, labor and seeds. Every month an expert is brought in from outside to talk to the group about issues, problems and new ideas for farming, such as nonchemical fertilizers, worming composts and other natural techniques to increase yields.

The pujaris spend eight hours working in the fields and the

evening hours discussing ideas, learning and studying from others. Business people and intellectuals who do not know about farming come as pujaris also. They learn about the earth and agriculture from those who can teach them during the day, and then contribute from their areas of knowledge during the evening hours of talk. "Dada provided us the opportunity to be detached from our house and our work and instead, to do selfless service. In this way we improve ourselves spiritually. We also have an opportunity to give back to Mother Earth what we take from her," said one white-bearded man tenderly gesturing to the trees around him.

When the crops are eventually harvested, they are sold to Swadhyayees at market prices. The demand is great, because they are, like the fishing catch from the matsyagandas, considered prasad. Remaining produce is sold in the regular bazaar. Profit goes back to the central Swadhyaya trust, which is used to fund similar purchases of land for other such experiments, the Swadhyaya universities and various projects.

The primary purpose of this shri darshanam experiment is to expand the notion of community and allow individuals to give of themselves selflessly, with no thought to their reward or gain. Men, women and children begin to think of more than themselves, their own families or even their own villages. They learn to respect the creator and the creations, like Mother Earth. But, in performing their work with love and absorption, Swadhyayees have also produced excellent harvests. It is the ultimate lesson of dedication to one's best effort, rather than the results of the work.

One Swadhyayee eloquently explained, "Our shri darshanam is proving that the statement 'man does not work without [monetary] incentive' is false. From twenty villages, we have made one community. Any sadness or need that exists in any other of these twenty villages is like it exists in our village. This is the community that has formed. This is above the sense of 'my' village. It is one level higher. It is about God's family."

ॐ

There are many compelling statistics to show the progress Swadhyayees have made in their communities in fighting discrimination, decreasing poverty and improving equality of income. But looking only at these statistics ignores the most important and often unquantifiable results: the self-respect that a Harijan feels in the same community in which he was discarded a decade ago; the pride a farmer feels when he shares his knowledge of the land with his seemingly different businessman neighbor; the wholeness of spirit and mind a woman feels when she leads a religious ceremony that she has been excluded from for hundreds of years. How can one measure inner peace, harmonious relations, or a new awareness of and respect for self? How, in other words, can one measure real empowerment?

The world is a diverse place, however, and Swadhyaya will certainly not appeal to everyone. Simply the fact that the central premise of Swadhyaya postulates a God (or at least some Greater Being) may exclude those who do not share such a belief. In some communities, for example, Muslims have taken offense to the worship of idols as a necessary part of the Swadhyaya rituals. The maulana's reaction at the end of our trip was very different, though. He stood up during our last meeting with Dada and stated in a quivery, emotional voice that he had "joined the Swadhyaya family." Just the day before, I had seen him enter a Hindu temple in one of the Swadhyaya villages and pray, an action that spoke volumes about his belief in Swadhyaya's philosophy of inclusion of Muslims into its fold. The rinpoche in our tour group, although expressing doubt that Buddhists could ever truly be incorporated into Swadhyaya's fold because of the movement's dependence on accepting God as a central figure (which Buddhists do not do), also voiced his support for Swadhyaya's philosophies and achievements.

There is also the question of whether Swadhyaya will appeal to those in the West who are so enveloped in materialism. Although for some, achieving material wealth may be the first opening to realizing there is more to life than just that, there are millions who are still caught up in "achieving" the skewed notion of progress that today's worldview promotes. But even if Swadhyaya were to stay simply at its current level, the magnitude of the transformation it is now achieving gives me more hope than anything else I have seen.

The success of the Swadhyaya path has been neither quick nor easy, however. The early Swadhyayees often doubted that anything would ever happen. It took eight to ten years for the beginning of any evidence of a changing consciousness. "The problems we have in society today will take at least two generations to resolve," says Dada, "and yet, we do not even have the patience to wait two years."

Dada's faith in the ultimate ability of Swadhyayees to establish a different kind of world continues to inspire and guide his followers. Few people I have ever met have Dada's courage to look beyond today's realities and believe in the seemingly extravagant possibility of a new world order. "I have nothing new to offer," Dada said at our last meeting, smiling gently. "I am only restating what has already been said."

These are almost the same words that Mahatma Gandhi used. What I saw in Dada and in the Swadhyayees was a living example of a real search for truth, a redefinition of individual happiness and societal progress, a world of relatedness lost in modern times. In the quest for individual truth, these Swadhyayees are creating truly dramatic transformations in living and thinking.

Villages

While I was living in India, the popular magazine *India Today* published a cover story called "What Indians Think." The magazine claimed to have conducted a comprehensive survey that would, for the first time, provide a true representation of the average Indian's attitudes on a variety of social and political issues. I was surprised by the responses. They seemed very different from the views of many of the villagers I had spoken with during my two years. Had I just spoken to a very small and unrepresentative sample? Then I read the fine print: The questionnaire had been administered only in India's large cities. *India Today's* editors had given a small disclaimer, without apology, that they had been unable to interview villagers. What they did not state is that villagers represent more than 70 percent of India's population, so a survey that focuses on the other 30 percent could hardly be called "representative"!

The mainstream hears very little about the opinions, lives and views of this enormous majority of the Indian population because, for the most part, this population remains outside the global economy that is built by and of interest to large corporate entities. And yet—as the well-known journalist-anthropologist Richard Critchfield reminded readers in his 1981 book, *Villages*—villages are "man's oldest and most durable social institution," a lesson that is too easily forgotten. For those who have spent most of their lives in cities, it is easy to be lulled into thinking that urban life is representative of all life. Until, that is, one steps out, even for a brief moment. Critchfield has commented that villagers who go to cities "travel through both space and time." The reverse is true as well. One enters a village, or even just leaves a city, and realizes instantly that cities represent one end of the continuum of change taking place in India. Villages, depending on how close or far they are from cities, dot that same continuum, showing in slow motion society's movement along this seemingly inevitable road of change.

ॐ

Our sea-green 1987 Matador minivan rattled its way through Varanasi's spewing, sputtering life to the relative calm of the Buddhist enclave, Sarnath, and on to the Gorakhpur National Highway. The "highway," a two-lane road, wound through agricultural fields, village bazaars selling fresh produce, small towns, periodic tea stalls and roadside *dhabas*, wooden shacks that displayed on rickety tables large steel containers of vegetables, dal and rice. We stopped and ate at one of these dhabas, mixing their potato and cauliflower concoction with homemade *rotis* stuffed with ground roasted lentils.

My hosts, Vidhu Chaturvedi and his mother, and I had started this journey from Varanasi at 1:30 on a pleasant December afternoon. Our 145-kilometer trip would take us to the village of Kamalsagar, deep in the interior of Uttar Pradesh, almost at the border of neighboring Bihar state. The Chaturvedis were from Kamalsagar originally, although they now lived in Varanasi. They were returning to the village to settle a dispute about their village lands.

The Gorakhpur highway closely followed the Ganges, and the fields next to the road were fertile. Lower-lying fields had flooded, and the water lay dirty brown in pools. Along the road, dung cakes were laid out to dry; dried cakes had been stacked on their sides in pyramids. Against the shacks, bundles of straw stood tall against the mud walls. The only sound I could hear came from our noisy diesel engine. Behind us the sun was sinking lower and lower into the curve of the river.

It took six long hours to travel the one hundred kilometers from Varanasi to the industrial town of Mau, about forty-five kilometers from Kamalsagar. Dark was falling and our engine had sprung a leak, so we decided to spend the night in the best hotel in Mau, a seedy concrete box filled with men who watched television at high volume and drank cheap liquor like water. The next morning we loaded ourselves into the van and searched for someone to fix our leak. After a stop at a string of auto mechanic shops en route, each one with their own specialty—brakes, engines, tires—we finally found an oil pipe "specialist." Some untangling of wires here, cutting of the pipe there, then 10 rupees into the mechanic's oil-smeared hand, and we were on our way.

Kamalsagar fell into the parliamentary district that had Kalpnath Rai as its minister to the central government. Rai, according to Vidhu, was "totally corrupt but much loved." As long as he continued to run, it was unlikely that anyone would challenge him. He had first been the Power Minister and then the Food Minister before he was expelled from the national Congress Party in 1996 during a wave of ministerial "house-cleaning" that followed a big corruption scandal. The scandal did not seem to hurt Rai much, however; he ended up winning the election from jail. (His opponent was also in jail for corruption.)

"People know he is corrupt," Vidhu said, "but he has done so much for this area. Before Rai, this place had no roads, no facilities, no electricity. The town of Mau is completely his creation. He turned it from a village into an industrial center, built proper roads and industrial complexes, brought in employment and business, and initiated countless power projects. According to Vidhu, some people even felt that Rai *had* to be corrupt to be as effective as he was in bringing change to the area, that if he had not accumulated so much money to contribute to the ruling national Congress Party, he would not have achieved such a high post.

Sugarcane stalks waved in the wind around us. From sugarcane villagers made *gur*, a dark brown sugarlike molasses. The sweet smell permeated the smoky air. It was toward the end of the sugarcane harvest; much of it had already been cut down. In the plots that remained, the fast-drying leaves drooped toward the brown earth.

Everywhere, people seemed busy. Men and women together shook wheat from old, worn dhotis to separate the grain from the chaff. On metal drums they thrashed the wheat and shredded the remains to feed to cattle. Several sugarcane crusher machines whirred noisily, chewing the sugarcane stalks and extracting a cloudy yellow liquid. In the fields children ran freely through the freshly plowed dirt, while their mothers bent over sowing seeds. Men pushed their buffalo- and cow-drawn plows through the fields, creating huge ovals in the square patches of land. On the roads next to us, horse-drawn carts jingled their way along, sometimes coming face to face with their modern relative: the red, new, shiny tractors decorated in gold and silver tinsel, carrying crops, supplies and passengers.

I had now seen the fields of India in all their seasons: first, in the heat of the summer when I traveled south from Lucknow to the Banda district along the Uttar Pradesh–Madhya Pradesh border. Then the fields were bone dry, not a flowering shrub nor a blade of grass to be seen. The land thirsted for water, seemed harsh and unforgiving. Next came the monsoons, when even in the deserts of Rajasthan, the land turned a verdant green. Everything was alive and fruitful. To the outsider it was unthinkable that production would not continue forever, that this bounty was indeed limited. With harvesting came a sense of richness. Villagers enjoyed festivals, marriages and the fruits of their hard labor, putting aside uncertain thoughts about the future. Now there was plenty for all. Finally, it was back to readying the fields again, stripping, plowing and replanting. The fields were turning to brown again—not the desperate brown of summer, but rather the hopeful brown of fruits to come. Time had come full circle.

With the notion of seasons passing, I felt a strong sense of the impermanence of time. I saw clearly how a villager's closeness to the earth keeps him or her grounded in an understanding of not just nature's cycle and rhythms, but also of human limitation. It may be certain that one has to plant seeds to attempt to reap a harvest, but it is not certain that those seeds will flower. One bad monsoon, one natural disaster can take away any certainty that might have existed. "Man proposes, God disposes," as the old saying goes. Here, more than anywhere, I was struck by how city-dwellers like myself have few reminders of how small humankind is in the entirety of the universe; we fool ourselves into thinking that so much in our lives is permanent and controllable. Villagers know better.

ॐ

Kamalsagar is set directly off a road, with no signboard to announce its existence. The "main strip" in Kamalsagar, stretching only about fifty yards, houses the *patshallah* (school), a small chai shop, which serves as the local gathering place, and a few assorted provision stores. Across from the chai shop is a now-defunct *ayurvedic* (the ancient system of medicine employing herbs, minerals and massage) hospital, set up by Vidhu's grandfather. A small stone plaque in his honor stands in front of the hospital.

We turned off onto a dirt road that eased itself through a clearing of bamboo trees. The van's clattering noises brought people running from their houses to see who had come. Accompanied by a large group, we made our way to the big wooden doorway across from where we had parked. A boy unlocked the padlock and chain on top of the door and let us into a courtyard shaded on the right by a huge still-flowering rosehip tree. The left wall of the courtyard was mud and served also as the side wall of the next-door neighbor's house. The wall was in its original state: mud topped with starting-to-rot but beautifully carved wooden beams sitting beneath a wavy, red-tiled roof. At the far right of the courtyard was a concrete area with a fairly new hand pump. Just beyond, another old wooden door led into the house's inner courtyard. Walking into this courtyard, I felt I had gone back in time. Inside, it was cool but sunny, with tiny narrow garden patches along the sides sprouting tall rose vines with full, ready-to-burst, ruby red roses. This was an area even in its current state of desertedness that conjured up memories of families and children playing, of peace and simplicity.

The ground floor of the house consisted of one big room, where the three of us would sleep, an adjoining room off one side used mainly for storage and another smaller room that opened onto both a front covered veranda and a little back courtyard and garden. This room was used as a kitchen, although there was also a small mud, fire-lit *chula* (stove) in an area off the front courtyard. "Usually, we cook all our food on the mud chula with a fire," Vidhu said, pointing to a huge tangled pile of firewood sticks next to the chula. "This time, though, it would have been difficult for my mother to manage on that chula alone, so we have brought a gas cylinder and single gas burner."

There were also two rooms with rusty grilled windows on the side of the front courtyard. This space was converted some years back into rooms for storing grains and crops, but now it lay empty because no one lived in the house permanently. One side of the back courtyard housed a simple, enclosed mud-pit latrine. On the other side was a small enclosure with a deep-well motor pump that was not working at the time. The house also had an upper floor reached by stairs from the front courtyard. There were two small rooms that opened onto a terrace. From here I could look down into the neighboring courtyards, across the sea of red-tiled roofs and beyond to the green and brown fields of Kamalsagar.

The land stretched out to meet the sky, hazy from the dust of village fires. The bright yellow of flowering mustard trees provided splashes of color amid freshly plowed brown fields. The small mud paths that divided the fields made the land into a maze, where one could wander around surrounded only by nature. From this perspective, Kamalsagar looked much like I imagined it had half a century ago.

ॐ

It had been six months since anyone from the Chaturvedi family had been back to Kamalsagar. Layers of dust coated the tables and chairs and cobwebs hung from the corners of the room. Leading the cleaning brigade were Baijnath and his wife, Baijnath-Bhu. They had worked with the Chaturvedis for more than twelve years, tending their fields and doing domestic work. They were Harijans, members of the lowest caste.

For the Chaturvedis, discrimination against Harijans had always been a social evil that they worked hard to change. Vidhu's infamous grandfather, Swami Satyanand Chaubey, was perhaps the first in a line of socially progressive Brahmins in his area. Swami was a rare combination: a politically-active sanyasi. He experimented with many social issues, the main one being the uplifting of Harijans. Through his work, land was donated to the Harijans so that they could settle in Kamalsagar. As a symbol of his support and to eliminate one of the biggest problems of discrimination faced by Harijans, Swami built a concrete deep well right in the Harijan *basti* (area of the village), so that they would no longer have to walk miles to fetch water because of banishment from Brahmin water sources. Despite severe resistance from almost all Kamalsagar families, Swami systematically broke the rules around caste pollution. In his house Harijans ate from the family's own dishes and came within scandalously close distances of Brahmins, sometimes even touching them. Later in life, Swami spent most of his time in a small town about forty kilometers north of Mau, where he had established a Harijan ashram.

Vidhu's parents had also taken an active interest in Harijan matters. During our visit numerous Harijans came to pay their respects to Mrs. Chaturvedi and to seek her advice. Just recently, a Harijan man had been killed by a bus, leaving children and the rest of his family behind. Representatives of the family came to visit, and Mrs. Chaturvedi gave them information on how to file insurance claims to receive compensation for the death.

To this day, the Chaturvedis' attitude toward Harijans remains a source of unspoken disapproval for many of their neighbors. I noticed that many people who came to visit did not drink tea from the Chaturvedis' cups. Vidhu told me later this was because they knew Harijans drank and ate from the same vessels. Although Vidhu and his mother always treated Baijnath and his wife with respect, and even considered them the managers of their land, I noticed how others treated them with a tangible air of condescension.

One night, a Brahmin visitor, who was a little drunk, peremptorily ordered Baijnath to make tea and then refused to take the tea cup from his hand, telling him to put it on the chair. Old habits die hard, I thought. Alcohol perhaps loosened the chains of "proper behavior" (or its village form of political correctness) enough to bring back true attitudes toward Harijans.

I mentioned the incident to Vidhu later, and he shrugged his shoulders. "Yes, it's still that way. At least he agreed to drink tea from the cup that had been touched by Baijnath. That, for him, is a big thing."

Had the situation changed for the Harijans over the years? Had "modernization" improved discriminatory attitudes of upper castes or the condition of Harijans? Most Brahmins answered with a resounding (sometimes resentful) yes. Most felt that the biggest change came in the Harijans' ability to choose their work and their employers. Previously, because of their low economic and social condition, Harijans often had to do whatever was asked of them by any upper caste person. Today, a Brahmin cousin of Vidhu's insisted, the "improvement of the lower class situation" meant that Harijans often dictated the terms even of labor.

In Kamalsagar, unlike many other villages across India, Harijans still work in the fields on a system of labor for crops. Traditionally, workers could take whatever they could carry. Today, however, agreements are more structured. Most Kamalsagar Harijans will not work for less than half of the harvest reaped in the fields they tend. Sometimes the deals are more lucrative. A landowner might agree to keep a certain amount of the harvest for himself, giving anything over and above this to his workers. Vidhu and his mother were even more generous, taking only what they needed for their own consumption and giving the rest to Baijnath and Baijnath-Bhu.

The labor-for-crops arrangement, originally known as the jajmani system, was an integral part of the caste system. Opponents and proponents of the jajmani system use it as an example of both exploitation and stability. In its original format, the jajmani system saw lower castes supply services or goods to higher castes in return for an annual wage paid in kind. The relationship extended back several generations and was part of a wider "patron-client" relationship. According to some scholars, this relationship provided certain rights for the workers: the right to work, to be paid for their work and to not have to compete with others for that work. These same scholars point out that these relationships were stable and long-term, that patrons protected the workers from exploitation and gave them economic backing in times of crisis. Other scholars have added that the jajmani system provided a clearer sense of identity regarding one's role in life. Occupations were fixed; it was certain that a son would perform the same tasks as his father for the same patron. With the decline of the jajmani system and the dissociation of castes and traditional occupations, however, specialist castes have been forced to train themselves for unfamiliar work with strangers—particularly a difficult task for lower, uneducated castes.

Critics of the jajmani system refute its billing as a generous system. They believe the system was nothing more than institutionalized oppression, that it took advantage of lower castes, ensured that they were perpetually kept "in their place," created a dependence on upper castes that was convenient for these castes to maintain their power and prevented any mobility among castes and occupations. With the breakdown of the jajmani system came an opportunity for the service castes to bargain for more equitable wages, to escape the grip of exploitative landowners, to seek new, greener pastures.

Although the original jajmani system has largely disappeared from rural India, modified versions (like the labor-for-crops exchange in Kamalsagar) still exist. However, the larger implications of the traditional system—such as links between a client and patron, or assurance of lack of competition—no longer remain. For the most part, today's generation of upper and lower castes only know of the old jajmani system from their grandparents and great-grandparents.

The Harijan basti in Kamalsagar, like those in villages across India, was situated an appropriate distance from upper caste lands. A clean, pleasant settlement, it was contained largely within the original acre or so of donated land. Some Harijans who did better for themselves, like Baijnath and his family of seven children, built their houses outside of, albeit next to, the original basti. The houses in the basti were clustered together around central shared facilities like the well-kept, concrete deep well, a hay shredder and a communal fisheries pond. The families tended to have many children, who ran around in thin clothes despite the cold winter weather. The houses were smaller and built lower to the ground than the Brahmin houses, but the difference in houses was much less than the perceived difference in social status between Brahmins and Harijans.

ॐ

I confess that I had the impression that life for Brahmins was quite easy, overall. They are at the top of a caste ladder that, despite assurances that the caste system is abolished, remains the critical social factor in India. But it is probably unfair to completely ignore the changing context of a Brahmin's life in today's India.

Traditionally, Brahmins used to hire lower caste people to do their work. Today, the rising cost of labor and the new independence of Harijans has forced many Brahmins to begin farming their own fields. Throughout India, the decline in agriculture has created a situation similar to the one I encountered earlier in my journey in Ladakj. Agriculture has become increasingly less profitable and holds little social status. Particularly for the younger generation, the lure of the cities, of blue-collar jobs, of "service" work (working for a company) is often too tempting to resist.

Add to this the true decline in the profitability of farming. Costs of agricultural inputs—labor, fertilizer, machinery, seeds—are rising. Average land holdings per family are declining as land is divided more and more among siblings who choose to farm separately rather than jointly. As in Ladakh, the issue is complex. Along with the idea that tending the fields is somehow inferior work, people's "needs" have increased. Whether it is the need to get a diesel-operated pump for agriculture, a car or motorcycle for transport or a television, today's generation seems to need more than the previous generation.

The oldest man in Kamalsagar, now more than 102 years, muttered to us in a quivery voice about days past when people used to walk for hours, even days, to reach their destination. Almost detailing history, he spoke about the changes that had come about in technology (such as irrigation devices), technology that cost significantly more to install or purchase but rarely produced sufficient increased yields to offset the increased costs. Even today's generation freely admitted that their needs, spurred on by exposure to television and easier access to urban areas and consumer goods, are greater than those of their forefathers and foremothers.

If a family has girls to marry off, its monetary needs are even greater. The concept of dowry is, unfortunately, still prevalent in too many parts of India, and in the growing consumer society, dowry no longer means only the mother's few gold ornaments. Dowry today includes ever-growing requirements for material objects: televisions, radios, motorcycles, furniture, even hard cash. Driving on the roads, I often saw jeeps loaded with these things. *"Dehez,"* Vidhu said to me the first time we saw one: dowry being transported from a girl's family to the in-laws. After that, I noticed these laden trucks quite often, early December being an auspicious time for weddings.

It is not, as many like to argue, just the economically poor and the lower caste people who give and take dowry. In fact, some of the most unforgivable and exorbitant requests for dowry come from those in the Indian Administrative Services cadre, the elite group of government officers that runs most of the large domestic and multilateral social development projects. Despite being well-educated and high-caste individuals, many of these officers feel that they are a "catch," that they earn too little money compared with their high status, and thus they have the right to demand outrageous dowries from their prospective brides.

In Kamalsagar, unlike other villages I have visited, Brahmin men were generally less educated than their female counterparts. Many of the men had not even studied up to high school, and only a handful had studied further. Because they no longer wanted to farm their fields nor had they the qualifications for any other occupation, these men remained largely unemployed and discontent. In contrast, the Kamalsagar girls were studying, had passed or were proposing to pass a bachelor's degree exam. Some were teachers, some had taken technical training.

Across India today, young men of high castes struggle to carve their place in society. Coming from Brahmin priestly families, many of the young men seem to be living according to a system that no longer exists, a system in which priests did not enter the formal education system but were accorded tremendous respect for their religious caste status. These men have not been trained as priests, however, nor have they been given the tools to find new careers. In the end, said one of the few college-educated youths in Kamalsagar, many of these men end up in cities doing "lowly work they would be embarrassed to do in their own villages. It is difficult being a Brahmin," he concluded wryly.

The Kamalsagar men I met were intelligent but frustrated with their lives. Few worked in the fields and those who did resented their duties. Arvind, Vidhu's cousin who came over regularly every evening, was a prime example. Asking us if we wanted to play cards one night, he plaintively said to me, "There is nothing to do here. We constantly have to find things to pass time." Handsome, quite articulate, the father of two, Arvind had not gone to college, did not work in the fields, nor was he particularly interested in agriculture. He spent his time, it seemed, roaming around. At night, he would while away hours in Vidhu's house, discussing politics or the latest village gossip. He had recently completed a course in auto mechanics at a local vocational college, but he had yet to find a job.

These evening chats, which I had first viewed as an expression of the camaraderie of village life, showed boredom too. Without real activities to keep them busy, villagers often gossiped cattily about village politics. Vidhu's land controversy and the so-called feud between his family and the relative who had encroached on their land, occupied everyone's mind. To them, there was little other excitement.

Pappu, another one of Vidhu's cousins, told me that he very much wanted to move to the city. "But," he said, "I would need to earn at least 3,000 rupees per month (about $90). I know I can live much better on less money here in the village, but there is no opportunity here." Pappu exemplified the conflict between tradition and modernity. The village, for Pappu and his friends, was stable, boring, the status quo; the city was glamour, opportunity, hope. I sensed some discontent in Kamalsagar, a struggle afoot to reconcile old and new, to make sense of a world that no longer consisted only of what was in one's immediate surroundings but also of what was possible further away. Stability and tradition could also be confining, and family connections too often burdensome.

ᛜ

By 2000, according to the 1996 United Nations report *An Urbanizing World: Global Report on Human Settlements*, almost 50 percent of the world's total population will be living in towns and cities. Over the next few years, people around the world will migrate in hoards to urban areas, running from their villages toward a brighter sun. Many of those will survive feeding only on their hopes and dreams, not on the real stuff like home-grown rice, dal and vegetables. But once gone, few will ever return to the villages, no matter how bad the situation may be in the cities. Loss of face? Constant hope that things will get better? Seeing another's child, the next-door neighbor in your slum, find himself a job—be it as rickshaw puller or grocery store clerk—that allows him to move "up"? That seems to be what life is about these days in many parts of the world, moving up. Up where, who knows? Is it really up, or does it only appear as up when the world has been turned inside-out, which is what happens when tradition and modernity conflict?

The U.N. report extols the virtue of urban areas for their role in the arts, education, culture, scientific and technological innovation. But it also warns that urban centers consume natural resources at an alarming rate. It suggests that one of the greatest needs, if one is to ensure that growing urban centers do not eat up the world's resources, is to "de-link high standards of living from high levels of resource use and waste generation." Is this possible? High levels of resource use and waste generation are the pillars upon which modern, technological society is based, at least currently. The countries of the world that have moved furthest away from a village-based society to an urban-based society are, the report points out, generally the ones with the most rapid economic growth and the most economic power. They are also the societies with the highest rates of consumption.

The very definition of community changes entirely from villages to urban areas. Individual survival overrides community sharing; responsibility for the community belongs to some anonymous centralized body like the city government; people no longer know, much less are related to, their neighbors. In cities people do their utmost to keep their own quarters clean but dump their garbage just outside their gates. Even a villager who comes to a city changes: He may throw his cigarette wrapper on the road instead of burning it, thinking that it is only a tiny part of the mounds of already-existing garbage. And, as long as poor people live in slums outside one's working and living radius, they can easily be forgotten.

Toward the end of our two years in India, my husband and I were invited to a conference in Delhi sponsored by a leading management consulting firm. The theme was "Building a New Vision for India," and the participants were supposed to represent the diversity of India's population. Perhaps the consulting firm did not know many rural people to invite; perhaps the poorer portion of the population that was invited felt uncomfortable attending a conference in the comfort of a five-star luxury hotel; or perhaps the organizers had just decided that these people would not really enjoy the high-flying conversation, good food and freezing cold air-conditioning. Whatever the reason, a few participants (equally urban, myself included) found ourselves in the position of trying to raise issues of poverty, rural life and other social matters that we felt applied to the majority of Indians who were ironically not represented that day. In the end, tired and not wanting to sound self-righteous, we listened while our table members talked about how we Indians are so inefficient, we must do something about the power outages. Here we are, having to buy expensive generators (which, by the way, pollute the thick Delhi air even more with noise and heat) so that we can run the air-conditioners in our houses. Me, me, me, that conference seemed to say. It is all about me and what will make my life easier.

With globalization and India's efforts to "liberalize" her economy, these attitudes are also seeping into villages. Take, for example, the issue of electricity in Kamalsagar. Thanks to Minister Rai, houses pay only 40 rupees ($1.20) a month for a legal electrical connection, no matter how much electricity they use. As a result, I noticed that houses, shops, schools keep their lights on all day and all night, regardless of whether anyone is there. The villagers have no connection with where the electricity comes from, how it is produced, how much of the earth's resources are taken when it is used. All they know is that they pay 40 rupees a month no matter what they use, so why not? If instead they had to build fires with wood they chopped themselves, they would make certain to use minimal amounts of wood so that they would not have to keep chopping down trees, either because they understand (as do most tribal and rural people) that they are using a valuable resource, or, at the very least, because they would want to minimize their own work. It would be beyond imagination to keep a fire going if one would not be there to enjoy its warmth or to cook over its blaze.

In cities it seems that almost everything has its equivalent of a big distant power plant with a flat fee. City-dwellers do not know the source of the amenities with which they are provided. They only know it is the anonymous city government's job to take care of everything; they have little sense of responsibility and therefore little guilt for their inaction or contributions to urban disrepair. Particularly after the rigid confines of village societal structure, the anonymity and lack of responsibility in the cities can be freeing, dangerously so.

When I arrived in Kamalsagar, I noticed how quiet the nights were. Vidhu, his mother and I would sit in darkness and feel night as it descended on us. There were no loud harsh sounds of generators, ever-present in cities. Even though I got varying accounts of how many households had televisions—some said four or five, others said at least half—I did not hear televisions or radios blasting. No sounds of automobiles or rickshaws, just the quiet sounds of nature, perhaps a rat as it nosed around the kitchen, a dog as it searched through the garbage piles for scraps of food, children playing or hushed voices in conversation. The village woke early in the morning, and by 8 p.m., it seemed, everyone was in bed.

"In cities, you are surrounded by artificial things," said Vidhu's cousin Arvind one night. "Here, we only have natural things." This was true, for the most part. People kept warm with wood fires; cooked on chulas, mud pits fueled with burning sticks from the fields; picked fresh vegetables out of their fields; grew their own wheat and made their own sweet, thick molasses syrup from burnt sugarcane residue. The well-known anthropologist Robert Redfield defined it this way: The peasant has "an intense attachment to native soil; a reverent disposition toward habitat and ancestral ways; a restraint on individual self-seeking in favor of family and community."

Walter Lippman, the journalist, called the city an "acid that dissolves the piety" of a villager and his knowledge that he is "obviously part of a scheme that is greater than himself, subject to elements that transcend his powers and surpass his understanding. Without piety, without a patriotism of family and place, without an almost plant-like implication in unchangeable surroundings, there can be no disposition to believe in an external order of things."

Walking through the fields in Kamalsagar reminded me of the simplicity of life. They were set apart from houses or other structures and formed their own peaceful world. The narrow mud paths divided the land into elegant, geometric designs. I could see around me the various stages of life: newly sprouted, half-bloomed, fully ripe and recently harvested. A few flowering mustard fields resonated their brilliant yellow for miles; purple eggplants peeped out from among tall leafy stalks. Women sowed seeds, men plowed the fields in rhythm with the earth, the sky, the world.

It felt like a long journey from Varanasi, farther from even the bigger cities of India and worlds apart from the life I know in urban America. I thought often, during my short stay in the village, of Mahatma Gandhi's words about the need for man to strive to fulfill his needs but not his greed; the world has enough resources for the former but not for the latter. Even though things are changing, villagers still seemed, not always of their own choice, to be living much closer to their needs.

Critchfield and Redfield, two authorities on village life, culled from their experiences of villages around the world the notion of a universal village culture. What I observed in Kamalsagar about the rhythm of life, the closeness to the real versus the artificial, was similar to what I have seen in other villages across India, in Africa, in Indonesia and in Thailand. In these villages there is a connection and reverence not only for nature and God but also a certain groundedness in family and relationships. People come together often, visiting, talking, establishing contact that disallows the isolation of an individual from her community. Grandparents, parents, siblings and relatives care for children and take responsibility for issues that urbanites might shun as being "not my concern." In these villages, everyone is ready without a trace of resentment to do tasks that, in urban areas or in the West, would more likely be seen as obligations or an invasion of one's personal time.

I am not trying to romanticize village life, though I confess, I am wont to do so. The grass is greener on the other side, or in Hindi, *"Dur ke dol souhavane hote hai,"* the sound of faraway drums is more pleasant. Like many of my Indian friends in Varanasi who talk nostalgically about village life and how they dream of someday going back, settling back into their village homes, eating vegetables from their own fields, it is much easier to utter these words than it is to live them. And, of course, our perspective on a situation always changes once we speak from within it rather than from outside. Like me, most of my friends will never move back to their villages. They have become accustomed to life in the city, and besides, stable and peaceful village life gets old fast. The slow-paced village rhythm and the lack of activities once agricultural work is over leads to an excessive interest in other people's lives, an over-analysis and tendency to judge people, a somewhat insular focus on the here and now, which can be as destructive as it can be productive.

But examining what city-dwellers find so appealing about village life illuminates what about our own lives withers the spirit rather than strengthens it and cuts community and heritage ties rather than honoring them.

Life in India is changing so rapidly that it is impossible for villagers not to see these changes, these new, puzzling, fascinating possibilities that did not exist for their parents and grandparents. Perhaps villagers know better than any others that life constantly changes: the strength of a monsoon from one year to the next, the social structure of caste that forces a Brahmin to do something that traditionally has been below his dignity in order to survive, or the access to brightly colored television pictures of life in such faraway places as America.

In many ways, Kamalsagar has been spared so far. Being in the country's interior, it has yet to experience many of the changes that have occurred in villages closer to urban areas. Much of the development that has reached Kamalsagar has been productive, in fact. Migration to cities has yet to destroy the village as it has other villages, the new roads serve people well in keeping family ties intact when migration happens, diesel pumps and electricity help to irrigate fields and increase yields without changing entire schedules and lifestyles. The challenge, it seems, is not to keep technology or "development" away, but to find ways to incorporate it into village culture that preserve the sense of relationship and interconnectedness that often disappears with modernization.

Critchfield, in his dynamic conclusion to *Villagers: Changed Values, Altered Lives* (written fifteen years later as the sequel to *Villages*), argues strongly for the need to preserve village culture. He poignantly asks, "Our lives are becoming a cacophony of ten thousand noises, and amidst these noises, what do we have for the inner ethical guidance religion once supplied?" It is debatable whether it is religion or tradition (perhaps Critchfield would not even have distinguished between the two) that provided the guidance that seemed to keep villagers so happy relative to their urban counterparts. Either way, villagers like those in Kamalsagar are now questioning their rural existence, wondering if there is more to life than sowing seeds and waiting for rain, striving to shake off the shackles of tradition, certainty, family responsibility and to run barefooted and free, like children, toward an urban paradise. This too is a process of change that has become inevitable. Perhaps these villagers will find paradise in the cities; perhaps they will return home and, discontent there, dream up another paradise; or perhaps they will realize they once had paradise and gave it up.

Diary of a Birth

Winter crept into Varanasi. Cold nights replaced humid, musty ones. Our fans became dusty from lack of use. In the early mornings and late evenings, fog settled over the city, creating a mysterious air. At night, cycle-rickshaw drivers covered their heads and necks with thick shawls and pedaled rapidly to keep themselves warm. People sought refuge inside their huts and houses before the sun went down to avoid the cold; those who had no shelters built small, smoky fires that created halos of glowing light on the broken pavement. Over the Ganga, the sun still rose golden but it was now hidden with thin films of white mist.

I had assumed, when I became pregnant, that I would have a trauma-free nine months. We would stay in Varanasi for the first two trimesters, my husband and I decided, and return to the United States in early March when I would be more than six months pregnant. This seemed appropriately cautious, and I looked forward to spending my last trimester finding a midwife in America to work with my family practitioner, taking birthing classes and easing back into what I knew would be a difficult culture shock.

First, however, I needed a gynecologist in Varanasi. Several people recommended the head doctor of a teaching hospital that was attached to Varanasi's best university. I was given a 9 a.m. appointment at the hospital's OB-GYN wards. Sheila, my landlady, who had taught at the university, kindly offered to accompany me through the enormous maze of campus buildings. We made our way through crowds of people and urinals that smelled like disinfectant, up winding stairs, to a paan-stained corridor where we waited for the doctor. She appeared half an hour late, with an army of younger students and doctors trying to get her attention. She cast me a marginal glance when I told her I had an appointment and ordered me to keep waiting. Ten minutes later, she emerged with a young assistant and gruffly beckoned me to follow her. I did so meekly, while Sheila waited in the cavernous, rather musty hall outside.

The examination room looked as if it had not been used in years. The walls were bare: no colorful prenatal charts, no comforting pictures of doctors cuddling newly delivered babies like those that fill my family practitioner's clinic in Seattle. I lay down on a table. The doctor, without asking my full name or medical history, proceeded to brusquely conduct an internal examination. She offered no explanation of what she was doing or why, and only grudgingly answered a few (not all) of my questions. Her replies and her silences all seemed to ask who I thought I was to question her. The rest of the appointment—a mere ten minutes—was equally miserable. I left the room feeling completely violated. My past work experience in women's reproductive health had heightened my sensitivity to a woman's right to good information and the need for a caring and respectful provider-patient relationship. I had received none of this today, and this was supposed to be the finest doctor in Varanasi!

Sheila could see I was upset. "She is the best doctor," she repeated soothingly. "If there was something wrong, she would have told you. Anyway, you have to understand, this is free treatment. You know, she has so many patients. What to do?" Her words, well-meaning as they were, sent me off on another tirade. What did it mean to say that this woman was the "best" doctor? Could she be so good that she knew my medical history without asking? As for free treatment, I was enraged by the idea that just because something is free, it should excuse deficiencies in quality. Sadly, I knew it was the poor who would suffer; people who could afford to pay would have other choices.

The next gynecologist I went to see was also highly recommended. She had a private clinic in a posh part of town and seemed to have better patient skills. As the months progressed, however, I began to have more problems with my pregnancy. I developed chronic bronchitis and severe asthma and was having to curtail my work and travel to villages because I could not breathe. When I spoke to my doctor about it, she gave me a medication that I knew was contraindicated for pregnancy and she refused to listen to my concerns. My Indian friends told me I was so sick because I was just doing too much. According to them, I should not carry a bag of groceries home or take rickshaws or exercise (other than a very slow walk if necessary). The advice was neverending and I ignored most of it. In my mind I pictured my American friends who while pregnant went running, carried on jobs and lived in ways that differed little from their lives before their pregnancies.

Underlying my desire not to fuss excessively over my pregnancy was the significant difference I saw in the treatment of pregnant middle- and upper-class women and that of lower-class women. Complete bed rest during pregnancy was often prescribed for middle- and upper-class pregnant women, who frequently moved in with their mothers. The mothers could control their daughters' diets, which often included enormous quantities of *ghee*, clarified butter, while the daughters did as little work as possible and received daily oil massages to keep them supple and relaxed. For the less fortunate, however, pregnancy was simply one more task. Their work—be it sweeping and cleaning or working in the fields—was never disrupted. One day in the train station bathroom, I saw a pregnant sweeper woman lifting a heavy pail of water and then sinking to her knees to scrub the floors. She was huge; her belly touched the floor as she scrubbed. "The baby's due in a few weeks," she told me proudly. No one was looking after her to ensure her health. She was expected to continue her backbreaking work regardless of her pregnancy. Like so many things in India, this did not seem fair.

I decided I needed a new doctor yet again. In sifting through the recommendations I had been given, I came across Dr. Amod Prakash. He had been highly recommended by several people, but I had avoided calling him because I preferred to have a woman doctor.

Now that I had exhausted my female options, I called him. Dr. Prakash had been trained in the United Kingdom and continued to practice abroad three months of every year. He explained each step to Alan and me in great detail and allowed us to pelt him with questions. After several visits, I began to relax. My respiratory problems abated, and the pregnancy progressed normally.

Our departure date from India had been set for March 9, 1997. By February, I was packing boxes of books to ship, giving away our few possessions and doing last-minute shopping. We planned our final nights, listened to music and watched the sun rise over the Ganges. But perhaps my planning tempted the gods too much. Intellectually, I knew that human beings have limited control over much of their lives, and I had admired villagers for their understanding of this. I did not fully understood this concept, however, until my son Janak was born.

෨෧෨

On February 18, at 5 a.m., I woke to find that I was leaking fluid. It occurred to me briefly that my water had broken, but I quickly dismissed that idea. After all, I was only twenty-five-and-a-half weeks pregnant. I was certain that it was just a weakened bladder. By 9 a.m., however, the leaking had not stopped. Alan and I walked five minutes to the nearest phone booth to call Dr. Prakash. He told me to go back to bed immediately and call him if I continued to leak or if I developed labor pains. I took complete bed rest, forcing myself to accept sponge baths from my visiting sister-in-law and even using a bedpan. I did this with frustration and impatience, certain that I was encountering some minor complication. I believed that, of course, I would return to America as planned.

After two days of leaking, Dr. Prakash made the first of many home visits to check on me. He concluded that I had developed a leak in my amniotic sac. Often the leaks seal off, he told me, but if it did not, the leaking could stimulate labor. "Let's hope that does not happen," he said gravely. "You are less than twenty-six weeks pregnant, and, quite frankly, a baby born here at that age stands no chance of survival."

I fell into denial. Perhaps we would not be able to return as planned on March 9, but surely this would resolve itself in a few weeks. Alan, the realist, tried gently to tell me that we should plan on spending the next few months in India, and even think about where in India we would want to deliver the baby. He convinced me that, at a minimum, I should ask my mother to fly to Varanasi from Bangalore in case my bed rest continued.

The flat that we lived in at the time was a simple two-room apartment on the second floor of a house. Our bathroom was a concrete structure off of the kitchen that had a squatter toilet. We had no shower and no hot water. To heat water, we would carry a bucket of water into the bedroom and stick an "immersion rod" into it, essentially an electric rod heater. When the water was hot (and it would get hot only if electricity was running at the time), we would carry the bucket of water into the bathroom and take a quick shower, gasping as the cold February air hit our chests in between mugfuls of hot water. The fact that we had no telephone was also of concern. If our landlady was home, we could receive incoming calls on her telephone. For outgoing calls, we had to go to the local telephone booth five minutes away. These conditions were far from ideal for a pregnant woman in fear of going into early labor.

On February 21 my mother flew to Varanasi. The leaking had continued, and it was becoming clear that this leak was unlikely to seal itself. We were worried, and we managed it in the only way we knew how—by trying to get information and gain some semblance of control. What did this mean for the baby? Should we be trying to fly back to the United States or at least to another major Indian city? What was the possibility that I would deliver soon? Dr. Prakash answered these and many other questions to the best of his ability, but we were still uncertain that we were getting full information.

Alan decided he wanted a second opinion. He called my mother's gynecologist in Bangalore, who was the retired director of the OB-GYN department at a well-respected hospital. This doctor was pessimistic about the baby's chances for survival and extremely worried about my health. "After so many days of leaking," he told Alan, "it is highly likely that both the fetus and the mother are infected. Forget about saving the baby's life and concentrate on the mother." He asked Alan if Dr. Prakash had started me on a course of antibiotics and steroids. The former was to control the infection; the steroids would help to mature the lungs of the baby in case of early delivery. Dr. Prakash had done neither. "Have you at least had an ultrasound done?" he asked. Another no.

Alan returned from the phone call in a panic. He was beginning to doubt Dr. Prakash, the one person we desperately needed to trust at that point. Lack of information and conflicting facts made us feel completely helpless. The logistics made it harder. We had neither phone nor car for an emergency, and I was not being continuously monitored (as would be standard procedure in the United States), so we would be unaware if the baby went into respiratory distress in the womb. But the most worrisome factor was that we knew if the baby was born in Varanasi, the chances of survival were almost negligible. Saving a twenty-six-week-old baby anywhere in the world presents challenges of morbidity if not mortality; in Varanasi, without appropriate facilities, it would be impossible. The only possible strategy was simply to try and keep the baby inside the womb for as long as possible. Every day made a difference.

We passed a tense day, waiting for Dr. Prakash. He arrived late that night, after completing another complicated delivery. He listened to our concerns and assured us that he had already decided that I should be started on antibiotics and steroids. Dr. Prakash also agreed that we should have an ultrasound done the next morning to determine the amount of water lost and the approximate weight of the baby. He had resisted doing this earlier, he said, because the ultrasound clinic was half an hour away on bumpy roads, and he did not want to exacerbate the leak. Now, however, we desperately needed to know exactly what was going on inside my uterus.

Because I was not allowed to move, we had to find a trained nurse to come to the house and administer the antibiotic and steroid injections at the odd hours of 5 a.m. and 10 p.m. (this schedule had to be strictly followed). Alan and a friend of ours visited several nearby clinics to find someone but had no luck. Finally, our friend found a man who was the neighborhood "compounder," the Indian equivalent of a physician's assistant. According to our landlady, he was "not very clean," but we had few other options. Alan watched him like a hawk to ensure he washed his hands, and then we provided him with clean, disposable syringes and needles. For 70 rupees (about $2), he agreed to come over for two days in the early morning and late night. In the mornings he would arrive looking as if he had just rolled out of bed, clothed in a bathrobe over a pair of white cotton pajamas and his hair sticking up on end. He was in his fifties and thrilled to be performing this service in a foreigner's house. After the injections he asked Alan very seriously about Alan's food habits in America! Smothering his laughter, Alan would conscientiously recite what he typically ate for breakfast, lunch and dinner.

The morning of February 24, I got out of bed for the first time in six days, climbed down the stairs and into a friend's old, rusted van to go to the ultrasound clinic across town. I could feel every pothole in the road slamming into my back. The ultrasound showed that, although my cervix had not started to efface and my water had not actually broken, 50 percent of the fluid in my sac had leaked out. However, it also predicted the baby's weight at 1.1 kilograms (about 2.4 pounds), above the accepted threshold for survival of 1 kilogram. This was the best news we had heard.

Dr. Prakash still hoped that we could keep the baby inside the womb for another couple of weeks. It would make an enormous difference to the baby's survival. But, he warned us, the possibility of an early delivery was still high. If I continued to lose fluid, the baby could go into severe respiratory distress. It was time to make some decisions. We considered trying to make it back to the United States, but Dr. Prakash advised against this, as it would be fatal for the baby if it was born in the air. In the end, the three of us decided the best option was to try to make it to Bombay. There, at least if the baby was born before thirty-two weeks, it would stand some chance of survival. Although Dr. Prakash told us the stress of even making this short flight could precipitate labor, he felt it was worth the risk.

The next order of business was to find a doctor in Bombay who would take us. Dr. Prakash had met a colleague at a conference, Dr. Rustum Soonawalla, who had an excellent reputation. He gave Alan the fax and phone number but warned us that many Indian gynecologists would refuse to take a case like this, where the chances of survival were not high. And, Dr. Prakash added, this gynecologist traveled a great deal, so currently he might not even be in Bombay. We would then have to go back to the drawing board.

Alan called immediately, and as luck would have it, Dr. Soonawalla was indeed in Bombay at the time and agreed to take me. "Fly to Bombay immediately," his secretary told Alan, "and check into a hospital."

"Which one?" Alan asked in confusion. The assistant gave him a few choices, and Alan took the one called Breach Candy, a good British-sounding name, that was described as "plush." This was not a time for scrimping.

For the next twenty-four hours we operated on sheer adrenalin. Alan called a friend in Bombay to arrange for an ambulance to meet us at the airport. We were to leave the following day at 1:30 p.m. on the one daily flight from Varanasi to Bombay. In order for me to travel, Dr. Prakash would have to do an internal exam and write a statement to the airline that I would not go into labor on the plane. He agreed to come to our flat the next morning before we left.

Often during this time, I silently thanked Dr. Prakash. He made many home visits, frequently late at night, and fielded dozens of phone calls. He gave unstintingly of his time and advice and responded willingly to our concerns. He encouraged us to fly to Bombay, a crucial decision. And he helped us to keep calm. Perhaps the greatest testament to my faith in Dr. Prakash is that if he practiced in America, I would use him again, despite the multitude of excellent men and women doctors in the States.

Without a goodbye to Varanasi, to the Ganges River, to the vibrant villages that had taught me so much, to our friends to whom we had given our hearts, we would leave for Bombay. We had never wanted to live in a large modern city before, preferring to spend our time in small towns and villages, but it was different now. We embraced rather than spurned Bombay's relative modernity and access to technology.

❀

The day of our proposed departure from Varanasi was exactly one week from the day I had begun leaking fluid. We readied small backpacks to carry on the flight and left everything else in our flat to be packed up at a later date. The airplane tickets were to be delivered to us in the morning. We would need to leave for the airport by noon.

At 11:30 that morning, Dr. Prakash arrived at our house to give me an internal exam. My cervix remained undilated, and he felt it was unlikely that I would go into labor anytime soon. Just to be sure, he gave me a labor suppressant that would last about five hours.

By 11:45, however, neither our tickets nor our friend Vidhu who was taking us to the airport had arrived. Alan paced up and down the terrace, and then up and down the lane. Finally, at 12:25, both arrived in concert. Vidhu was late because the students of Benaras Hindu University were rioting around political elections for the student unions, burning cars and creating roadblocks. He had gone back to his house to get a black scarf that he could wave out the window to show solidarity. The tickets were late just because they were late.

I made it only to the terrace before fainting. I came to on our sofa to a sea of worried faces. It was 12:40. Alan had called Dr. Prakash, who said that the fainting was probably due to lowered blood pressure, a side-effect of the labor suppressant. Although he thought we could still take the flight, he wanted to check me one last time to make certain there had been no other changes in my condition. We agreed to stop at his house on the way to the airport. When we reached Dr. Prakash's house at 12:55, he was waiting outside for us with his doctor's bag. He checked me quickly and blessed us as we left. It was 1 p.m.

I stretched out in the middle seat of Vidhu's old lime-green minivan. Alan crouched on his haunches in front of me, his head stuck between Vidhu and Vidhu's wife. My mother was behind us, gripping the tarnished metal bars on the door so tightly that her knuckles had turned white. It was boiling hot. Sweat gathered quickly on my upper lip and forehead.

The riots had blocked all of the city streets. Vidhu, waving his black scarf out the window, cursed as he swerved the wheel left and right, trying to make it through the crowds but eventually getting stuck in traffic jams for tens of precious minutes. The back of his shirt was drenched with sweat. The tension had mounted to unbearable levels in the car. Vidhu and his wife argued about which route we should take, and Alan and Vidhu argued over whether they should pull over to a phone and try and call the airline to ask them to hold the plane. Ultimately, we did not stop. At 1:20, we pulled up to the gates of the airport terminal.

In our two years in India, I had been on only one flight that departed on time. We were quite certain we would still be able to catch this airplane. Alan and Vidhu ran inside, while my mother helped me into a wheelchair and took me to the seats in front of the check-in counter. I could feel the fluid continuing to leak. To distract myself, I joked with one of the airport attendants I recognized from previous trips and waited for Alan and Vidhu.

I knew when I saw Alan's face that we had missed the flight. Although the plane was still on the runway, the doors had been closed and the airline staff refused to bring the plane back for us. Alan, Vidhu, and my mother had alternately pleaded and screamed, but to no avail. We would have to take the same flight the next day.

On the edge of tears, we packed ourselves back into the rickety van. Demoralization hung over us like a big heavy cloud. So that we would not have to go back through the rioting crowds the next day, we checked into a hotel about half an hour from the airport. That night my fluid leaked nonstop. I could not sleep. The following morning Dr. Prakash made the long journey to the hotel to conduct another internal exam (the airline required a new certificate dated on the day of travel). He said he could feel my cervix just beginning to open a little, but I should have no problem making it to Bombay. We decided against the labor suppressant this time, but Alan insisted that

Dr. Prakash show him how to deliver the baby, should it arrive unexpectedly during the flight.

The staff at the check-in counter remembered us and seemed more sympathetic this time. I was exhausted, as were my mother and Alan. I could no longer feel the baby moving; the amniotic sac had shrunk so much that the baby had no room to kick. More frightening, my stomach had become almost completely flat with the loss of so much fluid.

We passed time by playing cards and singing Hindi bhajans, devotional songs. The flight made one stop in Lucknow. Just after taking off from Lucknow, I went to the bathroom and found that I had started bleeding. All the control I had imposed on myself began to crumble. I thought at that minute that I had lost the baby. I toyed with the idea of not telling Alan for fear that he too would crumble, but I needed his support to help me think. He talked to the pilot and the flight attendant, who assured him that the airport ambulance would meet us upon landing and that we would be the first to deplane.

But the crew never made the announcement asking other passengers to stay in their seats and let us through. As is typical on all Indian flights, people leaped up as soon as the wheels touched the runway and began putting together their bags and standing in the aisles. Alan pushed his way through only to find there was no ambulance waiting. By the time I made it to the front with my mother, I could see Alan from the top of the stairs, screaming at the crew to get an ambulance. We were all dangerously close to breaking down.

Alan eventually got a wheelchair for me, and when we reached the terminal, to our great relief, the ambulance that our Bombay contact had ordered was waiting for us. It was a small minivan with a bench on either side in the back, very different from American ambulances, but at that moment it was the most wonderful thing I could have laid my eyes on. I lay down on the flattened, torn leather bench and grabbed a handrail for stability.

It was rush hour in Bombay, where traffic rivals that in the most congested cities in the world. The ambulance turned on a flashing red light, which helped minimally. Alan told me later that police had waved the minivan through when possible and some cars moved to let us pass. I remember little from the journey other than the siren's noise and the exclamations of Alan and my mother at one point because we were going down a one-way street the wrong way.

At the hospital I was carried in on a stretcher and put down in the middle of the reception area (there was no emergency room). People walked around me looking down curiously, until eventually I was taken up one floor to the labor and maternity ward. My room was cream yellow, air-conditioned and clean. I could feel my body beginning to relax, as I was finally close to medical help. Nurses in white starched uniforms and caps surrounded me and began taking my vital signs. Where was the doctor, Dr. Soonawalla? He will come soon, the head nurse replied.

An hour later, Dr. Soonawalla had still not arrived. It took several hours to find out that he had flown to Delhi that evening on an emergency call. He would not be back until the next night! "Rest now," urged his son, who practices with him. "Tomorrow, we will do the tests and see what is happening."

Surprisingly, I slept well. I was exhausted and, for the first night in many, felt that I was as safe as I could be. My room had no monitoring equipment, but during the night nurses came in every three hours or so to check the baby's heart rate and to take my vital signs, all of which seemed to be fine.

The next morning, as I ate my breakfast and looked out at the ocean through the open French doors in my room, I began once again to believe that this was just a bad dream. Soon I would be on the next flight to America. Just then, the head nurse came in and informed me that they were ready to do the ultrasound. It was a portable machine, the first I had seen in India. The technician expertly greased my stomach and began tapping away at the computer. I could see images from the side, but nothing that helped me determine what was happening to my baby. She told me little I did not already know: that there was hardly any fluid left in my amniotic sac.

Dr. Soonawalla's partner, Dr. Nagarwalla, came in shortly thereafter. "It looks like we will have to terminate the pregnancy," she said to me bluntly. My head was spinning. Terminate the baby's life? I asked, choked with tears.

"No, no," she said hurriedly, "Just take the baby out of the womb."

"What are the chances of survival?" I asked faintly.

"About 40 percent, given the strong likelihood that the baby is infected. The good news is that the ultrasound predicts a weight of 1.5 kilograms (about 3.5 pounds), which is a good weight for a twenty-seven-week-old baby. Rest now. Dr. Soonawalla will return this evening. Unless you go into labor or the baby is distressed, we will wait for him to decide what to do."

It was an endless day. For the first time since I had started leaking fluid, I cried. I cried because I was convinced that our baby would not live. I cried for failing this tiny being, for somehow forcing him out too early. I cried for the lost perfect birth I thought I would have. My mother and husband tried to comfort me, and I tried to comfort them by being as strong as I could. We were tied together that day more closely than ever before, by pain, fear, sorrow and love. I could not sleep. Alan and I sang bhajans to my mother, looked out at the water and agonized over whether we had done something to cause this.

Dr. Soonawalla finally arrived from the airport at 9:45 that evening. He had been briefed on my case on the way to the hospital. He was a young-looking seventy. Later, I discovered that he was one of the best gynecologists in the entire country and that we were exceedingly lucky to have him attending to me. After conducting an internal examination, Dr. Soonawalla confirmed that the baby would have to come out immediately. He gave us the choice of trying to have a normal delivery or a caesarean section, but he made it clear that the former would mean a 5–10 percent lesser chance of survival for the baby. It was not a difficult decision.

At 10:15, we told Dr. Soonawalla that we had opted for the C-section. He immediately prepared for the operation and asked the nurses to prepare me for a 10:45 surgery. As he left the room, I thought how ironic it was that just a week ago, I had such grandiose ideas about choosing the person who would deliver my baby. Now, here I was trusting myself to a man whom I had never even met until half an hour before—and feeling absolutely lucky that I had somebody to trust.

I was cleaned and prepared for surgery, a green cloth draped over me, and moved to a stretcher. Alan had decided, after some thought, to watch the surgery. He walked with me to the operating theatre and gowned himself for the surgery. A nurse hooked me to an electrocardiograph monitor and inserted a catheter into my bladder. The anesthesiologist introduced himself to me and asked if I was ready for the anesthesia to be administered. Because of a missing disc in my lower back, I had to be given general anesthesia instead of a spinal epidural. He began to administer the anesthesia. It was as if little pieces of ice were being inserted into my vein; as they melted, they flooded my whole body with cold. I did not have my contact lenses on; I could see only distant blurs. I thought I saw Alan's eyes smiling at me over his mouth mask from where he was standing about three feet beyond me. That was the last image I remember.

ᐰ

I awoke at about 5 a.m. My lower back felt like it had been tied to a wooden plank for days. I tried to move and winced in pain. I had an IV in one arm, and I could feel the needle in my skin as I attempted to change positions. I must have been moaning, because Alan came to my side immediately from the chair he had been sitting in.

"The baby?" I croaked, my voice hoarse from the anesthesia.

"The baby's okay," he said, stroking my head.

"Boy or girl?" I asked.

"Boy," he replied tenderly. And then, tentatively, "He is a little lighter than they thought. He's 850 grams." I could not comprehend what he was saying, could not understand that our baby, Janak Jayapal Preston, weighed one pound and fourteen ounces, about the same as a medium-size squash. All I knew was that he was alive.

Later, when I was fully awake, Alan told me about the operation. He dealt with it, he said, by not looking at my face, by pretending that it was someone else being cut up on the table. It took only fifteen minutes or so to bring Janak out, and double that time to stitch me up. There was so little fluid left in the sac, that the doctor had to actually scrape the membrane off the baby. Janak was immediately rushed to the Neonatal Intensive Care Unit (NICU), which was down the hall from the operating room. He was put on a ventilator and antibiotics were started immediately. Many days after Janak's birth, Alan told me he would never watch a C-section again, but he was glad he had been there. I too was glad. It provided a link between the end of my pregnancy and Janak's birth that would otherwise have been missing. To hear Alan talk about how Janak was born made it that much more real for me.

I wanted to see the baby immediately, although the nurses encouraged me just to rest. I could not wait, nor could I understand how they could think I would want to wait. The nurses finally agreed to wheel me to the NICU.

At the outside door, I left the wheelchair and my shoes and, leaning heavily on one of the nurses, walked through the small entry room. It had a sink, a refrigerator, a two-burner stove with a big sterilization pot and a large wooden closet. Underneath the closet were several pairs of rubber slippers. I put on a pair and walked through a door with a small window that led to the main room of the NICU. At the instruction of the nurses, I washed my hands in the sink near the door and put on a sterile gown.

Janak was being kept in a smaller room just off the main room. He was lying in one of two infant warmers in the room. The warmer was a small, plastic rectangular box crib with no cover, about two feet wide and three feet long. A couple of feet above the box was a radiant heater, electric rods that let off ambient heat. Janak was on a thin mattress in the middle of the crib.

I expected the worst. Alan had prepared me that Janak's skin would be shriveled and that he was tiny. Perhaps it is the essence of parenthood that even then, he seemed beautiful to us. I had never imagined that he would be as tiny as he was. He was 13.5 inches long, the length of about one and half of my hands. He was very fair, just bones with skin loosely laid over them. One arm was weighted down with an IV and a heavy splint so that he could not move it. He had a test tube attached to his penis, so that they could measure the amount of urine he was passing. His head looked huge compared with the rest of his body. His knees were bony protrusions in the middle of sticks. Over his head, he had a plastic oxygen hood that looked like a cake cover. It went down to his neck and had a small hole in the top where a tube was inserted that piped in supplemental oxygen. Three ECG pads almost covered his small bony chest. A feeding tube that led to his stomach was inserted into his nose.

I could not stay for more than five minutes. My stomach was screaming in pain, and my whole body was choked with emotion. This was my baby. I had not touched him yet, but I had seen him and he was alive.

⚛

The Breach Candy NICU had only five beds. Two were considered "critical" beds; Janak was in one of these. The other bed was occupied by another extremely premature baby who was hooked to a very modern ventilator. Because Janak also needed a ventilator, the NICU borrowed an older unit from another hospital floor. Each bed was connected to a three-lead ECG monitor, with capabilities for monitoring blood pressure and heart rate. Unlike most Indian hospitals, Breach Candy also had portable ultrasounds and X-ray machines.

The sanitation practices in the hospital were excellent. Cleaners came through the general wards and the NICU several times a day to sweep and mop the floors. All utensils were sterilized in a huge pot of boiling water for more than ten minutes. Detailed handwashing instructions were posted above the sink, and doctors, nurses and visitors had to carefully wash their hands before entering the NICU. Because the risk of infection to these tiny babies was extremely high, only the parents of NICU babies and hospital staff were allowed in.

Janak was in the NICU for two and a half months. During that time, we spent much of our days with him, leaving the hospital only to eat and sleep for a few hours. We slowly became used to the NICU environment, where alarms constantly sounded and monitors beeped. Janak, like most premature babies, often had apnea spells during which he would stop breathing for more than twenty seconds. The alarms would sound loudly, the ECG monitors showed flat lines, and we would see him go completely limp. The nurses would rush in to bring him back to consciousness by flicking his toes or palpating his chest. According to our doctor, the apnea spells occurred (simplistically put) because Janak's brain and lungs were not fully developed, and the brain would "forget" to send messages for the lungs to breathe. We learned to watch for these spells, and sometimes even palpated Janak ourselves. We steeled ourselves to watch as nurses pricked him with needles, clamped devices onto his arms and legs to measure blood pressure and blood oxygen levels, and stuck ECG leads on his chest. We learned to ask during that first month only how he was doing at that moment, because we knew it could change from minute to minute.

Janak was born with a severe infection that sent his white blood cell count soaring as his immune system tried to combat the infection. The infection raged on for two weeks, stubbornly refusing to respond to seven different antibiotics. Finally, on March 10, Janak's white blood cell counts slowly responsed to a new antifungal drug. During those first few weeks, we did not know if Janak would live or die. The doctors could offer little consolation. Our daily thought was simply that he would make it to the next day.

Once his infection was controlled, our attention turned to his feeding and weight. Because Janak's digestive organs remained undeveloped and unable to digest food, for more than two weeks he was fed only glucose. His weight dropped quickly to just over one pound. Slowly, he began to tolerate tiny amounts of milk, about fifteen drops of milk per feed. This amount was increased by about one cubic centimeter per day. It took two and a half weeks for Janak to regain his birthweight, and another six weeks to gain an additional two pounds. Every little bit counted; to talk of a time when he might gain many pounds in a week seemed unthinkable.

We struggled now with issues not of Janak's mortality, but of his morbidity. Just as we thought he had turned the corner, he would develop new problems: a sky-rocketing eosinophil (a type of white blood cell) count that could have signaled cytomegalovirus and toxoplasmosis, two serious infections, and a head size that was large for the rest of his body and could indicate hydrocephalus, water in the brain. He had made it through the first critical stage, but his condition was far from stable.

When we worried about whether Janak would live or die, little else had mattered. Once we knew that he would live, smaller frustrations and stress factors began to affect us. We ached to hold him, to touch him freely, to be his primary caregivers, to enjoy and love him without caution. We watched, week after week, as full-term babies came in and out of the NICU, or as nurses and glowing mothers carried their healthy babies outside in the maternity wards.

Compared with American hospitals, there were few formal support services at Breach Candy—no therapists to help process the myriad feelings I was experiencing, no team of physicians and nurses to constantly reassure and provide support, and no lactation consultant. The hospital had no electric breast pump, so instead I pumped manually six to eight times a day, a tiring and often painful process. The nurses, instead of encouraging me, disparaged my small quantity of milk. Underlying much of our tension was our distrust of the nursing staff. First, because the NICU was fairly new, Janak was one of only two or three babies of such low birthweight and the nurses, in particular, had little experience with such babies. Second, we had read dozens of articles sent to us by a close friend in Seattle who works at Children's Hospital. These articles discussed new findings that showed how handling of babies and their hospital environment can have long-term developmental effects. American NICUs today focus heavily on ancillary behaviors that can affect later development of premature babies, such as limiting noise, creating a warm and secure sleeping environment, speaking softly and handling babies gently. In India, however, the NICUs are too new and the nurses untrained as yet to incorporate these practices. The focus has been on "hard" technology rather than "soft" skills, on mortality rather than long-term developmental issues. Having read these articles, we were horrified to see the nurses try to wake up Janak by clapping their hands in front of his face or ears, flicking his feet to make him cry or holding him directly up to sunlight. They felt that he should learn to take milk through his mouth instead of using the nasogastric tube for feeding (in the United States, many premature babies are often released from the hospital with these tubes still in), so they would hold open his mouth and pour the milk in as he screamed. The discrepancy in how the nurses treated Janak and how these articles talked about treating babies was often too much for us to bear. We constantly weighed our discomfort about leaving him in the nurses' care with the risk of taking him out of the hospital too early.

Even our pediatrician, Dr. Mahesh Balsekar, recognized the gaps in this "soft" care. "We now have the hard equipment," he once told us. "Now we need to work on the nursing skills. In America nurses are equals to doctors, with their own areas of specialty and training. They interact on the same level, discussing issues and care. Here, nurses are generally afraid of the doctors and are merely following orders."

There were many other little stresses. The hospital did not keep many of the expensive and rarer medications that Janak needed; instead, they would call us at all hours of the night and we would rush out to try to find an all-night pharmacy. The hospital also required that we pay our bills in Indian rupees, not by credit card or check. It ended up being extremely complex to abide by foreign currency regulations and still get sufficient money in and out of the country. And although my mother was able to stay for much of the time, my grandmother contracted malaria and passed away unexpectedly the day that Janak was due to leave the hospital. Not having our friends and family nearby or a stable living situation were perhaps the most difficult for us. We moved several times and ended up renting a small room in someone's apartment, a far from ideal situation.

The last straw came when the U.S. embassy told me I would lose my permanent residence status (green card) if I did not return to the United States by April 20. If I lost the green card, I would have to reapply for permanent residence from India, a process that can take years. Alan paid several visits to the U.S. consulate to explain that we could not leave Janak at this stage, but it was to no avail. Through a State Department connection, we finally were able to get an expedited special visa to allow me back into the country when we could return. By the time we eventually returned to the States, I decided that I would finally take the plunge I have always resisted and apply for U.S. citizenship. My loyalty to India was great, but I had been beaten down by the only bureaucracy that easily rivals Indian bureaucracy: the U.S. Immigration and Naturalization Service.

ஃ

Our pediatrician, Dr. Balsekar, had started the Breach Candy NICU just three years before. He was trained in India and had also done some observation internships in London and in the United States. He had traveled abroad many times, spending three months at Johns Hopkins and other fine medical centers around the States. Although his knowledge of the field was excellent, Dr. Balsekar was not actually trained as a neonatologist (no formal training in neonatology was available then in India). Neonatology is a new field in India. The first NICUs opened in the early 1990s but remained quite sparsely equipped. Today, select Indian medical colleges have begun offering specialized training in neonatology.

During our entire experience and even today, I am most thankful for our relationship with Dr. Balsekar. From the beginning, he treated Alan and me like we too were his patients, not just Janak. He felt responsible for our well-being and forged a personal relationship with us, talking to us about America and asking about our lives. He was available to us day and night. At our first meeting, he gave us his home and cellular phone numbers so that we could call him any time. Especially early on, when Janak's condition was critical, he would visit the NICU a minimum of twice a day, often calling in between to get updates on Janak's status.

Dr. Balsekar went well beyond the call of duty. One incident stands out. Janak needed several blood transfusions. Dr. Balsekar had advised us that it was safer to use blood that we or our friends had donated, as blood testing in Indian blood banks was still suspect at the time. As it turned out, my C-section had rendered my hemoglobin levels too low to give blood, and Alan's antimalarial prophylactics barred him from giving blood. A family friend gave blood three times, but it was not enough. Janak needed a fourth transfusion and we had no blood to give. In desperation, we decided to use the hospital's blood bank.

The morning of the scheduled transfusion, I entered the NICU to see Janak's transfusion in progress.

"Whose blood is this?" I asked puzzled.

"Dr. Balsekar's," the nurses said, in wonderment themselves.

When I tried to thank Dr. Balsekar, he shrugged it off, saying lightly, "We often do this," a statement I knew to be false.

Dr. Balsekar took it upon himself not only to be Janak's doctor, but to be the guardian of our fragile psychological stability as well. A few days after Janak's birth, we were in the NICU when Janak's IV needle became dislodged. At his weight of just over a pound at the time, every drop of blood was critical. We watched anxiously as blood trickled out of his tiny veins. The nurses took off his splint to reenter the IV, but as they peeled the plaster from his arm, his tender skin also peeled off leaving raw flesh underneath. Janak, who could not even cry for many months after birth, gave a guttural, strangled scream that sounded more like a baby lamb bleating before slaughter. When I heard this and watched him draw his legs up to his chest in pain, the weeks of suppressed tension and accumulated stress exploded. I left the room crying uncontrollably, just as Dr. Balsekar was entering. He asked me what was happening, and I just shook my head, unable to answer.

Before leaving the NICU that day, Dr. Balsekar asked Alan and me to sit down with him. Gently, he discussed the need for us to do things that would relieve our stress. "This will be a long process. We have to take Janak's health one day at a time. Typically, what happens is that one's adrenaline kicks in for the first week, and you are able to continue. But long-term, the low-grade stress persists and will gradually build up and explode if it is not addressed. What kinds of things do you like to do?" he asked. Within minutes, he had arranged for us to swim at the beautiful club next to the hospital where he was a member, and to accompany him to a classical Indian music concert that weekend. "Don't worry," he said, guessing that we would be nervous to be out of contact for several hours, "you will be with me, and I will have my pager so we'll know immediately if anything is going on."

Over the course of the several months in Bombay, Dr. Balsekar and his wife Sheila took care of us in a way that I doubt most modern physicians in the United States do. They invited us to their house for dinner, helped us to find places to live in Bombay and put up with our barrage of questions. Dr. Balsekar encouraged us to call him at any time, day or night, if we had questions or concerns (we only did this a few times, because our Western attitudes to disturbing people unnecessarily were too ingrained). He was used to this, he said, because Indian patients considered it a right. When Janak was ready to leave the hospital, it was Dr. Balsekar who drove us home. A few days after coming home from the hospital, he and Sheila made a house call on their way back from a dinner engagement to relieve our worry about a fever Janak had developed.

Dr. Balsekar's genuine interest in us, the amount of time he spent with us discussing Janak's health or even in social conversation, and the little things he and his wife did for us, made us wonder if this was what the "family physician" of old (or perhaps that still exists in rural America) was like: providing medical care based on relationships, rather than on money and schedules.

My experiences during Janak's birth and his hospitalization showed me that medicine has two sides: technology and heart. It is far easier to find the former in the United States and the latter in India. And yet, when the chips are down, would any of us actually *choose* to be in India for a medical emergency? America's reputation as a leader in medical technology, information and knowledge is undisputed. Much of this has yet to filter to India; and many of the latest procedures and drugs will never filter there, simply because they are too expensive for the majority of Indians.

In describing Janak's birth and his hospitalization, I am also acutely aware of how completely unrepresentative it was of the care available to the general Indian public. Dr. Soonawalla's assistant had described Breach Candy as "plush," and although it might not seem that way compared to American hospitals, it earned its description compared with other Indian hospitals. As a private hospital and one of the best in the country, Breach Candy charges about $70 per night for a bed in a private room with an attached bath. The total bill for two and a half months of Janak's care (including bed charges, doctors' visits and medicines) was about $5,600. Although this sounds outrageously cheap by U.S. standards, it would be unaffordable for most Indians.

After two years of striving in India to live life without taking advantage of the privileged situation we knew we were in, it felt uncomfortable to be catapulted into a situation where we had access to services and technology only available to the rich. I thought many times about the thousands, maybe millions, of women who need but never get the access to medical care that we had. Part of the difference is in the results: Janak lived and thrived, while their babies are a fraction of the tens of millions of infant deaths that occur in India even today in the twentieth century.

༄

I have often thought it ironic that Janak was born in India. India, my partner, sometimes hidden but always alive in my mind. India, whose significant role in my life I had returned to reconcile. India, who brought me back to who I am as an Indian and ultimately as an American. Perhaps Janak wanted to be born in India. Perhaps he will go through his own struggles of identity with this strange, marvelous country, just as I have.

Those months in the hospital were some of the hardest of my life. The emotions I experienced were intermingled, difficult to separate. Anger, sadness, frustration, joy and healing: They were part and parcel of coping with Janak's birth and of the experience of India; Both pushed me to the edges of my emotions, forcing me to interact with an entire range of feelings.

I was most healed when I could cradle Janak in my arms for a few precious moments. I remember his silky soft skin against my breast; his ribs against mine as they rose and fell; his small hand against my chest like a soft breeze. I remember how he opened his eyes, large slate-gray circles below his furry eyebrows, with effort as if a heavy weight was on his eyelids. I remember the wrinkles of his furrowed brow that reached up and disappeared into his skull, like lapping waves on a sandy beach. And I remember, most vividly, thinking that Janak's birth was my final lesson that as powerful as we humans may think we are, ultimately, we do not control the events that matter the most. During those three months and even now, years later, I am profoundly conscious that Janak's life was in the hands of a greater force.

Yet this awareness did not stop me from trying to control what I could during that crisis. Control was my coping mechanism, one that went back to the way I had been raised, to my Western education and ingrained ways of thinking. I found it impossible not to want to make sense of what was happening around us, even though I innately knew that no sense could be made of it. Our friends in America sent us books; we talked to experts; we familiarized ourselves with the machines in the NICU so that we would know the meaning of every alarm. Order, order, give us order in chaos, we shouted. That, after all, is what life is: chaos that we try to order by imposing our own meanings and realities, changing a world we are physically incapable of grasping into something smaller and more manageable but not necessarily truer.

I believe that our efforts made a difference. My husband and I stayed by Janak's plastic box in the NICU, sang him Hindi bhajans, read him books, talked to him and finally, when we were able, held him close, skin to skin. I believe that the concrete actions the doctors took, with the help of technology, were also significant in saving Janak's life. But, still, I know that this alone would not have been enough. Janak could have died, despite all of our efforts. If I doubted this, I only had to look at Vinayak, the baby that lay next to Janak in the NICU. For every near escape that Janak had, Vinayak was caught and taken deeper into the problems of prematurity. Vinayak suffered severe hemorraging in his lungs and brain, and even today his prognosis is uncertain. Although some of the circumstances of Vinayak's birth were different than those of Janak's, the doctors cannot point to specific reasons that would have created such a vast difference between the ultimate results in the two cases. Vinayak received the same medical care at Breach Candy; he just was not as fortunate as Janak and we were.

Seeing Janak and Vinayak in the NICU like that made me angrily question karma and even religion. What could Vinayak or his parents have done that would merit this outcome? Vinayak's mother Seema regularly knelt before the statues of faith and prayed that her child would make it. I could not pray like that without feeling like a hypocrite. Unlike Seema, I had never been entirely sure how I felt about gods and prayer before Janak's birth. Even though I desperately wished I could ask for Janak's life in case someone was listening, I could not bring myself to do it now. Instead, I prayed simply that we would have the strength to bear whatever would come, that my son would have a chance to be on this earth whether this time or in the next incarnation.

Like everything else in India, Janak's birth and my reactions to it were not black or white. I will never know how much our efforts contributed to Janak's life. Had he not lived, I would have been able to take comfort only in knowing that we did our best and that the final results were out of our hands. This, and only this, is the real lesson of sorrow, of joy and of India.

✴

Janak is the name of the king of all kings, father of Sita, from the famous Indian epic *The Ramayana*. Today, Janak is healthy and happy, our miracle boy, truly the king of all kings in his parents' minds.

Every day, my husband and I give thanks for his life. We watch him dance—his toddler's celebration of life, so pure, unadulterated, spontaneous—and we exchange silent glances that only we understand. Crisis was a powerful experience that grounded me in a sense of being part of a bigger, churning process. In the wake of crisis, I continue to use meditation, spiritual exploration and writing to help me maintain that same sense. It is essential, I have come to understand, to respect life by understanding that ultimately we do not control it, even if we sometimes fall back on control as a coping mechanism, as I did many times. This perspective is not very American. American society prides itself on individual accomplishment, on being able to "pull oneself up by one's bootstraps" and take control of one's destiny. It is, after all, a country that has seen tremendous successes in the transformation of individual lives of refugees, of immigrants, of faceless, nameless people into Somebodies.

My life has been full of shining stars, kissed with luck, caressed with tenderness. Janak's birth was the deepest experience of suffering I have undergone. Although I can never compare this episodic experience to those who suffer every day—from drought, discrimination, violence—I have finally learned through experience what they knew long ago: that life involves surrender to one's limits as a human being; not in a passive negative way, but in a positive, life-celebrating acknowledgment of the greater universe.

Passage Beyond Place

I have arrived back in the United States to familiar Seattle rain, invisible drizzle falling from a gray sky. Unlike India's heavy monsoon showers, this rain has no sound and no form.

Our home is cozy, and though it is as transient a place for us as our many dwellings in India, the articles from storage that we have had for so many years provide a sense of security and familiarity. It strikes me as funny that there is more furniture in our living room alone than we ever had in our two-room apartment in Varanasi.

I sink into a rocking chair and warm my hands on a comfortingly solid coffee cup. Gazing out of our window, I see that the new owners of the house across the street have just painted the house bright blue with baby blue trim. Looking at the brightness of the color hurts my brain, and yet, had I seen a house that color in India, it would have fit right into the scenery. There, the colors—even those that seem not to mix gracefully, like pinks with reds or greens with blues—were a part of the setting. Here, it just seems loud, incompatible with the rest of life.

Remembering India is like watching a movie of a past life, images strong in my mind yet from such a different time and space. It is a space where there is vibrancy and unexpectedness in life, a space where community emerges organically instead of needing to be nurtured against the forces of the fast, efficient, modern American lifestyle. I miss the everyday, mundane events that were such a part of life in India, essential to my sense of completeness.

Like the act of buying yogurt from the local store. I would take a rickshaw to what looked like a small opening in a wall. The step up into the store from the street was so high, I would put my hands on it and then pull my legs up, scraping my knees as I went. I would wait my turn at the counter, under large black-and-white pictures of the owner's Brahmin ancestors, bare-chested except for the traditional string tied diagonally across their upper bodies. In front of me, a swarm of bees buzzed around a huge clay bowl filled with sticky-sweet fried dough balls. When my turn came, the owner would hand me my container of yogurt in the usual small clay cup covered with a banana leaf and tied with string. We would smile, exchange greetings and I would be off.

Or the pleasure of being hailed on the street to have a cup of chai with the owner of the small shop I had just passed. Maybe it goes against the principles of an active, healthy economy, but I loved the fact that people rarely seemed too busy for a cup of tea. The whole process of drinking tea could take anywhere from fifteen minutes to an hour or more. We would walk out to a chai stand nearby, sit on a rickety old wooden bench and watch the chai brew in a dented, blackened aluminum pot balanced on uneven stones in a charcoal pit. We would banter with each other and those around us, chewing on the grit of the clay from our cups that mixed in with the milky, sugary tea. And then, when we were finished, we would toss the little clay cup into the street and listen with satisfaction as it broke into a hundred blood-red shards on the black tar road. Once I heard a foreigner suggesting that the cups be washed and reused. The chai vendor was horrified. "Not clean, madam, very dirty." Besides, making the pots is the skill of a particular caste in the villages that survives from this trade.

In these small acts, there was a satisfaction of belonging to a community built on relationships. Whether it was the extended network of shop vendors and vegetable sellers or the more intimate connections with close friends and colleagues, I felt rooted by this network.

In the United States, I find I have to work much harder for that sense of rootedness. Here, the technological modern world does not encourage connection that has face and voice and smell and touch. Because we can move fast, easily and alone, we begin to think of this movement as our goal, slowly disconnecting ourselves from our inner and outer places.

It is too easy in America to forget to question what we are striving for and what we are willing to sacrifice to get it, because the dominant worldview of what our lives should look like is so overwhelming, blasted out in advertisements and billboards, glossy magazines and window displays. Participating in this culture of individual accumulation and autonomy seems to preclude us from thinking about others. Efficiency, technology, comfort, ease, luxury, independence, choice—each contains within its orbit an exuberant promise for an imagined "better" life. Yet, in seeing this world come to fruition, we are losing the promises of the other world, a world that was much more ecologically and spiritually sustainable because it maintained the web of living connections that this new world breaks down.

I am not advocating "going back" to the past. I myself have enjoyed and taken advantage of the many benefits of our technologically and scientifically advanced times. After all, my son might not have lived had he not had access to advanced technology. After being in India, however, I am convinced that we should be learning from some of the basic principles of villagers, of the indigenous people, of the communities that understand self-sufficiency as a necessity for preserving the earth and for maintaining a relationship-filled and meaningful life.

There are few people I know who love India who do not also recognize her dialectical opposites, who do not describe the country using antonyms like *beautiful* and *terrible* in the same sentence. In returning to the United States and contrasting my experiences in India, it is starkly clear to me that whatever promise this new technological world holds, it is also just as terrifying as it is beautiful. Perhaps more, because the terror is so easily cloaked in bigger houses and cars and bathrooms, in malls made for giants and growing stacks of paper money that people believe constitute real wealth. Environmentalists cry out that we are destroying our forests and arable land at alarming rates, former geneticists and biologists warn that our new genetically modified foods are killing living species around the world, social scientists write about the unprecedented rise in juvenile incarceration, young murderers, childhood depression. Our world is crying out to us, but we do not seem to hear it because the promise is so alluring. We have become so proficient at enclosing ourselves that we do not see anything we do not want to—except on the comfortingly numbing television set.

My two years in India exposed me to the reality that poverty and injustice are increasing despite the promises of the global economy. Ironically, many of the values and relationships Indians are beginning to give up in order to grasp for those promises are precisely those values and relationships that a growing number of Americans feel they need to recapture in their own lives.

And so, now back in the United States, the conversations and the shades of gray I found in India continue. Forward motion is inevitable, a part of the cycles of our universe; but how do we make it more conscious? Instead of accepting the notions of progress articulated by the world around us, how do we begin—as a global society—to question our directions and understand the values we are subscribing to and the effects of those values? It is only possible if we start to reassert our needs as a community of living beings that are interdependent, if we begin to live by Mahatma Gandhi's talisman of a half-century ago:

> Recall the face of the poorest and the most helpless man you may have seen, and ask yourself if the step you contemplate is going to be of any use to him. Will he be able to gain anything by it? Will it restore him to a control over his own life and destiny? In other words, will it lead to *swaraj* or self-rule for the hungry and also spiritually starved millions of our countrymen? Then you will find your doubts and yourself melting away.

Only then are we truly exercising real choice.

Shortly after I returned back to the United States, I took a trip to Oakland, California. I was heading to the heart of Oakland's Latino community. The shuttle bus I took was a spin-off from a Super Shuttle, a nondescript, rather beaten-up white bus with big red letters on it that said SHUTTLE. The driver was North Indian. He looked at me and smiled hesitantly, as if to wait to express himself fully in case I rejected the smile. I smiled back immediately and greeted him. I told him I needed to go to Oakland. He scratched his head and told me that his other customers were going to San Francisco, but he never liked to leave anyone waiting so he would drop me off first before heading into the city.

There were several others in the bus already. Behind me were two women in suits, and behind them, another two business men. The young African-American man next to me was the only one who smiled when I entered.

The driver had said he knew where I was going, a good thing since I did not. But when he got off the highway, it became clear quickly that he was lost. He began speaking to me in Hindi, asking me if I had other directions that might help. Meanwhile, my shuttle companions were getting annoyed. Tapping their feet on the floor to show their displeasure, they complained to each other about the detour. I apologized to them, although in truth we had been lost for only about five minutes.

We found the place eventually, the driver and I, by stopping and asking people along the way and poring over the map he had pulled from the glove compartment. The whole event had taken about fifteen minutes. I asked him to drop me in the middle of the street, across from the mobile home center of La Clinica de La Raza, where I was going. My companions looked at me strangely, a woman of color with several bags in the middle of a street dotted with taco vans and walls painted with Spanish-style murals.

As I was digging out my money to pay the driver, I heard one of the women behind me comment to her partner, "It's because she's from where he is, he's done this for her and made us late."

I stared at her silently.

It is just who he is, I thought. *It's not about place.*

☙

I did not realize it at the time, but I went to India to reconnect, with myself and with the world around me. India, because of my roots, was my passage. I went to India believing my search for identity was a search for place. Instead, I found, mine was a search for a way of looking at and being in the world that felt right.

The two are not disconnected, by any means. My Indian heritage—as much as I might have tried to disassociate from it in my early years—clearly influenced me. I often felt as if I was revisiting places I had been in some other life, that the connections I was able to make with Indian women, in particular, whom I had never met and had little in common with outwardly, had been established long before these physical meetings. I shed a skin in India, one that had both protected me and insulated me in the United States. In shedding that layer, I became vulnerable and open and alive. India and her influence on me are undeniable. There is no place that draws me as does India.

But my real lesson was this: In understanding India's influence on me, I no longer needed to try so hard to maintain it. There was nothing I needed to *do* to be Indian, to prove that I was inextricably linked to this country. Nor, importantly, could I lose my Indianness. I decided to give up my Indian citizenship when I returned to the United States. It was a monumental decision in that I had held on to that Indian passport for so long, as if it were my Indian identity card, proof of a principle of some sort. And it was mundane in that giving up that passport took nothing of my Indianness away. It was the ultimate reaffirmation of my trust in the Indian me. I no longer needed to prove anything, to myself or to others.

If I started with the connection between identity and physical place, I ended with the connection between identity and the kind of world I believe in and want to live in.

There are no geographic lines around what constitute healthy, happy individuals and societies. As human beings, we all yearn for relatedness and emotional connection. Parts of India offered me a reminder of the possibility of a world where people derive their energy and pleasure from inner strength, relationship with others and the earth and a profound belief in some greater force. They understand their limits as human beings, and this fosters a sense of responsibility. As an integral part of the chain of nature and evolution, of growth and decay, these communities seemed to understand balance in themselves and in the world in a way that too few of us in modern, technological societies do because of our detachment.

I loved the fact that in India, spirituality and discussions about it were not taboo. Unlike in the States, where I feel I must often offer examples of my rational mind to counterbalance my belief in spirituality, in India talking about spirituality and some greater force are part of everyday conversation. It does not detract from individual strength, but rather provides it.

India is not the only place to find communities that operate within an almost existential notion of relatedness. Across America, there are places where generations were raised with a similar sense of place, of respect for other living beings, of being part of a greater whole. But these places are under seige. Being in the United States, the innovator of modern, technological society, they are at the front of the bulldozer's path. It is hard to survive, to keep intact traditional ways of viewing the world that seem almost arcane, old-fashioned, distinctly un-hip in a very fast-paced, fashionable world.

India is struggling now with the same issues. But perhaps what is unique about India is that one can see the whole continuum of change happening before one's eyes. On one end, there are villages that have yet to be pulled into the grip of a global, modern society. One can see how these village societies both expand and limit the notions of individual and community. On the other end, there are urban areas that have all but embraced Western ideas of progress and development. Here, the wealthy use their wealth to further themselves, and the rest are left behind to grope and grasp. At the same time, there are better roads, opportunities for a better life, and voices for basic human rights and dignities. In the middle, there are societies slowly, inevitably moving along that continuum. But perhaps being sandwiched between the two extremes is what will ultimately give them the ability to create a new center, a center that is truly about choice and freedom and quality of life.

That India has a strong spiritual and philosophical heritage, a strong sense of kinship (for better or worse), and an enormously diverse population is hopeful. Ironically, so is the fact that we are able to witness firsthand in India the widening gap between rich and poor, and the obvious struggles that occur in embracing modernity and shunning traditionalism. Perhaps Indians will be pushed to evaluate and choose their destinies in unimaginable ways. I recently read an extraordinary piece of news: Four hundred Indian farmers who belong to the Indian Peasant Union were marching across Europe to "denounce the devastating effects of globalization on their agriculture." Like the Chipko movement, like the men and women in villages across India who are demanding a different kind of education for their children that honors agriculture as a viable life, this march inspires hope. In some strange way, that hope is coming from the fact that we see not just one but both extremes of the continuum.

Perhaps that is why India represents for me the ultimate struggle to find a middle ground, a place where progress can mean a positive change for Indians who live without their basic needs satisfied while simultaneously retaining the best of traditions, community structure and ties. It is a struggle to create, define and understand a new kind of human self that lives with a sense of responsibility rather than imposition, of interdependence rather than independence, of grace rather than right.

In Buddhist thought it is only through discovering ourselves that we can discover the universe around us. India encouraged me to look for spirit and soul, to experience the contradictions and wonders of the country and, in doing so, to discover India, myself and the universe. This is the ultimate gift of India.

Selected Bibliography

There are so many books on India, it is difficult to single out a few. These are books I have referred to in this book, or they are books that have stayed with me as exceptional portrayals of the India I came to know and love. There are hundreds more books that are both worthy and recommended for those who want to learn more, but there is no space to list them all here.

Anand, Mulk Raj. *Untouchable*. London: Arnold Associates, 1935.

Critchfield, Richard. *The Villagers: Changed Values, Altered Lives, The Closing of the Urban-Rural Gap*. New York: Anchor Books, 1994.

Critchfield, Richard. *Villages*. Garden City, NY: Anchor Books, 1981.

Dalmia, Vasudha and H. von Stietencron. *Representing Hinduism: The Construction of Religious Traditions and National Identity*. Delhi: Sage Publications, 1995.

Eck, Diana L. *Banaras: City of Light*. New York: Penguin Books, 1993.

Fischer, Louis. *Gandhi: His Life and Message for the World*. New York: Mentor, 1954.

Gandhi, Mohandas K. *An Autobiography: The Story of My Experiments with Truth*. Boston: Beacon Press, 1957.

Gandhi, Nandita and Nandita Shah. *The Issues at Stake: Theory and Practice in the Contemporary Women's Movement in India*. Delhi: Kali for Women, 1992.

Ghadially, Rehana, ed. *Women in Indian Society*. Delhi: Sage Publications, 1988.

Housden, Roger. *Travels Through Sacred India: Guide to the Soul and Spiritual Heritage of India*. London, San Francisco: Thorsons, 1996.

Hume, Robert Ernest, ed. *The Thirteen Principal Upanishads: Translated from the Sanskrit*. London, New York: Oxford University Press, 1877.

Jung, Anees. *Unveiling India: A Woman's Journey*. New York: Penguin Books, 1987.

Krishnamurti, J. *Questions and Answers*. London: Krishnamurti Foundation Trust, 1982.

Markandaya, Kamala. *Nectar in a Sieve*. New York: The John Day Company, 1954.

Nabar, Vrinda. *Caste as Woman*. New York: Penguin Books, 1995.

Nehru, Jawaharlal. *The Discovery of India*. Calcutta: Signet Press, 1946.

Norberg-Hodge, Helena. *Ancient Futures: Learning from Ladakh*. San Francisco: Sierra Club Books, 1991.

Osborne, Arthur, ed. *The Teachings of Bhagavan Sri Ramana Maharshi In His Own Words*. Tiruvannamalai: V. S. Ramanan, 1996.

Paz, Octavio. *In Light of India*. New York: Harcourt Brace & Company, 1995.

Srinivas, M. N., ed. *Caste: Its Twentieth Century Avatar*. New York: Penguin Books, 1996.

Srivastava, Raj Krishan, ed. *Vital Connections: Self, Society, God: Perspectives on Swadhyaya*. New York, Tokyo: Weatherhill Inc., 1998.

Zaehner, R. C., ed. *The Bhagavad-Gita*. London: Oxford University Press, 1969.

Acknowledgments

This book came out of a series of articles initially published by the Institute of Current World Affairs in Hanover, New Hampshire. I am grateful to Peter Martin and the ICWA trustees for the initial opportunity to spend two self-directed, often lonely but completely enriching years in India. It was a gift. Sincere thanks also to Gary Hansen and Ellen Kozak for their help along the way, and to my "avuncles," Warren Unna and Dick Morse for diligently reading and providing feedback on my articles.

To my mother, my thanks for pushing me for years to write a book, and for inspiring me through her own successful writing career. To both my parents, love and thanks for supporting me through the ongoing phases of my search for identity, even while wondering where it would lead.

There are many people in India who helped me navigate my way through places, and offered me friendship, spirited conversation and insights into complex issues. In particular, I thank: Vijayalakshmi Das; Pawan Gupta and Anuradha Joshi; Jitendra, Shobhan, Jagmohan and all the others at SIDH; Mahesh Shah; D.L. Sheth; Virendra Singh and his wonderful family; Roy Chacko; Pradeep Nair; Nishi Mehrotra; Priyankar Upadhyaya and Anju Sharan; Ranjana Narayan; Ramu Pandit; Vidhu Shekhar Chaturvedi and Mrs. Chaturvedi; Bhavany and Kutty Narayan; and Mahesh and Sheila Balsekar.

To Faith Conlon, my editor, my deep gratitude for having such trust in me and this book, for pushing me when I needed it and for tolerating my questions, needs and mood swings. Thanks also to all the other wonderful women at Seal Press who helped turn the book from concept to reality.

Being a writer, I have discovered, requires a superb support system to neutralize the ups and downs of writing. To these people who have provided that for me, I am eternally grateful: my book group— Regina Pacor, Kathleen Mullins, Aaliyah Gupta and Diana Bender; Joanie Warner; Jack and Gloria Bollens; Mary Jean Ryan; Tracy Rysavy for her careful and encouraging edits; Dean, Leslie, Kenneth and Linda Preston and Jenckyn Goosby; my wonderful sister, Susheela, and her family; John Melvin; Kevin and Julia Richards; Shannon and Sade Hayes; Jim Goebelbecker; Regan Warner-Rowe; Laura Hubbard for all the free lattes and inspirational conversations; and Rick Simonson, this book's guardian angel in its latter stages, for providing momentum, imagination and friendship.

Most of all, I celebrate my partner, Alan Preston, for his role in the creation of this book. He was an excellent editor, refusing to allow me to settle for anything less than what he sensed I wanted to say. He was with me through many of the experiences I describe, and displayed compassion, humility and grace as he interacted with a culture so different from his own as if it were indeed his. Perhaps it was in some other life. For all that we have gone through while I have been writing this book, he has been my guide and my support. For this, there are no adequate words.

Finally, I would like to express my deepest appreciation to the men and women across India who inspired me, shared their stories and allowed me to see a different possibility for the future. They have been my greatest teachers.

About the Author

Born in 1965 in Madras, India, Pramila Jayapal left the country when she was five and grew up largely in Indonesia and Singapore, coming to America at the age of sixteen and staying until her return to India in 1995. She has a B.A. in Literature from Georgetown University, and an M.A. in Business Administration from Northwestern University. Before her grant from the Institute of Current World Affairs (ICWA), she was the director of an international loan and technical assistance program that worked with health programs in developing countries, including India. She lives in Seattle, Washington.

Selected Titles from Seal Press

Beyond the Limbo Silence by Elizabeth Nunez. $12.95, 1-58005-013-1. A spellbinding novel tracing a young woman's journey from her Caribbean home to the United States during the civil rights struggle.

Blessed by Thunder: Memoir of a Cuban Girlhood by Flor Fernandez Barrios. $22.95, 1-58005-021-2. In this evocative memoir, Flor Fernandez Barrios tells the story of her childhood during the Cuban revolution and the irrevocable changes it brings to her family and hometown of Cabaigüán.

Bruised Hibiscus by Elizabeth Nunez. $24.95, 1-58005-036-0. A page-turning, hallucinatory novel that tackles the large themes of colonialism, sexism and racism in the 1950s on the island of Trinidad.

Chinese Medicine for Women: A Common Sense Approach by Bronwyn Whitlocke. $12.95, 1-58005-018-2. An informative and accessible guide for women exploring alternative health remedies.

Climbing High: A Woman's Account of Surviving the Everest Tragedy by Lene Gammelgaard. $25.00, 1-58005-023-9. The 1996 Everest disaster, recorded by a woman who made it to the summit and survived.

Nervous Conditions by Tsitsi Dangarembga. $12.00, 1-878067-77-X. Set in colonial Rhodesia in the 1960s, this evocative novel tells the story of a girl's coming of age and the devastating human loss involved in the colonization of one culture by another.

Tents in the Clouds: The First Women's Himalayan Expedition by Monica Jackson and Elizabeth Stark. $16.00, 1-58005-033-6. A spirited and vivid account of the 1955 all-female expedition to the Himalaya.

Where the Oceans Meet by Bhargavi C. Mandava. $12.00, 1-58005-000-X. A magical story that captures the lives of Indian and Indian-American women and girls, whose paths vividly intersect and gracefully glance off one another.

Seal Press publishes many books of fiction and nonfiction by women writers. If you are unable to obtain a Seal Press title from a bookstore or would like a free catalog of our books, please order from us directly by calling 800-754-0271. Visit our website at www.sealpress.com.